Microsoft 365™

PORTABLE GENIUS

Lisa A. Bucki

About the Author

An author, trainer, and content expert, **Lisa A. Bucki** has been educating others about computers, software, business, and personal growth topics since 1990. She has written and contributed to dozens of books and multimedia works, in addition to providing marketing and training services to her clients and writing online tutorials. Bucki is co-founder of 1x1 Media, LLC (www.1x1media.com), an independent publisher of books and courses focused on how-to topics for entrepreneurs, startup founders, makers, and other business professionals.

Acknowledgments

As I wrapped up the writing of *Excel® Portable Genius* and this book, my husband and I were deeply grieving the loss of two of our beloved dogs, Jack Black and Tucker, in a little more than three months' time. Associate Publisher Jim Minatel, Senior Managing Editor Pete Gaughan, Project Manager Kezia Endsley, and Technical Editor Joyce Nielsen—all of whom I consider both friends and colleagues—reacted with kindness, patience, support, and professionalism. I thank them for being wonderful human beings in addition to top professionals.

I would like to also thank additional team members for their excellent work on this project, including Copy Editor Kim Wimpsett, Content Refinement Specialist Saravanan Dakshinamurthy, Proofreader Louise Watson, and all the other Wiley employees or partners who had a direct or indirect role in this undertaking.

My gratitude also eternally flows to my excellent and patient husband, Steve Poland, and all of our beloved furry dog children.

Contents

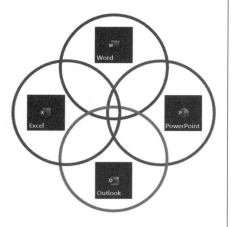

chapter 2

How Do I Develop Document Content in Word?   40

chapter 3

How Do I Make Changes in Excel?   62

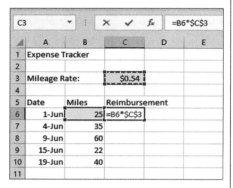

chapter 7

How Do I Use Graphics? 156

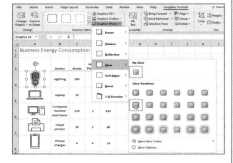

chapter 8

How Do I Manage Lists of Information? 180

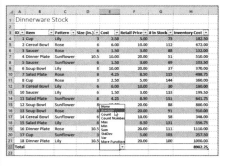

chapter 9

How Do I Present My Data in Charts? 200

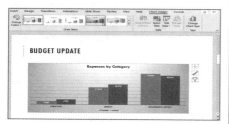

chapter 10

How Do I Manage Emails and Contacts in Outlook? 216

chapter 11

How Do I Print and Share My Content? 232

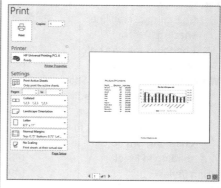

Introduction

Suites of apps designed to work together, such as Microsoft 365, offer many pros, including a common user interface, similar commands and features, and a robust set of tools that enables you to communicate effectively and explore your creativity to the max. Even so, some users can find the hundreds—if not thousands—of choices and features to be a little intimidating.

Microsoft 365 Portable Genius aims to help you answer 11 key questions you may come up against when using the top four Microsoft 365 apps—Word, Excel, PowerPoint, and Outlook. The book covers the features that you need to know, along with some others that you should want to know. I try to get right to the point in describing features and steps so you can power through, problem-solve on your own, and free up time for other activities.

A few special elements provide guardrails and inspiration. Notes help you delve a bit deeper into some topics, Cautions give advice and help you steer clear of problems, and Genius icons convey the pro tips that will make you more efficient, more productive, and (I daresay) more impressive in the results that you crank out from the Microsoft 365 apps.

I need to mention one last item from the "need to know" category before you dive in to Chapter 1. The screenshots for the figures in this book were shot at a low 1024 x 768 resolution to enhance their final appearance within the book's format. Most users now have their screens set to a much higher resolution, so you may see differences between the figures on your screen and those in the book, particularly with regard to the appearance of the ribbon. Also, users with touchscreen systems may see additional screen options and features not shown in the book's figures. Finally, there may be variations in screen features, depending on the type of Microsoft 365 subscription you have and your update cycle.

Thank you, reader, for adding *Microsoft 365 Portable Genius* to your library. You can find more bonus material in the Online Bonus Appendix for this book, available at www.wiley.com/go/ms365portablegenius.

How Do I Start Using Microsoft 365?

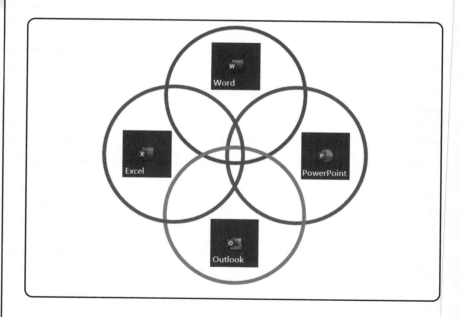

The Microsoft 365 applications, or apps, are easy to navigate yet loaded with powerful features designed to save you time and work. The core apps this book covers—Word, Excel, PowerPoint, and Outlook—share similar commands and procedures, meaning skills learned in one app translate smoothly to the other apps. Dialing in on all the basics will enable you to spend more time developing content. This chapter introduces you to the "must know" skills for your work in Microsoft 365, including essential command and interface navigation features, key techniques for creating and working with files, making selections, copying and moving information, and proofing content.

Starting and Exiting an App

Windows 10 gives you a few options for starting a program so that you can get to work. You may already have your preference for how to start up, but if not, you can try one of these methods:

● **Start button.** Click the Start button at the left end of the Windows taskbar. Move the mouse pointer over the right edge of the list of programs in the Start menu so that a scroll bar expands, and then use the scroll bar or the scroll wheel on your mouse to scroll down until you see the Microsoft 365 app that you want to start, such as Word, in the list. Then choose the app name. You also can pin a larger tile for starting an app to the right side of the Start menu. Right-click the app name in the list of Start menu programs, and choose Pin to Start. Then you can open the Start menu and click the large tile. If you need to remove the tile later, right-click it, and choose Unpin from Start.

● **Windows logo key.** Press the Windows logo key on your keyboard. Press the down arrow on your keyboard as needed until the app name is selected, and then press Enter.

● **Search box.** Click in the Search box to the right of the Start button on the taskbar. If a tile for the app appears in the Top Apps section, click it. If not, start typing the app name, such as **Excel**, and then choose the app when it appears under Best Match, as shown in Figure 1.1.

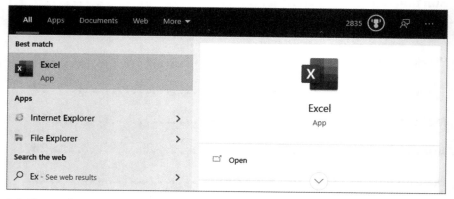

1.1 Choose the app name when using Windows Search to start a Microsoft 365 app.

Additionally, if you choose Office from the Start menu, an Office window with icons for all your apps opens. You can click an app's icon to be prompted to create a document and open the app, and you can leave this window open to launch other Microsoft 365 apps as needed.

Genius

If using the Start menu to launch a Microsoft 365 app isn't for you, then you can pin a button for the app to the taskbar. With the app open, right-click its button on the taskbar, and then choose Pin to Taskbar. Click the pinned button on the taskbar to start the program. If you decide you want to unpin the button, right-click it on the taskbar and choose Unpin from Taskbar.

When Word, Excel, or PowerPoint open, they prompt you to create a new document or open an existing one. (Outlook works a little differently when you start it.) The later section called "Working with Files" provides more details about those choices. For now, you could just click the Blank Document, Blank Workbook, or Blank Presentation thumbnail to create a new file.

When you've finished all your work for the day, you should close or exit the program. You could shut down Windows without closing open apps, but it's better to close the app first to ensure you've saved all your work. As when starting an app, you have these options for closing or exiting the program:

- Click the Close (X) button at the upper-right corner of the screen.

- Press Alt+F4.

To close the current file without exiting the app, click the File tab near the upper-left corner of the window, and then choose Close. If you have a file with unsaved work open and exit the app or close the file, a message box asks whether you want to save changes to the file. You can click the Save or Don't Save button as needed.

Caution

If you have multiple Word, Excel, or PowerPoint files open or multiple Outlook windows open, closing one of them doesn't close down the program overall. You have to close every open file or window to make sure you've completely exited the program.

Taking a Look Around

You interact with the Microsoft 365 apps through their *user interfaces* or *Uls*. Microsoft specifically designs the user interface in each of the Microsoft 365 apps to have similar features, making it easier to perform similar tasks from app to app. The apps still have their differences, which I'll highlight in the areas where I cover the individual apps. Let's start first, however, with the UI features that the apps have in common.

Note

The Account (or Office Account in Outlook) choice on the File tab takes you to a screen where you can sign in and out of your Microsoft 365 subscription and manage updates to the apps, among other choices. The Options choice on the File tab opens an Options dialog box where you can change settings affecting how the app appears and behaves.

Reviewing key screen features

The common interface features in the Microsoft 365 apps enable you to identify the file, give commands, work with the content in your documents, view status information, and change the document view. Figure 1.2 illustrates these common features. (I'll cover screen features specific to the individual apps throughout the book as needed.)

Here's what you need to know about the screen features shown in Figure 1.2:

- **Title bar.** The title bar identifies the name of the current file and holds other tools.

- **Quick Access Toolbar.** Found at the left end of the title bar, the Quick Access Toolbar (QAT) offers Save, Undo, and Redo buttons by default. The Undo and Redo buttons become active after you start performing actions. Clicking the down arrow at the right end of the QAT opens the Customize Quick Access Toolbar menu, where you can choose the name of another button that you want to add to the QAT.

- **Ribbon.** The ribbon below the title bar uses tabs to organize the majority of the commands that you'll use in your apps. Click a ribbon tab to see its commands. The names along the bottom of the ribbon identify commands that are grouped together because they have related or similar functions. In most cases, you click a button on the ribbon to choose a command, though clicking a button with a drop-down list arrow on it opens a list of additional choices. Still other ribbon buttons are split, with both a regular button on the top and a down arrow on the bottom part of the button. Clicking the top half of a split button executes the command immediately, while clicking the bottom part with the arrow opens a list of choices. Other buttons are split the other way, with the main button on the left and a drop-down list arrow on the right. Pressing the Alt key displays letters and numbers, sometimes called *keytips*, that you can press to choose a ribbon tab and then a command.

Quick Access Toolbar (QAT)

Ribbon tabs

Title bar   Search (Microsoft Search) text box

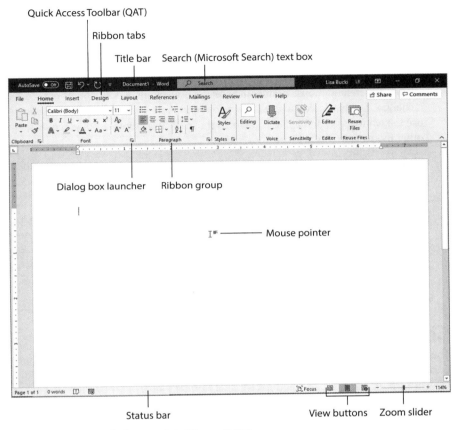

Dialog box launcher   Ribbon group

Mouse pointer

Status bar   View buttons   Zoom slider

1.2 You will work with these tools in Microsoft 365 apps.

Note

I'll use a type of shorthand throughout the book to tell you which ribbon command to choose, giving the tab, group, and specific button. For example, if I say "Choose Review → Proofing → Thesaurus," it means to click the Review tab on the ribbon, look for the Proofing group of commands, and in that group, click Thesaurus. Some command sequences can be longer if a list or menu appears.

- **Dialog box launcher.** Some groups on the ribbon include a small button called a *dialog box launcher* in the lower-right corner. Clicking one of these buttons opens a dialog box with more detailed choices, such as the Font or Format Cells dialog box.

7

● **Mouse pointer.** When you're using the mouse in various apps, the mouse pointer changes shape often to cue you when it's in the correct position to perform a particular action. By default, when the mouse pointer is over the document in Word, the pointer resembles an I-beam with lines of text beside it, as shown in Figure 1.2. However, it may change to a white arrow, a two-headed arrow, and other shapes. The default mouse pointer in Excel is a bold white plus, but at other times it changes to a black plus, a split black arrow, and more. PowerPoint and Outlook use the white arrow and a plain I-beam as the main app pointers, but you may see other mouse pointers in those apps, too.

● **Status bar.** This area below the main work area displays status information and has tools for changing the zoom that I'll cover shortly.

Note

The more recent Microsoft 365 app versions have made it easier to get help about a feature or task. Make sure your computer is connected to the Internet to receive the maximum results, and then press F1 or choose Help → Help → Help to open a Help pane at the right. Enter a command name, task, or other search keywords, and then press Enter to see matching results. You also can use Microsoft Search (Alt+Q) in the title bar to search for help.

Changing views

The View tab on the ribbon enables you to change the view and turn some view features on and off. The default view for Word, Print Layout, was shown in Figure 1.2. The default view in Excel, PowerPoint, and Outlook is called Normal. Figure 1.3 shows the View tab in Excel as an example.

1.3 Use the View tab choices to adjust screen appearance.

Generally speaking, the View tab in each of the apps has a main group with the overall view choices, plus additional groups with other settings. Here's the name of the group with the overall view choices for each app, plus a briefing on the available views:

● **Views group in Word.** Word's default Print Layout view approximates how the document will look when printed in hard copy, showing margins, spacing between pages, headers and footers, and so on. It also includes Web Layout view so you can see how the document would look when published as a web page. Outline view, which you will learn more about in Chapter 2, enables you to organize or reorganize a document. Draft view shows just the text, without any of the features in Print Layout view. Finally, Read Mode hides most of Word's screen features, so you can read a document more easily.

- **Workbook Views group in Excel.** In addition to the default Normal view, which is shown later in this chapter, Excel offers Page Break Preview view. Use it when you want to print and think you might need to adjust how the contents break between separate pages. The Page Layout view not only shows page breaks, but also shows how headers and footers will appear when printed.

- **Presentation Views group in PowerPoint.** Beyond the default Normal view, this group in the PowerPoint View tab has an Outline View choice, like Word. It also has a Slide Sorter view for rearranging the order of the slides, or pages, in the file. The Notes Page view enables you to see a speaker notes layout for presentation slides. As in Word, you can choose the Reading View to see the presentation without app tools getting in the way.

- **Current View group in Outlook.** Even though Outlook has a Normal view and a Reading view, this group doesn't offer those choices. Instead, you can choose Change View to adjust aspects of how messages are displayed, or View Settings to change details such as which columns of message information display.

Note The buttons near the right end of the status bar (refer to Figure 1.2) also enable you to change between views. In Outlook, these buttons are the only way to change between Normal View and Reading View.

You also can tinker with whether the ribbon is fully visible. The small up arrow button in the lower-right corner of the ribbon is called the Collapse the Ribbon button. You can click it or press Ctrl+F1 to hide everything but the ribbon tabs, allowing more of the file's contents to appear on-screen. When you need to choose a command, just click a tab to expand the ribbon temporarily, choose the desired button or item, and then continue working. The ribbon will collapse again on its own. To return the ribbon to its normal appearance and function, click a ribbon tab, and then click the Pin the Ribbon button—it has a pushpin on it—in the lower-right corner of the ribbon or press Ctrl+F1 again. You also can double-click a ribbon tab to collapse the ribbon or pin it back open.

The button in the lower-right corner of the Outlook ribbon looks like the Collapse the Ribbon button in the other apps, but its name is Switch Ribbons. Clicking the button toggles between a one-line Simplified Ribbon or the Classic Ribbon that looks like the ribbon in Word, Excel, and PowerPoint.

Zooming

Today's trend of computers offering ever-higher screen resolutions has its pros and cons. While graphics and video look gorgeous in hi-res, screen features and content in business-oriented programs can look small and difficult to read. Whether you've forgotten your glasses or just have eyestrain from a full day of screen time, increasing the zoom or zooming in can make screen contents easier to read. On the other hand, decreasing the zoom or zooming out allows more of the file's contents to appear on-screen at once, which can be handy in some situations. For example, you might want to zoom out when working in Excel to show more rows and columns, which would make it easier to select a large set of data for a chart. Or, you might want to zoom in when performing design tasks in Word or PowerPoint, such as aligning graphic objects, and then zoom back out to see how your changes look in context with the rest of the contents.

The Zoom group of the View tab holds choices for changing the zoom. Word offers the most preset zoom choices, enabling you to zoom to One Page, Multiple Pages, or Page Width size. In Excel, you can select an area on the worksheet and then click the Zoom to Selection button in that group so the selection will fill the screen, usually by zooming in. PowerPoint has a Fit to Window choice that zooms the slide in or out as needed to fill the available space on-screen. To return to the normal zoom in Word and Excel, click the 100% button in the group. Clicking the Zoom button in Word, Excel, or PowerPoint opens the Zoom dialog box, which enables you to choose a preset zoom percentage or enter your own setting in the Percent text box (Word and PowerPoint) or Custom text box (Excel); click OK to apply your choice and close the dialog box. Outlook's View tab doesn't really have zoom settings per se, but you can choose the Use Tighter Spacing button in the Layout group to see more messages on-screen.

All four apps have the Zoom slider shown in Figure 1.2. Use it to change the zoom on the fly. You can drag the slider "thumb" to the left to zoom out or to the right to zoom in. Or, you can click the Zoom Out (-) or Zoom In (+) buttons at either end of the slider to zoom out or in at preset 10% increments. When you change the zoom using any method, the change applies to the current file only, and normally only to the current sheet in Excel.

Genius

A zoom setting of 120–125% strikes a good compromise between increasing the zoom enough to reduce eyestrain and allowing plenty of the work area to appear on-screen at once.

Working with Files

Now that you've had an overview of how the Microsoft 365 apps tick, it's time to turn to the practical business of starting to work with files in Word, Excel, and PowerPoint. But what does the term *file* mean when it comes to the various apps, anyway? Generally speaking, you can refer to any Microsoft 365 file as a *document*. And in fact, Word files are called documents. However, an Excel file is called a *workbook*, with the name stemming from how Excel enables you to organize your data in an orderly fashion on separate *worksheets*. Because PowerPoint files are intended for a speaker to use while giving a presentation, PowerPoint files are called *presentations*, each holding individual *slides* of information.

When you click the File tab on the ribbon, a screen loaded primarily with choices for working with files appears. This screen is sometimes called Backstage or Backstage view. You can use the choices on the File tab to create, save, export, and print files, among other actions.

Note

While Outlook has a File tab and you can save messages as files, using the app to create and manage email messages differs substantially from how you use the other three apps covered in this book. If you're eager to learn more about Outlook, skip ahead to Chapter 10.

Creating a blank file

You learned at the start of the chapter that when you start Word, Excel, or PowerPoint, the app prompts you to open or create a file. You can click the Blank Document, Blank Workbook, or Blank Presentation thumbnail to create a new blank file at that point. If you've already started the app and opened a file (blank or otherwise), you can click the File tab and then choose Blank Document, Blank Workbook, or Blank Presentation (Figure 1.4) to create another blank file. But for my money, it's fastest to press Ctrl+N to create a new file. No matter the method, the app assigns a placeholder name to each blank file you create until you save it under a new name. The placeholder names reflect the app's file type, so Word assigns Document1, Document 2, and so on; Excel assigns Book1, Book2, and so on; and PowerPoint assigns Presentation1, Presentation2, and so on.

11

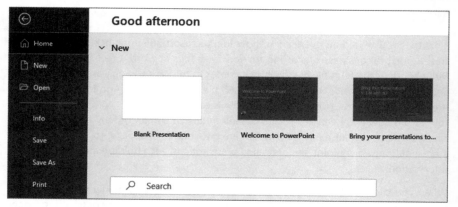

1.4 Click the File tab and then choose Blank Document, Blank Workbook, or Blank Presentation to create a new blank file.

Caution

If you work in Word, Excel, or PowerPoint for the web, the cloud-based versions of the apps, you might have gotten very comfortable with how the cloud apps automatically save the file for you as you work. Unfortunately, the desktop versions of the apps aren't as helpful, so you should make sure you save your work frequently. See the later section called "Saving and Closing a File" to learn how to save.

Exploring templates

If starting from a blank slate sounds like too much work, if you're looking for design or content ideas, or if you're fairly certain someone else has already created just the type of file you're looking for, then you might find what you need in the huge selection of templates offered through the apps. A template is simply a pre-made file that typically includes section or slide titles and labels, placeholder content or prompts, formulas, and formatting. When you use a template file, which has a slightly different file format than a regular file, it creates a new file with the same contents as the template. You fill it out with your own content from there and save the copied file. Thousands of business and personal templates are available for download, including resumes, flyers, brochures, planners, calendars, budgets, invoices, inventory lists, sales pitches, and financial or scientific results presentations. PowerPoint also enables you to download a new presentation theme and create a file from it. "Understanding Themes" in Chapter 6 covers themes in more detail.

To find and download a template after starting an app, follow these steps:

1. **Choose File → New.** The options for creating a new file appear. To display only themes and not templates in PowerPoint, you also need to click Themes under the Search for Online Templates and Themes text box.

2. **Scroll down to see thumbnails for suggested templates.**

3. **Click a template thumbnail to select it.** As shown in Figure 1.5, a larger preview of the template appears, along with a description and the download size information.

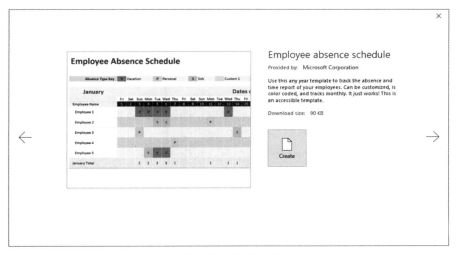

1.5 You get to preview a template before downloading it.

4. **If the template looks like what you want, click the Create button.** The template downloads to your computer, and a new file based on the template opens in the app. You can then add your own content and save the copy of the template file.

If you didn't see a template that looked promising in Step 2, you can scroll back up and click one of the Suggested Searches choices under the Search for Online Templates text box (called Search for Online Templates and Themes in PowerPoint). Or, you could click in that text box, type a search term or brief description, and press Enter. The screen displays thumbnails for matching templates in the search results. At that point, continue with Step 3 to select and download a template.

Caution | The templates you download through the Microsoft 365 apps are from a trusted source, so they should be free from viruses. If you obtain a template from another source, make sure to check it for viruses and other malware.

Each app automatically stores each template you download into a subfolder of your Windows 10 user folder so that you can reuse it. The next time you choose File → New, downloaded templates will appear at the top of the screen to the right of the Blank Document, Blank Workbook, or Blank Presentation thumbnail. If you've downloaded numerous templates, you may have to click an arrow button to scroll right to find the one that you'd like to reuse. To remove a template from the choices at the top of the screen, right-click it and choose Remove from List.

Opening an existing file

When you start one of the Microsoft 365 apps or click the File tab, the initial screen that appears includes a Recent list, which includes previously saved files you've worked on during the not-too-distant past. Click a file in that list to open it immediately.

If the file to open is not on the Recent list, click the Open choice at the left (below New). Toward the middle of the screen, a list of locations appears. Depending on the type of Microsoft 365 subscription you have, there might be OneDrive and Sites locations for cloud-based storage. You can choose a location like that to look for files.

Lower, under Other Locations, the This PC and Browse choices appear. If you click This PC, the list at the right changes to show the files in the same folder as the currently opened file (if any). You can use the up arrow button to the left of the folder breadcrumb trail at the top to navigate a bit and display different files.

I prefer to click Browse and use the good old Open dialog box (Figure 1.6) to navigate to the location holding a file and open it. As shown in Figure 1.6, when you move the mouse pointer over the Navigation pane at the left, arrows appear to the left of the listed locations so that you can expand and collapse the listing. Clicking the right arrow beside This PC would show all the storage locations under This PC, including available disk drives on your computer. Double-click an item in the Navigation pane to show its contents in the file list at the middle of the dialog box. If you need to open a folder from the file list, double-click it. The Address box at the top of the dialog box shows the path to the current folder. When the file you want to open appears in the file list, either double-click it or click it and click the Open button.

Navigation pane   Folder path

1.6 Use the Open dialog box to locate and open an existing file.

Genius

Glitches happen. Your laptop might lose power and shut down before you save your file, or the system might restart on you after a Windows update installed in the background. To try to recover an unsaved file in an app, choose File → Open. Below the list of files at the right, click the Recover Unsaved Documents, Recover Unsaved Workbooks, or Recover Unsaved Presentations button. The Open dialog box that appears lists any unsaved files. Click the file to reopen it, and then click the Open button.

Switching to another file

You may encounter situations where you need to be working with two or more files at once. With multiple files open, you can use the View tab shown in Figure 1.3 to switch to another file in the same app. On the View tab, click the Switch Windows button in the Window group, and then click the name of the file. If you like using the taskbar, you can move the mouse pointer over the app's button. When a thumbnail for each open file appears, click the desired thumbnail.

15

To use the keyboard to display another file, press and hold the Alt key, briefly press the Tab key while still holding Alt, use the arrow keys to select the thumbnail for the file to display, and then release the Alt key. This is one of the methods you can use to switch between open files in different apps. Alternatively, you can move the mouse pointer over the other app's taskbar button, and then click the thumbnail for the desired file. If only one file is open in the other app, click its taskbar button.

Another method is not really "switching" files exactly. You can change the size and position of windows on-screen, such as when you might want to be able to see contents from two files at the same time. The Minimize and Restore Down/Maximize buttons sit to the left of the Close (X) button in the upper-right corner of each file window, as shown in Figure 1.7.

Minimize   Close

Restore Down/Maximize

1.7 You can also work with a window's size and position to facilitate working with multiple files.

Here's how those buttons work and come into play when working with multiple files:

- **Minimize.** Clicking this button collapses the file down to the app taskbar button, effectively switching you to the next open file.

- **Restore Down/Maximize.** A window is maximized when it fills the computer screen, and clicking this button on a maximized window reduces the window to a smaller (but still visible) size. The button changes from Restore Down to Maximize when the window is not maximized. When you need to see information in two separate files at the same time, click the Restore Down button for each window. To resize each window, move the mouse pointer over the window border so that it changes to a white double-headed arrow, and then drag until the window reaches the dimensions you want. Then drag each window by its title bar to position it on-screen as desired. Click the Maximize button to return a window to full screen size.

Note

The Window group of the View tab offers additional choices for viewing and sizing file windows, such as Arrange All, which opens a dialog box with choices for arranging the open windows. You also can right-click the Windows taskbar and use some of its choices, such as Show Windows Side by Side, to arrange the open windows. Keep in mind, though, that the taskbar shortcut menu choices apply to open windows from all programs.

Typing in a Word Document

Whether you are a two-finger hunt-and-peck typist or a fluid touch typist, Word makes it fairly easy to create content in a document. If anything, many people overthink how to type in text and cling to outdated ways of doing things. For example, if you're old enough to have learned touch typing on a relic called a typewriter, like (yikes!) me, you may have learned to press the typewriter space bar twice between sentences and the carriage return twice between paragraphs. Modern proportional fonts (letter styles) and the inclusion of extra spacing between paragraphs in Word's default paragraph style have rendered those manual double spacing and lines obsolete. Additionally, many professional writing style guides also call for single spacing between sentences.

The upshot is, just start typing in the document. As you type, a blinking vertical line called the insertion point appears to indicate where the next typed character will appear. Press the Spacebar once between words and sentences. Press the Enter key once to start a new paragraph. When you type enough content to fill the current page, Word creates a new page for you automatically. Keep it simple for now.

Caution

Ongoing confusion surrounds the terms *insertion point*, *mouse pointer*, and *cursor*. Decades ago, before the invention of the mouse and similar input devices, *cursor* referred to a blinking box or line on-screen, similar to the insertion point described here. Windows settings use *cursor* for the blinking vertical line. However, in some instances, Microsoft (and other) online documentation calls the mouse pointer a *cursor*. For the record, I'm using *insertion point* for the blinking vertical line and *mouse pointer* or *pointer* for the mouse.

Figure 1.8 shows a basic document with some text in Word's Print Layout view. Even though it's not obvious, even a blank Word document uses a default template called Normal.dotm that defines some document basics like the page size, margins, and document styles. Text you type uses the default Normal style, which uses the Calibri font, 11 pt. size, 1.08 spacing between lines, and 8 pt. spacing after paragraphs. (Later chapters explain more about settings like these.) This is why you don't need to overthink while typing. The Normal.dotm template applies attractive and legible settings for you.

Beyond just typing, Word includes a feature called Click and Type that enables you to add text anywhere on a page. Move the mouse pointer over the blank area where you want to place the text. When lines of text appear with the I-beam mouse pointer, as shown in Figure 1.8, double-click to place the insertion point there, and then start typing. Be advised that using this method sometimes inserts a tab stop for the newly created paragraph. Once you have text in the document, you may need to move around by changing

17

the location of the insertion point. If the area where you want to place the insertion point is visible, just click that spot with the mouse. You also can use numerous other keyboard shortcuts to move around, changing the location of the insertion point. Table 1.1 lists the main ones that I use.

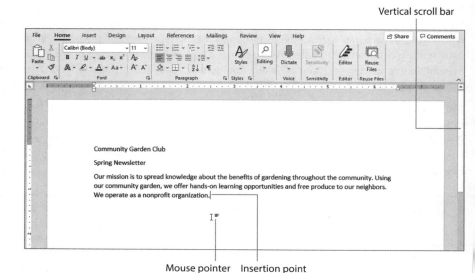

Vertical scroll bar

Mouse pointer   Insertion point

1.8 Word's default formatting settings make attractive, legible text.

Table 1.1 Word Keyboard Shortcuts

Key(s)	Description
Arrow keys	Moves the insertion point one character or line in the direction of the arrow.
Home and End	Moves the insertion point to the beginning or end of the line currently holding the insertion point.
PgUp and PgDn	Moves the insertion point up or down by one screenful.
Ctrl+Home and Ctrl+End	Moves the insertion point to the beginning or end of the document.
Ctrl+left arrow and Ctrl+right arrow	Moves the insertion point by one word in the direction of the arrow.
Ctrl+up arrow and Ctrl+down arrow	Moves the insertion point up or down by one paragraph. If the insertion point is within a paragraph, Ctrl+up arrow moves the insertion point to the beginning of the paragraph.

Caution

If the PgUp and PgDn keys on your keyboard are integrated with a 10-key keypad, you must press the Num Lk (Number Lock) button to turn off having the keys enter numbers and activate the alternative functions of the keys. Press Num Lk again to return to number entry.

You also can use the vertical scroll bar to change the area of the document currently displayed on-screen. The vertical scroll bar at the right controls up and down movement. When the document uses a wide page format or a higher zoom, the horizontal scroll bar appears at the bottom for controlling left and right movement. Figure 1.8 shows the vertical scroll bar. Drag the scroll box in the scroll bar to move more quickly, or click an arrow at either end of the bar to move in smaller increments. Be sure to click to move the insertion point as needed after you scroll.

Chapter 2 explores content and document development in more detail. Note that you can use many of the same techniques you'll learn in Word to add content to the body of an Outlook message. Chapter 10 covers Outlook.

Genius

If you're slow at typing, have painful hands, or create many or lengthy documents such as medical records or legal documents, try plugging a microphone into your computer and using Word's dictation feature. Choose Home → Voice → Dictate (main part of the button) to toggle dictation on and off. Click the arrow part of the button to change languages. Just be patient with the lag between saying the words and seeing them in the document.

Making Your First Cell Entries in Excel

As you just learned, when you're writing a document in Word, you can get away with just typing a lot and not knowing the nuances of how to get around. Excel is trickier than that. Some of the interface's features are important to being able to work accurately in the program, especially when it comes to creating formulas that calculate or organizing data effectively. This section covers a few unique Excel interface features that offer powerful shortcuts and introduces you to the nuances of making various types of cell entries in Excel.

Exploring the Excel screen

At first glance, the Excel screen can look a bit busy with an extreme number of buttons and letters and numbers and boxes. Each worksheet or sheet in an Excel file has more

19

than 16,000 columns and 1,000,000 rows, for a total of more than 17 billion cells! That sounds overwhelming, so I'm going to zero in on the key screen features you need to know to work in Excel, which are shown in Figure 1.9. Later parts of the book will cover other features of the Excel interface in discussions about particular tasks and actions.

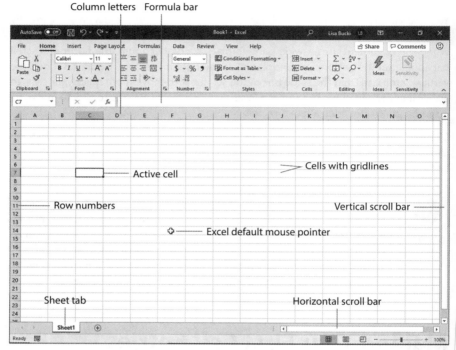

1.9 These screen features facilitate your work in Excel.

Excel's mouse pointer is a large white plus by default, as shown in Figure 1.9. Here are other unique features you'll use when working in Excel:

- **Formula bar.** You will use this area to enter and edit cell contents. The Formula bar also displays the contents of the active cell. Or, if the active cell contains a formula, the formula appears in the Formula bar, while the formula result appears in the cell itself.

- **Row numbers and column letters.** The working area in Excel is organized into rows and columns of cells. The column letters across the top of the grid and the row numbers down the left side identify the address or location of a cell or range. The bands with the letters and numbers are also called *row and column headers*.

- **Cells and gridlines.** A *cell* is formed by the intersection of a single worksheet row and column. The column letter and row number combined identify the *cell address*, also called the *cell reference*. For example, the address for the cell in column C of row 7 is C7. Knowing the cell address comes in handy when you need to jump to a particular piece of information in a worksheet, as well as when you are building formulas. Gridlines identify the cell boundaries.

- **Active cell.** A bold outline, sometimes called the *cell selector*, identifies the active or currently selected cell. When more than one cell is selected, the bold box surrounds the entire selection.

- **Sheet tab.** A tab appears for each worksheet in the file.

The Show group of Excel's View tab has Formula Bar, Gridlines, and Headings check boxes that you can use to toggle those screen features on and off. (*Headings* is another name for row and column headers.) When you want to finalize a workbook file and discourage other people from making edits, you might click the Formula Bar check box to uncheck it, thus hiding the Formula bar. It's common to turn off the gridlines and headings displays for some types of worksheets, such as an executive dashboard that shows summary information and a few charts. In particular, hiding the gridlines makes some sheets more legible and attractive. Keep in mind that these settings in the Show group of the View tab control only the on-screen display of gridlines and headers. If you want to control whether gridlines and headers print, you'll have to adjust the page setup, which is covered in Chapter 11.

Moving around the sheet

Excel holds a few surprises for you when you're moving around and making different types of cell entries. I'll highlight the shortcuts and the pitfalls for you. When you move around the worksheet, you change the cell that's the active cell. Any entry that you make will then appear in the active cell, which is why I'm covering moving around as a prelude to making cell entries. The most obvious way to move around a worksheet is to press the down, up, left, and right arrow keys, moving the cell selector one cell in the arrow direction. Or, you can click a cell that appears on-screen to make it active immediately.

Genius

If you know the address for a cell that doesn't currently appear on-screen that you want to select, press Ctrl+G or F5, or choose Home ➜ Editing ➜ Find & Select ➜ Go To. In the Reference text box of the Go To dialog box, type the cell address, and then click OK. Boom, cell selected! In Word, launch Go To using Home ➜ Editing ➜ Find ➜ Go To, Ctrl+G, or F5. In an Outlook message, press F5. PowerPoint does not have Go To.

You also can use the vertical and horizontal scroll bars (refer to Figure 1.9) to change the area of the worksheet currently displayed on-screen, as for a Word document. But—this is important—moving with the scroll bars does not change the active cell. So after you use a scroll bar, be sure to click the cell you need to select.

My other favorite keyboard shortcuts for moving around in Excel include the PgUp and PgDn keys, which move the active cell up or down by one screenful of rows. (Keep in mind that the number of rows may vary depending on your zoom setting and row heights in the sheet.) I also like Ctrl+End, which selects the cell at the bottom-right corner of the range that holds data on the sheet, and Ctrl+Home, which jumps back to cell A1.

Adding text and values

Once you've selected a cell, you can type in various types of information. This section covers the most basic types of entries, while Chapter 4 will cover how to enter and create formulas. After you type an entry in a cell, to finish the entry and select the next cell, press Enter if you want to move down the column or press Tab if you want to move across the row. Keep these notes about the different types of entries in mind as you begin to populate a worksheet with data:

- **Text.** Also called labels, text entries can serve as items in a list of data, column or row headings and other types of identifiers, or notes or instructions on the sheet. Excel considers any alphanumeric entry that begins with a letter to be text. Text entries can include entries that begin with a number, such as 10 Handbags or A123. By default, text entries align to the left in the cell.

- **Values.** These are the numeric entries you make in a sheet and are typically the values used to perform calculations. By default, value entries align to the right in the cell. If you have an instance where you need for Excel to store a numeric entry as text, type a ' (single quote) at the start of the entry.

- **Hyperlinks.** If you type a website address or email address into a cell, Excel automatically converts it to a hyperlink. (The same thing happens in Word, PowerPoint, and Outlook messages.) You can click the hyperlink in a cell (when you see the hand mouse pointer over the hyperlink) to open the linked web page or create a new email message to a contact. You have to click and hold on the cell to select the cell itself. Note that you also can insert other types of hyperlinks, such as a link to a contract or other relevant resource document, by pressing Ctrl+K or choosing Insert ➔ Links ➔ Link (choose the top part of the Link button) and then using the Insert Hyperlink dialog box to select the file to link.

Figure 1.10 shows examples of text, value, and hyperlink entries in a sheet. Any entry that is too long to fit in its cell automatically spills over into the next cell to the right, like the email address entered in cell B2. Chapter 3, "How Do I Make Changes In Excel?," will present a few techniques for addressing how entries fit in cells, such as increasing the column width. Excel also provides shortcuts for entering series of information. See "Using Auto Fill and Filling Series" in Chapter 3 to learn more.

E4	▼ :	× ✓	fx	Disc. %	
▲	A	B	C	D	E	F
1	Order Summary					
2	Operator:	name@example.com				
3						
4	Order #	Date	Customer	Total	Disc. %	
5	1		Ryan			
6	2		Miller			
7	3		Smith			
8	4		Acton			
9	5		Ryan			
10	6		Casper			
11	7		Smith			
12	8		Phillips			
13	9		Yelton			
14	10		Miller			
15						

1.10 You can make basic entries like these in sheet cells.

Genius

Despite that little inconvenience of sometimes having to toggle Num Lk on and off, I love having a 10-key keypad on my laptop or keyboard to speed up numeric data entry in Excel. It's much easier to use to the compact keypad layout than to stretch for the number keys near the top of the keyboard, especially if you've had any 10-key typing training. If you're a heavy Excel user looking to up your data entry game, check out some online 10-key tutorials.

Adding dates and times

Excel treats dates and times differently than other types of entries. It converts each date or time entry into a date serial number behind the scenes, even though the date and time continues to display as usual in the cell. Because it stores dates as serial numbers, you can create formulas to do date-related actions, such as finding out how many days fall between a start date and an end date. As a practical matter, you don't have to worry about the serial number. All you have to do is type the date, time, or a combination of the two in a format that Excel recognizes and then press Enter or Tab. Figure 1.11 shows examples of acceptable date and time entries. Don't forget to include AM or PM when you're typing a time according to the regular 12-hour clock. In some cases, Excel automatically changes the width of the column when you make one or more date entries.

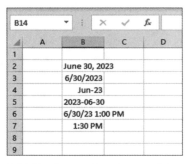

1.11 Excel recognizes dates and times typed using these and other formats.

If you use a format that Excel does not recognize as a date or time, Excel will either display an error or treat the entry as text (left aligned) rather than a date (right aligned). In other cases, Excel might recognize a date or time you enter but convert it to another format when you finish the entry, based on location settings for dates and times in Excel and other default date settings in the Windows operating system. Don't worry, though. Chapter 6 explains how to change the number formatting manually for dates and other numbers in the section called "Changing the Number or Date Format in Excel."

Number formatting on the fly

You've just seen how Excel can interpret date entries in cells and adjust the formatting. Similarly, Excel can recognize certain types of number formatting depending on what other characters you include with the number. Knowing how this "on the fly" formatting works can save you some typing time, as in these cases:

- **Decimals.** If you type a . (decimal point) when entering a number followed by additional numbers, that sets the number of decimal places displayed in the cell. So, if you type 11.1234, Excel displays the entry with all four decimal places. However, if the last number entered after the decimal place is a 0 (zero), Excel truncates that digit. That is, 11.1230 would be displayed as 11.123.

- **Thousands (and beyond).** By default, if you type 1000 in a cell, Excel displays it as 1000. But if you include the thousands separator and enter 1,000, Excel displays it as 1,000. If you enter 1,000,000, Excel displays 1,000,000. You get the drift.

- **Currency.** You can type a currency symbol such as the $ (dollar sign) or € (Euro symbol) at the beginning of an entry, and Excel will recognize it as currency. Include a decimal point and two decimal places, and comma separators if needed, as well.

- **Percentages.** Now, this is where things get a little trickier because of how percentages work in math. A percentage is part of the whole. In math, the "whole" value is 1.00 or 100%. So .25 is 25%, .75 is 75%, and so on. Years ago in Excel, you had to enter the decimal value (such as .25) in the cell and then apply a number format to change it to a percentage. Now, you can just include the % (percent sign) when you type the value in the cell, and Excel automatically interprets it as a percentage. However, in formulas referencing the cell holding the percentage, Excel uses the corresponding decimal value to make the calculation.

Figure 1.12 shows some dates entered in column B, some values with two decimal places included in column D, and some discount amounts entered with the % (percent sign) in column E.

E14	▼	:	×	✓	fx	10%	

⊿	A	B	C	D	E	F
1	Order Summary					
2	Operator:	name@example.com				
3						
4	Order #	Date	Customer	Total	Disc. %	
5	1	6/20/2023	Ryan	99.99	15%	
6	2	6/20/2023	Miller	129.99	10%	
7	3	6/24/2023	Smith	80.95	10%	
8	4	6/28/2023	Acton	65.25	5%	
9	5	6/29/2023	Ryan	349.58	15%	
10	6	6/29/2023	Casper	79.99	5%	
11	7	6/30/2023	Smith	58.75	10%	
12	8	6/30/2023	Phillips	275.89	5%	
13	9	6/30/2023	Yelton	105.75	5%	
14	10	7/1/2023	Miller	79.99	10%	
15						

1.12 The way you type some number entries helps Excel apply a number format automatically.

Caution

When a number format has been applied to a cell, even by typing as just described, the cell keeps that number format even if you later delete the cell contents. This may lead to unexpected results if you need to type a number that needs a different format later, so you'd need to clear the cell formatting or apply another number format as described in Chapter 6.

25

Adding Slide Content in PowerPoint

PowerPoint uses a third arrangement or method to add and organize content in each page or slide in a presentation. Each slide uses a *slide layout* that establishes where the main slide contents appear through predefined *placeholders*. Some placeholders just prompt you to enter text, while content placeholders enable you to add either a bulleted list of text or an object such as a table, chart, picture graphic, and more to the slide. Another type of content placeholder limits you to inserting a picture. Figure 1.13 shows a slide that uses the Title and Content slide layout. I've added a title into the title placeholder, while the content placeholder shows the icons that can be used to add one type of object to the slide.

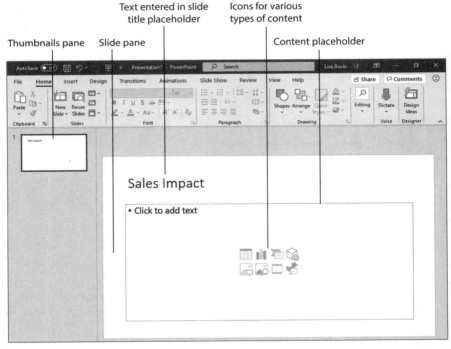

1.13 Add content to placeholders in PowerPoint.

To add text in a title or other text placeholder, click in the placeholder and type, and then click outside the placeholder. To type a bulleted list in a content placeholder, click in the placeholder, type bullet text, and press Enter to add the next bullet. Press Tab and Shift+Tab to change the bullet levels. Once you've added all the needed bullets, click outside the placeholder to finish.

Once you add more than one slide to a presentation, you can use the PgDn and PgUp keys to move between slides. In the default Normal view, you can move between slides by clicking the thumbnail for the desired slide in the Thumbnails pane at the left. (Some other views also enable you to navigate between slides by clicking thumbnails.)

Chapter 5 provides the detailed discussion of adding slides, using slide layouts, and adding various types of content in a content placeholder.

Making and Working with Selections

You've already seen how to move around in the different types of files so that you can add content or make small changes. For other operations, such as when you want to copy or move data or work with data formatting and layout, you will usually need to make larger selections, and you have your choice of using the mouse, the keyboard, or a combination of the two. Let's run through how to do that next.

Selecting content in Word

As usual, making selections is easiest in Word. OK, and Outlook messages, too. To make a selection of any set of content, just drag diagonally over it with the mouse. When you release the mouse button, selection highlighting identifies the selection. You also can click to place the insertion point at the beginning of the text to select, and then Shift+click the end of the area to select. Double-clicking a word selects it, Ctrl+clicking a sentence selects it, and triple-clicking selects the whole paragraph.

Caution

This brings up one of my biggest tech writing pet peeves. Some tech content uses the term "click and drag" rather than just drag. By definition "click" means to press and release the mouse button, while "drag" means to press and hold the mouse button while moving the mouse, so a "click and drag" action isn't really possible. To make selections, just drag, please.

If you move the mouse pointer in the margin area to the left of the text, the mouse pointer changes to a white arrow that tilts to the right. When this arrow appears, clicking it once selects the line of text that's to the right beside it. Double-clicking selects the paragraph that's to the right. Triple-clicking selects the whole document.

The keyboard shortcut Ctrl+A also selects the entire document. You also can press and hold the Shift key plus any of the arrow keys to start and expand a selection in the direction of the arrow. To use the mouse and keyboard together, click or use an arrow key to move the insertion point to the beginning of the selection, then Shift+click the end of the selection. You also can select a noncontiguous selection. This is a selection that basically includes two or more selected areas with space in between them, meaning they are nonadjacent. Select the first area using any technique; then press and hold the Ctrl key while dragging to select additional areas as needed.

Click in the document away from a selection to deselect it.

Selecting content in Excel

Any selection you make beyond a single cell in Excel is considered a range. A *range* encompasses a rectangular group of cells, such as multiple cells holding sales data down a column or across a row. A range also can include multiple columns or rows of information. The *address* or *reference* for a range includes the address for its upper-left cell, a : (colon), and the address for its lower-right cell, as in F10:H25. If you refer to Figure 1.12, the range D5:D14 holds the Total amount for each order. The range A7:E7 holds the information for Order 3. And the range A4:E14 holds all the order information, including the labels or headers identifying each column of data.

Selecting a range

Most users prefer to use a mouse to make selections in Excel. Just drag diagonally over the range to select it. The bold selection border or cell selector expands accordingly, and shading appears over all the cells within the border. Alternatively, you can click the upper-left cell and then Shift+click the lower-right cell. Figure 1.14 shows an example, with the range of order numbers and dates in cells A5:B14 selected.

If you're out in the field with your laptop, you may not have a mouse with you and may be stuck using the trackpad. I admit it, when it comes to making Excel range selections, I'm pretty trackpad incompetent, so I tend to switch to using keyboard shortcuts to make range selections. Using the keyboard is also more efficient when the range you need to select is wider or taller than the area that can show on-screen at once. Just select the upper-left cell for the range using the method of your choice, and then press and hold the Shift key while using the right and down arrow keys to expand the selection as needed.

| A5 | ▼ | : | ✕ | ✓ | fx | 1 |

◢	A	B	C	D	E	F
1	Order Summary					
2	Operator:	name@example.com				
3						
4	Order #	Date	Customer	Total	Disc. %	
5	1	6/20/2023	Ryan	99.99	15%	
6	2	6/20/2023	Miller	129.99	10%	
7	3	6/24/2023	Smith	80.95	10%	
8	4	6/28/2023	Acton	65.25	5%	
9	5	6/29/2023	Ryan	349.58	15%	
10	6	6/29/2023	Casper	79.99	5%	
11	7	6/30/2023	Smith	58.75	10%	
12	8	6/30/2023	Phillips	275.89	5%	
13	9	6/30/2023	Yelton	105.75	5%	
14	10	7/1/2023	Miller	79.99	10%	
15						

1.14 Range A5:B14 is selected.

If you know the range address for the range you want to select, click in the Name box, type the range address, and press Enter. For example, you could type **B2:C7** in the Name box and press Enter to select the range B2:C7.

As in Word, you can select a noncontiguous selection. Select the first range as needed, and then press and hold the Ctrl key while dragging over an additional range or ranges to add with the mouse.

To deselect a range (including a selected row or column), click any cell on the sheet.

Selecting a row or column

You might select an entire row that contains column labels to apply identical font formatting to all the cells, or you might select an entire column when you want to adjust the column width or fill with a different background color. You also can select multiple rows or columns when needed. To select one or more rows or columns, follow these steps:

1. **Move the mouse pointer over the row or column header for the (first) row or column to select, until the mouse pointer changes to a black right arrow or down arrow.** (See Figure 1.15.)

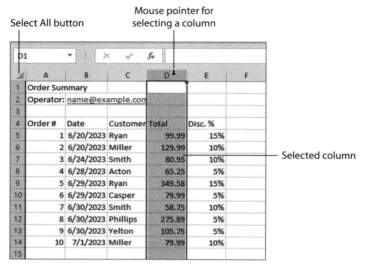

1.15 You can select one or more rows or columns.

2. **Perform one of the following actions:**

   ◉ **Click the header for the row or column to select it.**

   ◉ **Drag down to select multiple rows or right to select multiple columns.**

Genius

If you want to select all cells in a worksheet, such as to adjust the formatting for all the cells, click the Select All button. It's in the upper-left corner of the sheet where the row and column headers intersect and has a triangle on it that points to the sheet cells (see Figure 1.15). You also can press Ctrl+A to select all the cells. Depending on the sheet contents, sometimes you need to press Ctrl+A twice to select absolutely every cell.

Selecting content in PowerPoint

PowerPoint in some ways is the trickiest app when it comes to making selections, because the slide placeholders add another selection "layer" to navigate. The first layer, clicking the box around the slide placeholder, selects the placeholder itself. This enables you to perform actions that apply to the placeholder itself, including adding a fill color or design style and, in some cases, changing the font for all the text in the placeholder.

The second layer of selection in PowerPoint means selecting the placeholder content itself. For example, if you click within the text in a placeholder, you can use the same selection techniques covered earlier for Word to select all or part of the placeholder text to make changes such as formatting and edits. For other types of placeholder content, you might select the placeholder and then click an individual item, such as the legend in a chart.

Click a blank or empty area of the slide to deselect the placeholder and/or its contents.

Copying or moving a selection

The ability to copy or move existing content in an app means you don't have to retype and reformat new content. As easily as you can pick up and move a pen on your desk, you can copy or move a selection from one spot to another in an app, or even between apps in many instances. The method you use to make the copy or move depends somewhat on location.

If you just need to copy the information or move it on the current page, sheet, slide placeholder, or email message within an area that's visible on-screen, drag-and-drop editing with the mouse works well. In Word, PowerPoint, or Outlook, select the text to move on a page or in the placeholder or message window. Point to the selection with the mouse, drag it to the desired new location, and then release the mouse button to drop it into place. As you drag, the mouse pointer changes to include a rectangle, as shown in Figure 1.16, and a black vertical bar appears to show the destination spot for the moved material. In Excel, select the cell or range to move, and then point to the selection border so that the mouse pointer changes to include a black four-headed arrow. To move the selected cell or range, just drag it to the new location. To copy the selection or range, press and hold the Ctrl key while dragging so that the mouse pointer changes again to include a small plus sign, and then drag until the copy of the selection or range reaches the destination you want.

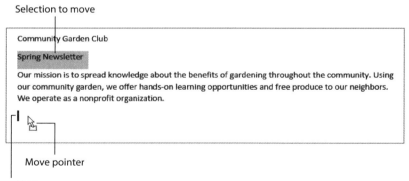

Selection to move

Community Garden Club

Spring Newsletter

Our mission is to spread knowledge about the benefits of gardening throughout the community. Using our community garden, we offer hands-on learning opportunities and free produce to our neighbors. We operate as a nonprofit organization.

Move pointer

Vertical bar

1.16 Using the mouse works well when copying or moving a selection within the visible area.

Moving or copying with the mouse becomes impractical for distances beyond the current Word or Excel screen, because Word tends to hang up and not scroll when you try to drag down to another page and Excel tends to scroll too quickly or sometimes jump by a full screen at a time. PowerPoint doesn't let you use the mouse at all to move or copy material between slides. And using the mouse to copy between Excel sheets or different app files is an obvious no-go unless you want to spend a lot of time resizing and positioning windows. In these scenarios, you should use the Copy, Cut, and Paste commands, as explained in these steps:

1. **Select the content to copy or move.**

2. **Choose Home → Clipboard → Copy to copy the selection or Home → Clipboard → Cut to move the selection.** You use the Cut command when moving the selection because you want to remove it from its original location.

3. **Navigate to the new location for the copied or cut information, whether elsewhere in the file, on another Excel sheet or PowerPoint slide, or in another file.**

4. **Click to position the insertion point in the document page or slide placeholder, or click the upper-left cell in the range where you want to place the copied or cut selection.**

5. **Choose Home → Clipboard → Paste.** Be sure to click the top or main part of the Paste button. The copied or cut selection appears in the new location.

Caution

When you paste in a workbook file, Excel will replace existing contents in the destination location. Make sure that when you click a cell in Step 4, there's a range of empty cells below and to the right that's big enough to hold the selection you made in Step 1. In the other apps, content is replaced only if you select the content before pasting.

Purists maintain that using a mouse to choose commands slows you down because you have to take your hand off the keyboard. In case you subscribe to that opinion, as I tend to because I type a lot, the keyboard shortcuts for the Copy, Cut, and Paste commands are Ctrl+C, Ctrl+X, and Ctrl+V. These three keyboard shortcuts work in Windows and most Windows programs.

Genius

The Clipboard is a memory holding area that Windows uses when you copy or paste information. Microsoft 365 has an expanded Clipboard that holds up to 24 items that you've copied during your current work session. Click the dialog box launcher in the Clipboard group of the Home tab to open the Clipboard pane, and then double-click a copied item to insert it at or near the insertion point, at the active sheet cell, or in a placeholder, as applicable.

Using Undo and Redo

As you begin to make changes in your files, you may have the occasional "Darn! I didn't mean to do that" moment. Lucky for you, the apps have Undo. When you've made a change that you decide you don't want, click the Undo button (with the left-swooping arrow) on the QAT or press Ctrl+Z. After you've undone at least one action, the button for Undo's pal Redo also becomes active on the QAT. You can click it or press Ctrl+Y to redo the change that you just undid.

Undo tracks all actions you take during the current work session, which can be dozens. If you want to backtrack and undo numerous actions, click the Undo button's drop-down list arrow, move the mouse pointer over the oldest action to undo, and then click the action. This undoes that action as well as all the others above it in the undo history. The Redo button's drop-down list works the same when you want to redo multiple actions that you've undone.

Refining Your Content

We all make typing mistakes, and some of us routinely mistype the same word over and over, almost like an unfixable glitch in the brain's typing circuitry. And there are some of us who just have more training in grammar and punctuation than others. Microsoft 365 offers many tools to help you clean up content glitches so that your documents reflect well on you.

Note

In addition to the tools described in this section, the Review tab in Word, Excel, PowerPoint, and an Outlook message window include other choices for refining your text, such as using the Thesaurus to choose another word or translation capabilities.

Spell checking your work

You may have noticed that in Word, PowerPoint, and an Outlook email message body, wavy red underlines sometimes appear under words. This means that the word doesn't appear in the dictionary and is likely misspelled. In such a case, you can right-click a word with a wavy underline and choose a suggested correction from the menu that appears. Word also flags possible grammar errors with double-blue underlines, which you can right-click and then choose a suggested fix.

In Excel, you have to check spelling manually. It's a great practice to run a manual spell check in PowerPoint or an Outlook message, too, just to enhance the professionalism of your communications. Follow these steps to run a spelling check in one of those three apps:

1. **Select a single cell or a range of cells to check in Excel, or specific text to check in PowerPoint or the Outlook message.** When you select a single cell in Excel, the spelling check feature checks the whole sheet. If you don't make a selection in the other two apps, the spelling check feature checks the entire contents of the file or message. Otherwise, the spelling check reviews only the selected content.

2. **Choose Review → Proofing → Spelling (Review → Proofing → Spelling & Grammar in Outlook) or press F7.** If an error is found, the Spelling dialog box opens in Excel. In Outlook, the dialog box is called Spelling and Grammar, and in PowerPoint, the Spelling pane opens at the right.

3. **Click the desired fix in the Suggestions list and then click either Change or Change All.** You also can use other buttons to ignore the spelling, add the spelling to the dictionary, and more. Repeat changing and/or ignoring words that the spelling feature flags as needed.

4. **If you see a message box asking whether to continue from the beginning of the file or message, click Yes.** If you made a selection in Step 1, you also may see a message asking if you want to check the rest of the document. Respond as desired.

5. **Click OK in the message box telling you the spell check is complete, if it appears.**

Caution

You might find that the AutoCorrect feature automatically "fixes" some entries that aren't typos. You can edit the entry to avoid unwanted corrections. Choose File → Options, click Proofing at the left side of the app's Options dialog box, and then click AutoCorrect Options to adjust these corrections. In Outlook, choose File → Options, click Mail at the left, click the Spelling and Autocorrect button, and then click AutoCorrect Options.

Word offers a completely new tool for reviewing document contents called the Editor. It suggests spelling and grammar corrections, as well as ways to improve factors such as text clarity and vocabulary. You can open the Editor pane by choosing Home → Editor → Editor, by choosing Review → Proofing → Editor, or by pressing F7. The Editor pane opens at the right, as shown in Figure 1.17.

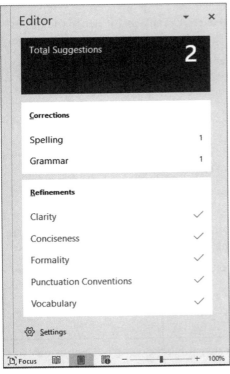

1.17 Word's Editor suggests corrections and refinements.

When a number appears to the right of one of the items listed under Corrections or Refinements rather than a green check mark, click the item in the pane to see and select specific suggestions. Click the right arrow (back) button at the upper left to return to the main Editor pane, and click the Close (X) button in the upper-right corner of the pane when you've finished using the Editor. If a message box saying that you've finished reviewing the Editor's suggestions appears, click OK.

Using Find and Replace

You might need to change entries throughout a file, such as when you learn you've misspelled a product name. In a case like this, the Find and Replace feature is your friend. You've probably performed a find and replace operation in another word processing program, so here's a refresher of the basic steps to run through a find or replace in the Microsoft 365 apps:

1. **Press Ctrl+F to start a find and Ctrl+H to start a replace.** The ribbon commands for Find and Replace vary from app to app, so if you want to know them, here goes:

   - **Word.** Home → Editing → Replace, and then use either the Find or Replace tab. In Word, Ctrl+F and the Find command open the Navigation pane, which you can use to perform a find and then click matches to display and select.

   - **Excel.** Home → Editing → Find & Select → Find or Home → Editing → Find & Select → Replace.

   - **PowerPoint.** Home → Editing → Find or Home → Editing → Replace. PowerPoint uses a separate Find dialog box and a separate Replace dialog box.

   - **Outlook message.** Format Text → Editing → Find or Format Text → Editing → Replace.

2. **Enter the word, phrase, or value to find in the Find What text box, and if you're replacing it, enter the replacement information in the Replace With text box.**

3. **Use the Find Next or Replace buttons to review or replace entries one by one.**

4. **Click Close.**

Genius

Most dialog boxes are *modal*, meaning while the dialog box is on-screen, you can only work in the dialog box. The Find and Replace dialog box, in contrast, is *nonmodal* or *modeless*. This means that while the dialog box is open, you can click in the file and make changes, such as if you see a typo after clicking the Find Next button, and then click anywhere in the dialog box to return to using it.

Saving and Closing a File

You can save your file and give it a unique name any time after you create the blank file or create a new file from a template. This is your opportunity to establish an orderly system for naming files, just as you should use an orderly system for naming and organizing folders. After all, how are you going to find your work later if you can't navigate to the right folder and don't know what you named the file? For example, if you work with a variety of clients, you could create a folder for each client using File Explorer in Windows 10. Then each file for a particular client could start with a project number and include the client name and year and month, as in *0123 BestClient 2023-06.*

From there, saving a file will seem similar to the process of opening a file covered earlier in this chapter. Follow these steps:

1. **Choose File ➔ Save As.** (You also can choose File ➔ Save the first time you save a file.) The Save As screen that appears again gives you the option of working with recently used folders or working with the other save locations. Again, I'm going to stick with the traditional method of using the Save As dialog box. Feel free to explore other methods the screen presents on your own. As noted earlier in the chapter, you can save an email message when selected either in the main Outlook screen or in an open message window. Starting the save opens the Save As dialog box immediately, so you can skip to Step 3.

2. **Toward the middle, under Other Locations, click Browse.** Because the default save location is the Documents folder for your Windows 10 user account, the address that initially appears at the top of the Save As dialog box reads This PC > Documents >.

3. **Use the Navigation pane and file list to navigate to the folder where you want to save the file.**

4. **Edit the name in the File Name text box as desired**. Figure 1.18 shows the Save As dialog box.

5. **Click Save.**

To resave a file as you periodically add data or make changes, choose File ➔ Save, click the Save button on the QAT, or press Ctrl+S. After saving the file, you can choose File ➔ Close to close the file without exiting the app, assuming you have finished working with the file.

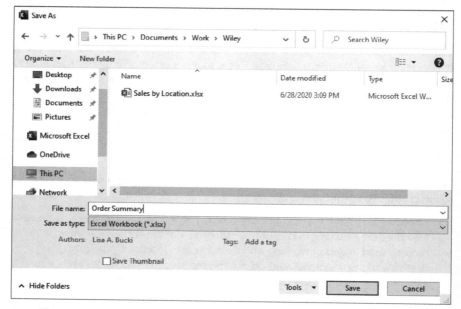

1.18 Files have generic numbered names until you rename them.

Another Way to Save

When you save a new file for the first time, clicking the Save button on the QAT or pressing Ctrl+S works a bit differently than the File ➔ Save or Save As command. A Save This File window opens. You can enter a name in the File Name text box and then choose a default or recently used location from the Choose a Location drop-down list. (For at least one of my Microsoft 365 accounts, the default location listed is OneDrive in this list.) After choosing a location, click the Save button. This can be a good way to save new files if you frequently save to the default location or one or two other folders.

How Do I Develop Document Content in Word?

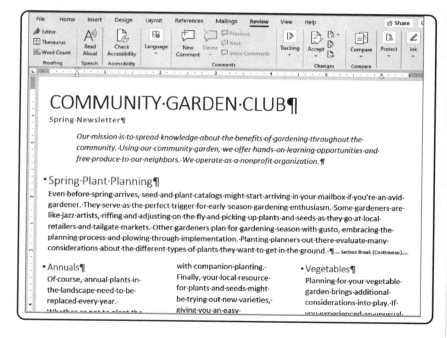

1 2 3 4 5 6 7 8 9 10 11

If you write infrequently, a blank Word document screen can feel as daunting as a blank piece of paper. How do you start? What if your written thoughts have errors or seem out of order? Word makes writing a more flexible, forgiving process than writing on paper. This chapter shows you how to use outlining and editing to get your words in order. From there it covers presenting information effectively in bulleted and numbered lists, tabbed and indented paragraphs, pages, sections, and columns. The chapter finishes with a look at review and reference tools that can help you improve your writing.

Using Outlining to Organize Your Thoughts

For shorter documents like letters, many of us are familiar with the convention of typing the date, recipient's address, greeting, body, and closing. Flyers, invitations, cards, and other short documents also seem familiar and accessible. But longer documents such as reports, contracts, marketing plans, newsletters, and even book chapters (!) need more structure. Including *headings* to organize and identify different parts of a long document not only helps the reader but also may be required by various writing style guides or common practice within an organization or profession.

Usually, each heading is a brief phrase in its own paragraph in the document. To use the proper method for defining headings in a document, you use the heading styles Heading 1, Heading 2, and so on to define the outline levels in the document. (Chapter 6 discusses styles in more depth.) While you can apply a heading style in Print Layout view by clicking in a heading paragraph and then choosing the desired style in the Styles gallery in the Styles group of the ribbon's Home tab, not only does working in the Outline view make it easier to apply heading levels, but you can also see the document outline even if you've already added some body text.

Note

Word typically doesn't show all nine heading styles in the Styles gallery of the Styles group on the Home tab, because most documents need only two or three heading levels. If you need to see more heading styles, click the Styles group dialog box launcher to open the Styles pane. Click the Options button, open the Select Styles to Show list, and choose All Styles. You can then see and apply additional heading styles in the Styles pane.

Choose View ➜ Views ➜ Outline to change to Outline view. You'll notice immediately that a style area appears to the left to identify the style applied to each paragraph and that an Outlining tab appears. If the document already includes other text, click to position the insertion point where you want the first header to appear, press Enter, and then click back in the paragraph. Then in the Outline Tools group of the Outlining tab, open the Outline Level drop-down list and click Level 1. (Alternatively, you could click the Home tab, open the Styles gallery if needed, and then click the Heading 1 style in the Styles gallery.) Note that the numbered outline levels in the Outlining tab correspond to the heading style numbers so that the style area will show the Heading 1 style for the heading you just created. To display the style area, choose File ➜ Options. Click Advanced at the left, scroll down to the Display section, change the entry in the Style area pane width in Draft and Outline Views text box to something like 1 (for 1 inch), and then click OK.

From there, it's even easier to build the outline. If you click at the end of the first Heading 1 heading and press Enter, Word automatically assumes you want the next paragraph to be another Heading 1/Level 1 heading. From there, you can just type additional headings for the document, pressing Enter at the end of each one. After you press Enter, you can either use the Outline Level drop-down list to change the level or press Tab to indent or demote the heading to the next level down, such as going from Level 1 to Level 2. Pressing Shift+Tab outdents or promotes the heading to the next level higher, such as going from Level 2 to Level 1. You also can use the buttons to the left and right of the Outline Level drop-down list to promote or demote headings as you build the outline. Figure 2.1 shows a short in-progress outline and the tools on the Outlining tab.

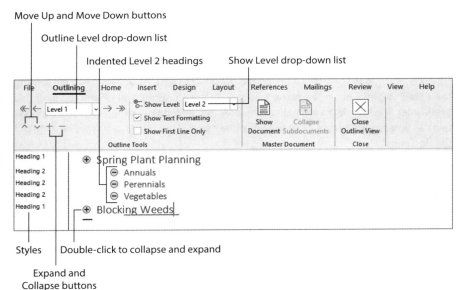

2.1 Word's Outline view and Outlining tab make it easy to outline and reorganize a document based on styled heading levels.

If you rethink the location of one or more headings, you can make a selection and either drag it to a new location or use Cut and Paste, as you learned in Chapter 1. The Outline Tools group also has Move Up (Alt+Shift+up arrow) and Move Down (Alt+Shift+down arrow) buttons. When the small circle to the left of a heading has a plus in it, that means that the heading has content within it. Move the mouse pointer over the circle until the pointer changes to a four-headed black arrow, and then double-click to collapse (hide) or expand (redisplay) the contents under the heading. You also can use the Expand and Collapse buttons in the Outline Tools group to expand and collapse a single heading. To expand or collapse the entire outline, choose a heading level from the Show Level drop-down list in the Outline Tools group. Choosing All Levels at the bottom of that drop-down list expands the document to redisplay all of its contents, including regular text.

Caution

Be sure you collapse the contents of a heading at any level before moving it up or down in the outline. This ensures the heading's contents—whether lower-level subheadings, body text, or something else—move along with it. If the heading is not collapsed, moving it in the outline moves only the heading and not the contents.

When you finish working on your outline, you can choose Outlining → Close → Close Outline View to change back to Print Layout view and redisplay the document's entire contents. You can then further work on the document's text. If the document file is using the default Normal.dotm template, you can click at the right end of any heading and press Enter. The template automatically applies the default Normal style (for regular body text), so you can just start typing to add content below the heading, further fleshing out the document.

Genius

Developing a document outline or hierarchy first is considered a top-down method of planning. When you map out a document's contents in advance, it can make your writing more efficient, focused, and complete. That said, some writers resist being "constrained" by an outline. As with any other good habit, after you give outlining a chance for more documents, developing an outline first will feel more natural.

More on Navigating, Selecting, and Editing in Word

It's rare for me to create a great document on the first try. Maybe I used inelegant phrasing, left out a few important points, or just ran out of steam at the end of the day and needed to revisit the work later. Thankfully, Word lets me edit a document as many times as I need to, until I'm satisfied with the product.

You can edit a document immediately after creating it or reopen a document. When you reopen a document you've worked on, a Welcome Back! pop-up prompt like the one shown in Figure 2.2 may appear and then resize to a smaller prompt with a bookmark icon in it. Click the pop-up to scroll the document and

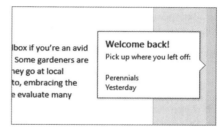

lbox if you're an avid
Some gardeners are
hey go at local
to, embracing the
e evaluate many

Welcome back!
Pick up where you left off:

Perennials
Yesterday

2.2 When you reopen a document, Word prompts you to return to the location of your last edit.

position the insertion point where you made your last edit before saving and closing the document. I've found that this feature—sometimes called *resume reading*—seems to work primarily on documents with more than one page that I've saved during a prior day, but sometimes it works if I exit and restart Word and then reopen the document.

Depending on what you're doing in Word, sometimes the vertical scroll bar automatically hides itself. If you don't see the scroll bar and need to use it to move around, move the mouse pointer over to the right edge of the screen, and it will reappear. When you drag the scroll box on the vertical scroll bar, a ScreenTip appears to show you what page you've scrolled to. When the ScreenTip shows the page number you want, release the mouse button and then click on the page to position the insertion point there.

Genius

Having the right screen zoom also makes editing less of a strain. I like to choose View ➔ Zoom ➔ Page Width to at least fill the screen. Others prefer a zoom of 125% or more, depending on their screen resolution and other factors.

Chapter 1 explained the keyboard shortcuts for moving around in Word, along with how to add text to a document, how to make selections, and how to use copy and paste. You'll use all of those techniques when editing a document, too, but there are a couple of additional key points to know:

- **By default, new text you type is inserted at the insertion point location and pushes existing text to the right.** Make sure you position the insertion point correctly to add text at the right location.

- **If you make a selection, any text you copy or paste replaces the selected text.** This means it's a good habit to deselect text after you've finished an action such as formatting it, just to ensure that you don't accidentally delete or replace it.

Genius

Word does enable you to change these editing behaviors if they don't work for you. Choose File ➜ Options, and then click Advanced at the left side of the Word Options dialog box. Under Editing Options, you can change the Use Overtype Mode and Typing Replaces Selected Text check boxes. Change other editing behaviors in the Word Options dialog box, too, if desired, and then click OK.

There are a few more keyboard keys and shortcuts that I find come more into play when I'm editing than when I'm initially drafting text. Backspace deletes the character to the left of the insertion point, and Delete deletes the character to the right. Using the Ctrl key with these keys makes them even more powerful. Ctrl+Backspace deletes the word to the left of the insertion point, and Ctrl+Delete deletes the word to the right. Pressing Shift+F5 moves the insertion point between the most recently edited locations, although I sometimes have to press that keyboard combo a few times before it works. (Note that Word has many more keyboard shortcuts for moving around and editing than can be covered in this book. To learn more, check out the Help topic "Keyboard Shortcuts in Word.")

Another super editing shortcut is the ability to change the case of the words in a selection. Whether you've simply failed to press the Shift key to cap a word when typing it, need to change the case of material copied from another source, or want to give your headings a trendy ALL CAPS look, you can do it without retyping. Just select the word(s) or heading to change, choose Home ➜ Font ➜ Change Case as shown in Figure 2.3, and then click the capitalization style to apply. Pressing the Shift+F3 keyboard shortcut cycles through the options.

Change Case button

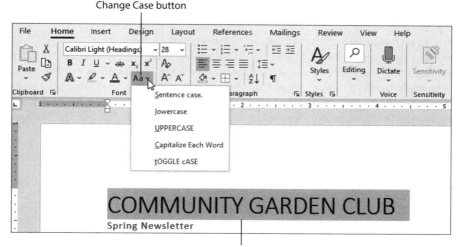

Uppercase capitalization applied

2.3 Use Change Case to apply a new capitalization style to selected text.

Creating Bulleted and Numbered Lists

If you have a set of related items that you want to set off from normal body text in a document, you can format them as a list. Word enables you to create three types of lists, which I now present to you *in* a list:

- **Bulleted.** In this type of list, each item is set off with a small symbol called a bullet. This list is a bulleted list. The default bullet style in a document using the Normal. dotm template is a black dot. The items in a bulleted list do not necessarily have to be presented in any type of hierarchy or order.

- **Numbered.** In this type of list, each item by default begins with a number identifying its position or order in the list, though you also can change to other "numbering" styles that use letters or Roman numerals. It's most common to use this type of list to present a sequence of actions or events.

- **Multilevel.** Bulleted and numbered lists by default have one level of indentation. Multilevel lists have more indent levels, as when using outlining as described in the first section of the chapter. Each list level uses a different style of bullet, numbering, or labeling, and some styles alternate between numbers and letters.

47

If you want to convert existing text to a list, each item in the list needs to be a separate paragraph, whether it's a single word or multiple sentences of text. (That is, press Enter after typing each item.) Then, select all the text to convert to the list, and then click the Bullets, Numbering, or Multilevel List button in the Paragraph group of the Home tab (Figure 2.4). Word automatically adds tabs and indentations to the list paragraphs as needed, along with the bullets and/or numbering. For a multilevel list, you then need to take the additional step of clicking at the beginning of list items and pressing Tab as needed to indent or demote the items one or more levels. As when outlining, Shift+Tab outdents or promotes items in the list. Lists work similarly in PowerPoint content placeholders.

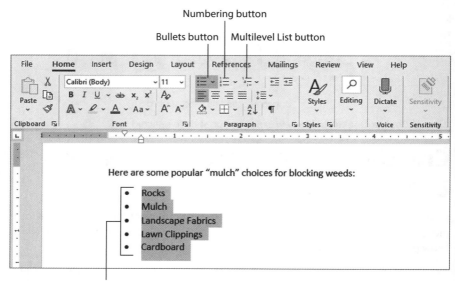

2.4 Use these Paragraph group choices to create simple lists in Word.

You also can create a bulleted, numbered, or multilevel list while typing. After you press Enter to finish the previous paragraph, click the button for the desired type of list in the Home tab, and then type each list item, pressing Enter after each. Use Tab and Shift+Tab as needed before typing a multilevel list item to change the list level. Word automatically adds a bullet, number, or other label as needed to the beginning of each item as you go. To finish the list, press Enter twice after the last list item.

Word's AutoFormat As You Type feature also enables you to create a basic bulleted or numbered list by typing. These are called automatic lists. Start by typing ***** (an asterisk) and pressing Tab, or a **1.** (with or without the period) and pressing Tab. Word immediately converts the * to a bullet symbol in the case of a bulleted list. Type the first list item, and press Enter. Add additional list items as needed, and then press Enter twice to finish creating the list.

You can change the bullet or number style after you create and select a list or before you start typing it in. To do so, click the drop-down list arrow for the Bullets, Numbering, or Multilevel List button in the Paragraph group of the Home tab (see Figure 2.5), and then click the new style to use. Note that each of the three galleries includes a Define choice for creating a custom bullet, number format, or multilevel list.

Chapter 8 covers how to create more advanced types of lists in the Microsoft 365 apps.

2.5 You also can choose another bullet or number style.

Working with Tabs and Indent Settings

While I've emphasized the ease with which you can just stick with basic typing and create a perfectly fine document, some situations call for a different arrangement. For example, sometimes you need to align separate words or entries on multiple lines, as in a price listing. Certain writing styles and document types also call for indentation in specific situations, such as to set off the beginning of a paragraph. In many journalistic styles, the first paragraph in a story or article may not be indented, while subsequent paragraphs are. This section covers how to use tabs and indents to align paragraph content. Chapter 6 covers how to adjust line spacing as needed, which is another paragraph setting.

Note

Some of the tab and indent techniques covered next require the horizontal ruler. If you don't see it, choose View ➔ Show ➔ Ruler to display it. You also can toggle the display of formatting marks such as tab, space, and paragraph marks by choosing Home ➔ Paragraph ➔ Show/Hide or pressing Ctrl+* (asterisk).

Setting tab stops

Word has left *tab stops* every .5" from left to right by default. That means each time you press the Tab key, the insertion point moves .5" farther right on the current line. But there are instances where you may want to set your own tabs to create a custom alignment for information you type. You can create five types of tabs in a document:

- **Left.** Lines up the left side of text at the tab stop.
- **Center.** Centers text on the tab stop.
- **Right.** Lines up the right side of the text at the tab stop.
- **Decimal.** Aligns the decimal points in numeric values on the tab stop.
- **Bar.** Places a vertical bar at the tab stop to create a visual break.

A tab stop also can include a *leader*, which is a dotted, dashed, or underscored line before the tab stop (and usually used after another tab stop to the left) to help with visual tracking along the row. Follow these steps to set and use tab stops:

1. **At the location where you want to insert the text that will use the tab stops, press Enter twice and then press the up arrow once.** This ensures that the tab stops will start at the blank paragraph, while the blank paragraph below will still use the default tab stops. Alternately, you could select some paragraphs of text where you've already entered tabbed content and use this process to apply custom tabs instead.

2. **Click the dialog box launcher in the Paragraph group of the Home tab and then click the Tabs button.** The Tabs dialog box shown in Figure 2.6 opens. Note that you also can just double-click the horizontal ruler to open the dialog box, but because that also tends to add a perhaps unwanted tab stop, I usually stick with using the dialog box launcher.

3. **Type a measurement for the horizontal position of the tab stop in the Tab Stop Position text box near the top of the dialog box.** Enter the measurements in inches by default, including decimal values such as .25 or .5 if needed. Enter the value only, without any inches symbol.

Change tab type

Indent markers

Show/Hide button

2.25" Decimal tab stop

1" Left tab stop

3.5" Center tab stop

4.5" Right tab stop

Right indent marker

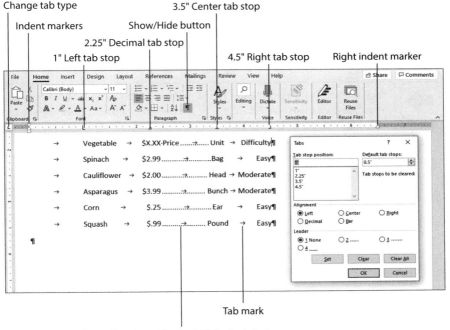

Tab mark

Dotted leader set for the 3.5" Center tab stop

2.6 You can use the Tabs dialog box or the ruler to set tabs.

4. **Click an option under Alignment.** Your choice specifies the tab stop type.

5. **Click an option under Leader if needed.**

6. **Click Set.** This sets the first tab stop.

7. **Repeat Steps 3 through 6 to set additional tab stops.**

8. **Click OK to finish setting tab stops and close the dialog box.**

51

9. **Type a line of text, pressing the Tab key as needed to move between tab stops and pressing Enter at the end of the line.** When you press Enter, Word creates a new paragraph that already has your custom tab stops applied, so you can simply repeat the process to add additional lines (paragraphs) of text using the custom tab stops.

10. **When you've finished adding all the lines, click the empty paragraph below the text with the custom tab stops.** The blank paragraph will have the default tab stops, ready for typing as usual or a change to other custom tab stop settings for subsequent document text.

Note

You can select a tab stop in the Tab Stop Position list of the Tabs dialog box and then click Clear (see Figure 2.6) to remove it from the currently selected paragraph(s). Clicking Clear All removes all of the custom tab stops in the currently selected paragraph(s).

For simplicity, Figure 2.6 shows already set tab stops and has formatting marks displayed so that you can see where I pressed the Tab key to align the example text and decimal values to the custom tabs stops. It also shows the markers that appear on the run for four of five different types of tab stops.

You also can use the ruler to set and remove tab stops for a paragraph. To set a tab stop, click the box at the left end of the ruler that shows a left tab by default until you see the type of tab that you want to apply. Then click the bottom part of the ruler at the location where you want to set the new tab stop. To remove a tab stop, drag it off the ruler.

Note

When setting tab stops or indents for a single paragraph, you can just click in the paragraph. It's not necessary to select the entire paragraph.

Setting indents

Indentation or *indent* refers to extra space between the paragraph and the left or right margin. If you press Tab at the beginning of a paragraph, AutoFormat As You Type creates an indent rather than a tab stop. The type of indent created, a first line indent, is one of two types of special indents you can create. The other is a hanging indent, where the first line is not indented, but the rest of the paragraph is. Bulleted and numbered lists with multiline paragraphs have hanging indents by default.

You also can set a left or right indent for all the lines in the paragraph. For example, if you're including a long quotation in a formal document, by convention you should include the quotation in its own paragraph and indent it .5" from both the left and right margins.

Follow these steps to create indents for one or more selected paragraphs:

1. **Click the dialog box launcher in the Paragraph group of the Home tab.** This opens the Paragraph dialog box, with the Indents and Spacing tab selected by default. Figure 2.7 shows this dialog box.

Left and Right indent values entered

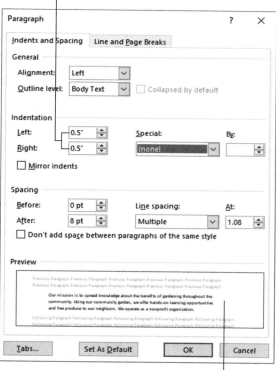

Preview of the indents

2.7 Create indents to set a paragraph off from the left or right margin (or both).

2. **Specify the desired settings under Indentation.** You can apply different types of indentation as follows and can apply any combination of the three types:

- **Enter a value in the Left text box to apply a left indent to all lines in the paragraph.**

- **Enter a value in the Right text box to apply a right indent to all the lines in the paragraph.**

- **Choose an indent type from the Special drop-down list and then enter the desired amount of indentation in the accompanying By text box.**

3. **Click OK to finish.**

As for tabs, you can use the ruler to adjust existing indents or apply new ones. Drag the indent markers near the left end of the horizontal ruler (refer to Figure 2.6) to set and adjust indents along the left side of the selected paragraph. The white square marker at the bottom controls the left indent, the top white down arrow controls the first line indent, and the bottom white up arrow controls the hanging indent (and drags the left indent marker with it when you move it). If you refer back to Figure 2.4, you can see how the indent markers near the left end of the ruler correspond with the appearance of the hanging indents in the bulleted paragraphs. The second white up arrow marker that sits on the bottom edge of the ruler nearer the right margin controls the right indent for the paragraph.

Working with Line, Page, and Section Breaks

When Word wraps the text at the end of the line for you and creates a new line in the paragraph, that's known as a *soft return*. (Chapter 1 explained that pressing Enter creates a new paragraph, also called a *hard return*.) Similarly, a page break created by Word is a *soft page break*. You will inevitably reach a point in your document creation journey where you need to take control and determine where a line or page breaks yourself. For example, if a two-line heading breaks at an awkward place, you could use a *soft return* at a better location. You might need to create a *hard page break* to make sure that the next heading appears at the top of the next page if too little of that section would appear at the bottom of the current page.

To insert a soft return at the insertion point while typing or editing, press Shift+Enter. This kicks the next line of the paragraph's text back to the left margin or left indent so that you can continue typing the paragraph. If you have formatting marks displayed, the mark for a soft return looks like a bent arrow pointing to the left. You can click at the beginning of the next line after a soft return and press Backspace to remove it.

To insert a hard page break at the insertion point when typing or editing, you can press Ctrl+Enter or choose Layout ➔ Page Setup ➔ Breaks ➔ Page. Figure 2.8 shows both the Breaks choices and the formatting mark for a hard page break. To delete a hard page break, you can click at the beginning of the next page and then press Backspace. Or, if that's not practical for some reason, such as having a table at the beginning of the next page (Chapter 8 covers tables), you can select and delete the formatting mark.

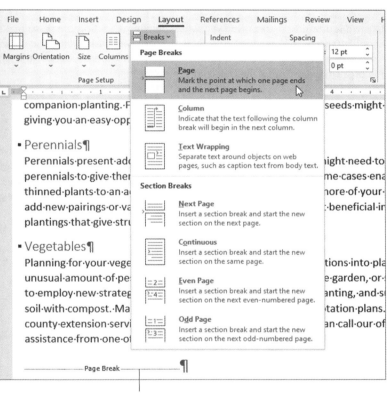

Page break formatting mark

2.8 The Layout tab enables you to insert various types of breaks in a document, including page breaks.

Section breaks strike many users as being very complicated, but they're really not once you get used to them. You create new document *sections* so that you can apply different types of formatting in each section. For example, you may want to change the header or footer contents for each section to include the section name. Or, you may need to include a page that uses a different page orientation than the rest of the pages. (Chapter 11 covers headers, footers, and orientation.) To insert a section break at the insertion point, choose Layout ➔ Page Setup ➔ Breaks, and then click the desired type of break under Section Breaks. As shown in Figure 2.8, a detailed description for each break type and a preview icon appears for each break type, so I won't repeat that information. From there, you can make the desired formatting changes within each section as needed.

You need to have formatting marks displayed when deleting a section break, so make sure you've toggled those on. A section break mark has a double dashed line, and it says Section Break with the break type in parentheses, as shown in Figure 2.9. Click to the left of the section break mark and press the Delete key to delete it.

Creating Columns of Text

Creating multiple columns of text can make certain types of documents more attractive and legible. Many of us are familiar with newspapers, magazines, newsletters, brochures, and other publications that present text in two or more columns and sometimes use different column layouts on different pages and sections. You can easily create columns for all or part of a Word document, using the following steps:

1. **Select the text that you want to format in columns.** For example, in a newsletter, you might select just the article text so that the newsletter name and issue information at the top remains as a single column. To format all the text in a document, select all of the text. Or, if you're starting a new document and want to use the same number of columns throughout, specify the number of columns immediately after creating the document.

2. **Choose Layout ➔ Page Setup ➔ Columns, and then click the desired number of columns.** Figure 2.9 shows the available Columns choices.

If you selected text before applying columns, Word inserts a section break before and after the column text. You can delete the section marks or use the Columns menu if you want to return the text to a single column. If the text breaks awkwardly between columns, position the insertion point where you'd like to insert a better break, and then choose Layout ➔ Page Setup ➔ Breaks ➔ Column (refer to Figure 2.8).

Text previously formatted in three columns   Section break mark

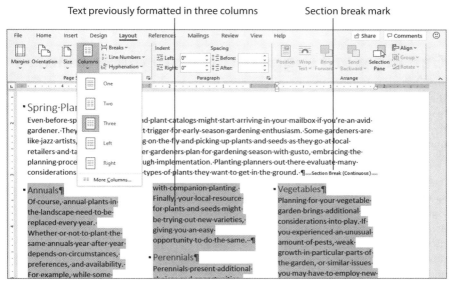

2.9 It takes only a single command to create columns in a document.

Genius

When working with page and column breaks, watch out for widows and orphans. A *widow* is a heading without any text after it or a line or two from the beginning of a paragraph on the bottom of a page or column. *Orphans* are also lines from the prior page's last paragraph that break to the top of a page or column. Fix these by inserting breaks, usually before the widow or orphan heading or paragraph.

Using Review Tools to Improve Your Writing

The Review tab rounds up numerous Word features that can help you refine a document's contents. Whether you need to discover a better word choice or comment about document information, Word offers numerous intelligent research and collaboration tools.

57

(Check out the References tab to find even more advanced choices for refining a document.) A brief introduction to some of the Review tab tools comes next.

Getting word suggestions from the Thesaurus

The Thesaurus is a tool that finds synonyms for the selected word. As a professional writer, I've leaned heavily on Word's Thesaurus feature over the years. It's stupid easy to use the Thesaurus to find a better word.

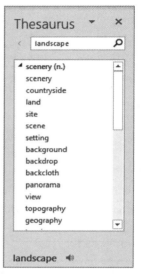

To use the Thesaurus, select the word to replace in the text. Choose Review ➔ Proofing ➔ Thesaurus. In the Thesaurus pane that opens (see Figure 2.10), scroll to review matching synonyms as needed. When you see the one you want to use, move the mouse pointer over it so that a down arrow appears at the right, click the arrow, and then click Insert. The synonym replaces the selected word in the document text. Click the pane Close (X) button when you are finished.

Tracking changes and commenting

In my experience working with numerous clients outside the world of publishing, I've found that Word's ability to track changes is one of the most underused and underappreciated features.

2.10 You can use the Thesaurus to replace a word with a better synonym.

tures. When collaborating and editing someone else's document, you should turn on the Track Changes feature as a professional courtesy at the very least so that they can readily see what you've changed rather than having to compare multiple document versions manually.

To turn on Track Changes, choose Review ➔ Tracking ➔ Track Changes. (Be sure to click the main part of the button.) Or press Ctrl+Shift+E. From there, any changes you make will be marked up in the text. By default, Track Changes marks insertions and deletions, as well as formatting changes. As shown in Figure 2.11, which is in Print Layout view, inserted text is underlined in the document, while deletions are moved to balloons in the Markup Area at the right. Formatting changes also appear in markup balloons. When you receive a document with tracked changes, you can right-click a tracked insertion in the text and choose either Accept Insertion or Reject Insertion. Likewise, right-click the balloon for a tracked deletion or formatting change, and then choose the appropriate command to accept or reject the change. You can also use the choices in the Review ➜ Changes group to navigate between and accept or reject the markup. Toggle the feature off using the same command or shortcut for toggling it on.

Comment

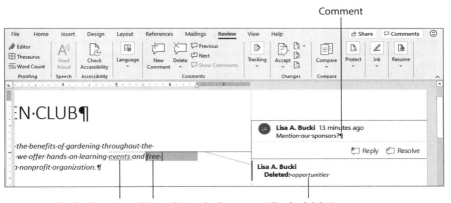

Tracked insertion   Text with attached comment   Tracked deletion

2.11 You can track changes and comment on a document.

The Comments feature enables you to ask questions or note potential changes to selected text without actually changing the text. I also like to include comments with links to online sources I've consulted while writing, especially in documents that don't require any sort of formal sourcing or source citations. To add a comment to selected text, choose Review ➜ Comments ➜ New Comment. Type the comment text, as well as pasting information such as a web page link in the comment, and then click outside the comment to finish. Figure 2.11 also shows a simple comment in a comment balloon. If you're having a back-and-forth collaboration with many versions of the document, you can reply to a comment by moving the mouse pointer over it and clicking Reply, or right-clicking it and clicking Reply To Comment. Type your reply, and then click outside the balloon. You also can click Resolve in the comment balloon if you've made requested changes or verified requested details or right-click the balloon and click Delete Comment if you no longer need the comment. Use the tools in the Comments group of the Review tab to navigate between and delete comments.

How Do I Make Changes in Excel?

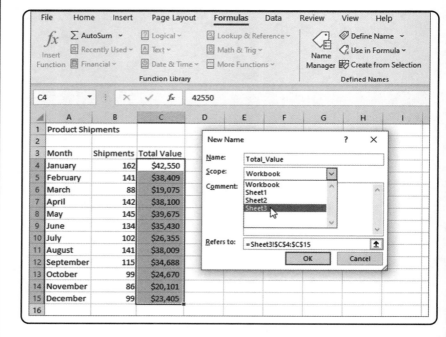

Often, your initial stab at entering information into a workbook file in a workable arrangement is just a first draft. You may need to add sheets to organize the data. Some values may have changed since you made your initial cell entries, you may need to add new data, or you may need to make a few adjustments to make navigating the sheet easier. Excel includes numerous tools to make updating and improving your sheets a breeze. In this chapter, I show you how to handle some of those cleanup tasks so your Excel content is more accurate and easier to use.

Working with Sheets

In recent versions of Excel, the default number of sheets in a new workbook file is one. Yep, one. That means if you want to expand to other sheets at all, you have to add the sheets into the workbook file. Theoretically, the number of sheets you can add and use in a given workbook file is limited only by the amount of memory in your computer. As a practical matter, unless you're a data scientist or other analyst working with a large data-set like U.S. Census data or world weather data, a typical workbook file for you might need anywhere from a handful to a dozen sheets.

Adding, renaming, and jumping to a sheet

Fortunately, you can add a new sheet to the workbook with a single click. Just click the New Sheet button to the right of the existing sheet tab(s). The new sheet appears immediately. Excel assigns generic names (Sheet1, Sheet2, and so on) as you add sheets. Renaming sheets to use more meaningful names is a good practice, particularly if you will be sharing the workbook file with other users who need to understand what sheet holds which data. Follow these steps to rename a sheet:

1. **Right-click the sheet tab.**

2. **Choose Rename from the shortcut menu.** Instead of Steps 1 and 2, you also can double-click the sheet name to select it.

3. **Type a new name to replace the generic name or any previous name you assigned to the sheet.** Figure 3.1 shows the new sheet name I typed.

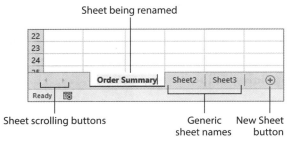

3.1 Sheets have generic numbered names until you rename them.

4. **Press Enter.**

To move from one sheet to another, click the destination sheet tab to make it the active sheet. If your workbook file has more sheets (tabs) than can display on-screen at once, the sheet scrolling (arrow) buttons to the left of the first sheet tab become active so that you can scroll the desired sheet into view using one of these techniques:

- Clicking one of the buttons scrolls one tab at a time in the direction of the button arrow.

- Ctrl+clicking either button displays the first or last sheet tab.

- Right-clicking either button opens the Activate dialog box, where you can click the name of a sheet and then click OK to display that sheet.

If you want to see more sheet tabs on-screen at a time, move the mouse pointer over the button that has three dots on it to the left of the horizontal scroll bar. When the mouse pointer changes into a pair of black horizontal arrows with two vertical lines (also known as a *split pointer*), drag to the right to make more room for tabs.

Genius

You can include multiple similar sheets in a workbook file, such as if you use the same layout to collect sales information from each quarter. After you add the sheets, click the first sheet tab, and then Shift+click the last sheet tab to group the sheets. When sheets are grouped, cell entries or formatting appear in the same locations on the other grouped sheets. (This is sometimes called working with a *3-D selection*.) When finished, right-click a grouped sheet tab and choose Ungroup Sheets.

Moving or copying a sheet

You can move a sheet to change its order among the sheet tabs. Simply use the mouse to drag the sheet tab left or right. As you're dragging, the mouse pointer changes to an arrow with a sheet on it. When the little black triangle above the tabs reaches the desired new sheet location, release the mouse button. Given that moving sheets becomes more difficult if you have to scroll the sheet tabs at all, take the desired sheet order into account when planning your workbook so that you can create your sheets in a solid order from the start.

Copying a sheet presents another opportunity to save data entry and formatting time. These steps lead the way:

1. **Right-click the sheet tab of the sheet you want to copy.**

2. **Choose Move or Copy from the shortcut menu.** The Move or Copy dialog box opens.

3. **Select the Create a Copy check box near the bottom of the dialog box to check it.**

4. **In the Before Sheet list, click the name of the sheet before which Excel should insert the sheet copy, or click (Move to End).** I often use the (Move to End) choice, as shown in Figure 3.2, to build a workbook a sheet at a time.

3.2 Copy a sheet to reuse its information.

5. **Click OK.** You also can Ctrl+drag a sheet to copy it.

Note

You can use the Move or Copy dialog box to move or copy a sheet to another open workbook file. Select the destination file from the To Book drop-down list at the top of the dialog box, and then continue with Step 3, shown previously.

Cell Editing Basics

Editing the cell entries in your workbook files is another core task because, well, typos happen and the circumstances driving data change. You might identify an error in a formula that you need to correct. Or, consider a project schedule being tracked in Excel. If a team member misses a deliverable date, then the cell holding that deliverable date must be changed.

Making changes

Fortunately, changing cell contents in Excel is as easy as typing the contents in the first place. And, Excel gives you a few options for making changes:

- **Replacing a cell entry.** To replace the contents of a cell, click the cell, type the new contents, and then press Tab or Enter.

- **Editing in the cell.** Click the cell or select it using the keyboard, and then either press F2 or double-click the cell's contents to place the insertion point in the cell. Use the keyboard keys to make changes (including arrow keys to move the insertion point, and Backspace and Delete to remove characters), and then press Enter or Tab.

- **Editing in the Formula bar.** Click the cell, and then click in the cell contents in the Formula bar using the keyboard as just described for editing in the cell. You can then press Enter or Tab or click the Enter button on the Formula bar, which appears in Figure 3.3.

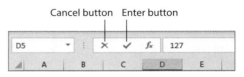

Cancel button Enter button

3.3 Click the Enter button on the Formula bar to finish editing a cell.

Note

The Formula bar also has a Cancel button, which cancels your changes to the cell. You also can use the Cancel and Enter buttons when you're making your initial entries in cells.

Clearing cell contents

You may need to delete or clear cell contents, such as when you're rearranging information on a sheet or deciding how to organize information on a new sheet. You can clear either an individual cell or a range that you've selected. Click the cell or select it with the keyboard, or select the range of cells to clear, and then perform one of these actions:

- **Press Delete, and then press Enter or Tab.** Pressing Backspace also works when you're clearing a single cell.

- Right-click the selected cell or range, and then choose Clear Contents (see Figure 3.4).

- Choose Home ➜ Editing ➜ Clear ➜ Clear Contents.

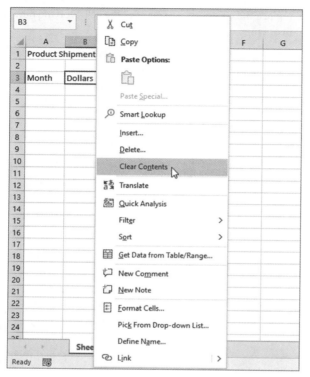

3.4 You can use a shortcut menu to clear the contents from a cell.

Caution

Clearing a cell's contents doesn't clear the formatting applied, and in the case of number formats, this can cause surprises if you need to make an entry in the cell later. The Home → Editing → Clear menu also has Clear Formats and Clear All choices for clearing more than just the cell contents.

Using Auto Fill and Filling Series

While you're free to arrange and track your information any way that you want to in Excel, there are some common conventions that people generally follow. In business, it's typical to track results by the month or quarter, for instance. Excel's Auto Fill feature can automatically enter some lists of information for you, including the following:

● **Days of the week.** *Mon, Tue, Wed. . .* or *Monday, Tuesday, Wednesday. . .*

● **Month names.** *Jan, Feb, Mar. . .* or *January, February, March. . .*

- **Quarters.** *Q1, Q2, Q3. . .* or *Qtr1, Qtr2, Qtr3. . .*

- **Other labels with a number added.** *Week 1, Week 2, Week 3. . .* or *Quintile 1, Quintile 2, Quintile 3. . .*

Caution

For the first three types of Auto Fill lists noted here, Excel correctly restarts the list when needed after it fills the first full set of entries, such as filling *Monday* after *Sunday* or *Q1* after *Q4*. For the last numbered label type of list, it keeps incrementing the number. So even though Quintile indicates five groups, Excel mistakenly follows *Quintile 5* with *Quintile 6*, *Quintile 7*, and so on. Bottom line: Always double-check your Auto Fill entries for accuracy.

When you want to Auto Fill label entries down a column or across a row, follow these steps:

1. **Enter the first label in the desired cell and press Enter or Tab.** If you prefer, you can stop before pressing Enter or Tab and skip to Step 3, but I find I usually press Enter or Tab out of habit and have to reselect the cell anyway.

2. **Reselect the cell with the first entry.**

3. **Move the mouse pointer over the small box, called the *fill handle*, at the bottom-right corner of the cell selector until the mouse pointer changes to a small black plus.**

4. **Drag down the column or across the row to fill as many cells as needed.** Figure 3.5 shows an Auto Fill operation in progress. As you drag, a ScreenTip appears with the mouse pointer showing the entry being filled (December in this case). Check it out, and when it shows the last label you need in your list, release the mouse button to stop dragging. If you go too far before you stop dragging, simply reverse directions.

You can Auto Fill formulas, too, a subject that I cover in Chapter 4 in the section called "How referencing works when filling, copying, or moving a formula."

Genius

If Auto Fill can't fill the desired list, you can create a custom list. Choose File ➔ Options. Click Advanced at the left side of the Excel Options dialog box, and then scroll down to the General section. Click the Edit Custom Lists button, and leave NEW LIST selected under Custom Lists. In the List Entries text box, type each text entry for the list and press Enter. Click Add to make the list, and click OK twice to close both dialog boxes.

A4	▼	:	×	✓	*fx*	January

◢	A	B	C	D	E
1	Product Shipments				
2					
3	Month	Total Value			
4	January				
5					
6					
7					
8					
9					
10					
11					
12					
13					
14					
15					
16		December			
17					

Fill mouse pointer with
ScreenTip

3.5 Use Auto Fill to enter a series of labels by dragging.

The fill handle by default just repeats a numeric entry in a single selected cell if you fill it down the column or across the row. That seems counterintuitive, but it makes sense because as you saw with filling labels, Excel has to know what pattern it's repeating. A single numeric entry can't form a pattern, so you have to make and select at least two numeric entries to establish the pattern or increment between values. For example, if you entered 1 and 1.25, selected the two cells holding those entries, and then dragged the fill handle, Excel would fill *1.5*, *1.75*, *2*, and so on, based on the .25 increment between the first two values.

The fancy name for this activity is filling a series of numbers. By default, the filled series is a *linear* trend, meaning the fill assumes the same increment, or step value, between each of the entries you select as the basis for the fill. Excel adds the step value to each item in the series to determine the next value. If you enter and select more than two values and the increments aren't the same, you won't get the fill results you expected, and it may be a little tough to interpret the results.

Showing Growth with a Series Fill

You can fill a growth series or trend rather than a linear series, such as when you're trying to make business or economic forecasts. In a growth series, Excel multiplies each value by the step value to determine the next value. For example, if you entered 1 and 5 in two cells and then selected those cells and filled a growth series, the next entries would be *25, 125, 625, 3125,* and so on. The first two entries, 1 and 5, established that each subsequent value should be multiplied by a step value of 5. The easiest way to fill a growth series is to enter and select the first two values and then right-drag the fill handle. (Press and hold the right mouse button while dragging.) In the shortcut menu that appears, choose Growth Trend.

Inserting and Deleting Rows, Columns, and Cells

You can change the layout of your worksheets as needed when your reporting and communications needs change. For example, your boss might ask you to include a column for another metric in a sheet you've already created. Or, if a colleague provides you a workbook file with data exported from another source, such as your company's inventory database, you might need to delete rows or columns with nonrelevant information.

You can insert and delete one or more cells, rows, or columns as needed. Working with rows and columns is easiest, and there are a couple different techniques you can use to get the job done:

- **Right-click the header for a single row or column in the location where you want to insert or delete, and choose Insert or Delete in the shortcut menu, which is shown in Figure 3.6.**

- **Select multiple rows or columns in the desired location, and then right-click and choose Insert or Delete.** Or, rather than using the shortcut menu, you can choose Home → Cells → Insert or Home → Cells → Delete.

Note

The Home → Cells → Insert and Home → Cells → Delete buttons each have a drop-down arrow that you can click to open a menu with additional choices, but that's often not necessary when inserting and deleting rows and columns as just described.

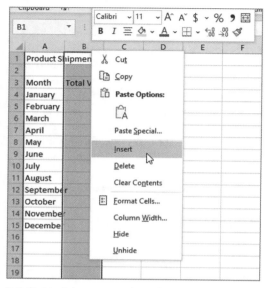

3.6 Right-click a row or column header and then click Insert or Delete.

When you insert one or more new rows, the rows below shift down. When you insert one or more new columns, the columns to the right shift further right. When you delete rows or columns, the opposite happens: rows below shift up, and columns to the right shift left.

Caution

Excel doesn't give you any warning when you're deleting rows and columns, so check carefully when you're deleting rows and columns and remember to use your friend Undo, if needed.

Inserting or deleting a range of cells takes a little more thought, as Excel asks you to choose how it should shift information in the worksheet. To insert or delete a range, follow these steps:

1. **Select the range where you want to insert or delete cells.**

2. **Right-click the selection and click Insert or Delete.** The Insert or Delete dialog box appears, prompting you to specify how to shift the cells. Figure 3.7 shows the Delete dialog box. The Insert dialog box looks similar.

3.7 Excel prompts you to specify how it should shift cells when you're inserting or deleting a range.

3. **Click the option button for the way you want the data to shift.** For example, when deleting, Shift Cells Left will move all the cells on the same rows as the selection to the left to replace the deleted data, while Shift Cells Up will move all the cells in the same columns as the selection up to replace the deleted data. When you're inserting data, the Insert dialog box has Shift Cells Right and Shift Cells Down choices.

4. **Click OK to finish and close the dialog box.**

If you choose the Home ➔ Cells ➔ Insert or Home ➔ Cells ➔ Delete button directly when inserting or deleting a range, Excel doesn't display a dialog box. It immediately inserts or deletes the cells, shifting the other cells on the same row as the selection to the right when inserting or left when deleting.

Genius

You can hide rows or columns holding sensitive data. First select the rows or columns. Then right-click the selection and choose Hide. To redisplay the hidden rows or columns, select the rows above and below the hidden area or the columns to the left and right of the hidden area. Right-click the selection and choose Unhide. The Home ➔ Cells ➔ Format ➔ Hide & Unhide submenu also has choices for hiding and unhiding rows, columns, and sheets.

Working with Column Width and Row Height

When you apply some number formats or other formatting, Excel automatically adjusts the column width and sometimes the row height. When you're entering data, however, this isn't the case. If you make a text entry that's too wide for the cell and there's an entry in the cell to the right, the text entry can't fully display and is cut off at the right. Or you may see ##### (a series of pound signs) within a cell holding a value or formula, which means the number is too wide to display in the column. (The number is still there; you just can't see it at the moment.) You also might just want to adjust row height or column width to suit your own taste and add some spacing between information in various rows or columns of the sheet.

Note

The series of pound signs filling a cell is sometimes called a *hash tag error*, because the # (pound) sign is also known as a hash sign and used in hash tags.

73

There are at least four ways to change the column width or row height, and the best method depends on whether you want to resize one row or column at a time or select multiple rows or columns and make them all the same size for consistency. Here are the three main methods, along with my thoughts on when it's best to use each:

● **Double-clicking the column header or row header divider.** If you move the mouse pointer over the divider line to the right of the column letter or below the row number, the mouse pointer changes to a black double-headed arrow with a vertical or horizontal line through it (see Figure 3.8). When you see that pointer, you can double-click the divider line, and Excel snaps the column width or row height to the optimal size for the cell contents. This is my preferred technique in most cases given its no-brainer appeal. Excel even calls this feature AutoFit, appropriately.

Caution

Given that it's typical to enter the title for a worksheet in cell A1 and worksheet titles can get pretty long, you probably don't want to double-click the column A heading border to widen the column because you'd end up with a massively wide column. Dragging the border or using another method gives you more precision.

● **Dragging the column header or row header divider.** Do the same maneuver with the mouse to get the special pointer, and then drag the column or row divider until the column or row reaches the size you want. As you drag, a ScreenTip shows you the current Width or Height, displaying both character and pixel values for Width and pt (point) and pixel values for Height. This method works fine if you just need the cell contents to display correctly but aren't trying for a precise column width or row height, which is more difficult to achieve when dragging.

● **Using the Column Width or Row Height dialog box.** If you want to set multiple columns or rows to a uniform width or height, this is the way to go. It also works for a single column or row. Start by selecting the column(s) or row(s) to adjust. Then, either right-click the header and choose Column Width or Row Height, or choose Home → Cells → Format → Column Width or Home → Cells → Format → Row Height. Enter or change the Column Width or Row Height text box value as applicable (character values for column widths and pt values for row height), and then click OK. Figure 3.8 shows the Row Height dialog box as an example.

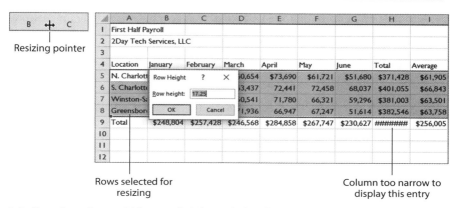

Resizing pointer

Rows selected for resizing

Column too narrow to display this entry

3.8 Changing column width or row height can help cell entries display properly and add spacing to the layout of information in a sheet.

Creating Range Names

In Excel, you can assign a range name to any range, even a one-cell range. Why would you want to take the time to do this? Convenience, plain and simple. When a range has a name, you can select the range quickly using the Name box at the left end of the Formula bar. And, as the Chapter 4 section titled "Using Range Names in Formulas" explains, you can use a range name rather than a range address in some formulas. Descriptive range names make working in the file more user friendly.

Range names can be up to 255 characters long, but within that broad guideline, there are some additional rules you have to follow. Short, descriptive names are the best, and you generally cannot duplicate the same name within the workbook file. The range name can't be the same as a cell address, like C4. Range names can be a single letter, but you cannot use the letters *R* and *C*, which are used in Excel for an alternate cell reference style. The range name must start with a letter, _ (underscore), or \ (backslash), and cannot include spaces. You can use the . (period), ? (question mark), _ (underscore), and \ (backslash) symbols within the name, but not as the first character, with

75

the exception of _ (underscore) and \ (backslash). It's common to use the _ (underscore) character rather than a space. If you happen to try to use a range name that's the same as another range name that Excel might be using, Excel may prevent you from assigning the range name.

Genius

After you assign the range name, you can reselect that range at any time by typing the name in the Name box and pressing Enter or by clicking the down arrow at the right end of the Name box and choosing the range name. Even if you capitalize range names when you create them, range names are not case sensitive. Typing the range name in all lowercase letters when using the Name box to reselect the range works.

Using the Name box

As with many of the other Excel operations you've seen so far, Excel lets you choose from a few different methods to assign a range name. First, here are the steps to follow if you want to use the Name box to name a range:

1. **Select the range to name.** If the range you're naming contains values and has an identifying label above it or to the left, you should omit that label from your selection as a best practice. This is because including the label with the numeric values might create an error if you try to use the range name in some formulas.

2. **Click in the Name box to select its contents.**

3. **Type the range name in the Name box, as in the example in Figure 3.9.**

4. **Press Enter.**

Note

If you make a change that shifts the position of the range you selected and named, the range retains the name you assigned, even in its new location. So if you add a column to the left of the named range, the named range just shifts one column to the right. If you add rows or columns within the named range, the range expands to encompass them, so there's no need to repeat the steps for naming the range.

New range name
entered in the Name box

| Shipments | : | × | ✓ | *fx* | 162 |

◢	A	B	C	D
1	Product Shipments			
2				
3	Month	Shipments	Total Value	
4	January	162	$42,550	
5	February	141	$38,409	
6	March	88	$19,075	
7	April	142	$38,100	
8	May	145	$39,675	
9	June	134	$35,430	
10	July	102	$26,355	
11	August	141	$38,009	
12	September	115	$34,688	
13	October	99	$24,670	
14	November	86	$20,101	
15	December	99	$23,405	
16				

Selected range

3.9 You can create a range name using the Name dialog box.

Using the New Name dialog box

By default, a range you create with the Name box has a Workbook scope assigned, meaning it can be used throughout the workbook file. That is, if the named range is on Sheet1 and you want to reference the range in a formula in a cell on Sheet2, you could. In other cases, you might want to limit the use of a range name within the sheet holding the named range. You might create a range with a scope limited to the current sheet if you want to use the same range name on multiple sheets within the workbook file.

The New Name dialog box enables you to assign a scope when naming a range. To create a range name using the New Name dialog box, follow these steps:

1. **Select the range to name.** Again, it is advisable to not include any label in the range of values.

2. **Choose Formulas → Defined Names → Define Name.** The New Name dialog box appears. As shown in Figure 3.10, Excel may suggest a range name for you in the Name text box, basing that name on the label beside or above the selected range.

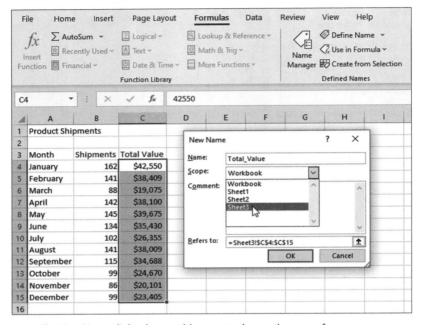

3.10 The New Name dialog box enables you to choose the scope for a new range name.

3. **Edit any suggested name in the Name text box as desired or type a new name.**

4. **Open the Scope drop-down list and click the name of a sheet to limit the scope of the new range name to that sheet.** Of course, this step is optional, as is making an entry in the Comment text box.

5. **Click OK.**

Deleting a range name

You don't have to keep the range names you've assigned in a workbook file. You can delete a name if it becomes obsolete, such as if you delete the data from the range. To use the Name Manager dialog box to delete a range name, follow these steps:

1. **Choose Formulas → Defined Names → Name Manager or press Ctrl+F3.**

2. **In the list of range names (Figure 3.11), click the range name to delete, if needed.**

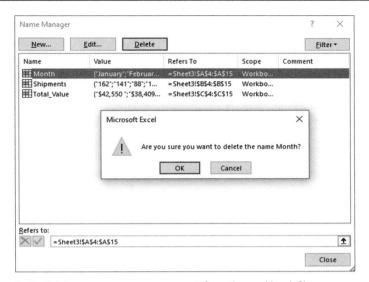

3.11 Deleting a range name removes it from the workbook file.

3. **Click the Delete button above the list.** A message box asks you to confirm the deletion.

4. **Click OK.**

5. **Click Close to close the Name Manager dialog box.**

Caution

Click the Edit button in the Name Manager dialog box to open the Edit Name dialog box. However, in that dialog box, you are limited to changing the name and the range that the range name refers to. You cannot change the scope of the range. If you need to change the scope, first delete the range, and then re-create it using the Formulas ➔ Defined Names ➔ Define Name command and the resulting New Name dialog box.

Freezing Rows and Columns On-Screen

Terms such as *business intelligence* (BI), *data analytics*, *data mining*, and *data visualization* have become very "buzzy" in the last several years. Generally speaking, those terms refer to using various techniques to tease meaning and insight out of very large datasets, especially for decision-making in a large organization.

You might not be working with a massive dataset, but you might have a sheet with a few dozen columns of product details or a few hundred rows of sales transactions. In those instances, it can be hard to keep the detail data in context if the important column or row label information scrolls off the screen as you move around to review and edit the data. The solution? Using the Freeze Panes choices to freeze vital row or column information (or both) on-screen, while retaining the ability to scroll around the other nonfrozen data. You have three basic Freeze Panes choices, each of which apply on the current sheet when used:

● **Freezing the top row only.** To do this, choose View ➔ Window ➔ Freeze Panes ➔ Freeze Top Row. With the top row frozen, when you scroll down, it remains on-screen.

● **Freezing the left column only.** To do this, choose View ➔ Window ➔ Freeze Panes ➔ Freeze First Column. With the left column frozen, when you scroll right, it remains on-screen.

Caution

The commands for freezing the top row or left column cannot be used together and essentially switch between each other. If you want to freeze one or more rows *and* columns, you have to use a different command. To do this, choose View ➔ Window ➔ Freeze Panes ➔ Freeze Panes.

● **Freezing one or more rows and columns.** To do this, click the cell that's both below the row(s) you want to freeze and to the right of the column(s) you want to freeze, and then choose View ➔ Window ➔ Freeze Panes ➔ Freeze Panes. For example, in the worksheet shown in Figure 3.12, I clicked cell B13 before choosing View ➔ Window ➔ Freeze Panes ➔ Freeze Panes, which froze rows 1 through 12 and column A on-screen. Notice that I've scrolled down and right so that row 109 displays below row 12 and column G appears to the right of column A. Slightly darker gridlines also identify the frozen panes.

To unfreeze panes, choose View ➔ Window ➔ Freeze Panes ➔ Unfreeze Panes.

Columns jump from A to G
because column A is frozen.

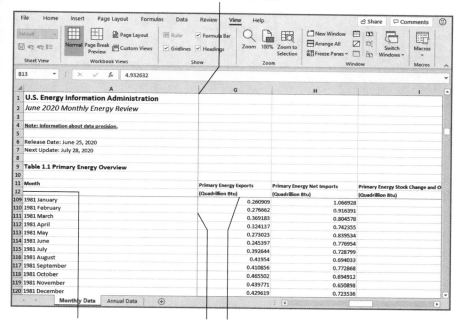

Rows jump from 12 to 109
because rows 1 through 12
are frozen.

Slightly darker gridlines
identify the frozen panes.

3.12 Rows 1 through 12 and column A are frozen on-screen in this sheet.
Source: U.S. Energy Information Administration (July 2020).

How Do I Do Math with Excel Formulas and Functions?

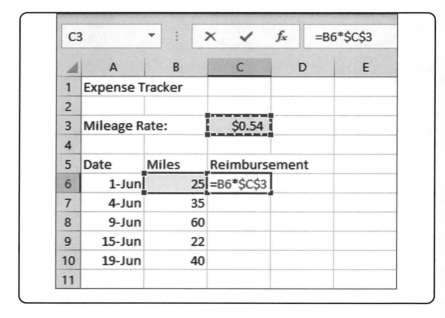

Costly, room-filling mainframe computers from the 1970s had a fraction of the processing power of today's typical home or business computer. And with sophisticated software like Excel installed, your computer becomes equipped to perform hundreds or thousands of complicated calculations—once you've set up those computations. This chapter introduces you to creating formulas in Excel. It covers how to enter a formula and how to use operators and functions correctly and otherwise structure the formula to calculate correctly. It also covers using different types of cell references and range names and handling minor errors.

Entering a Basic Formula

A formula is a special type of cell entry that performs a calculation or produces another result. You can almost think of a formula as a tiny little computer program that (usually) does one specific thing. Many formulas calculate numeric values, but formulas can return a text result, tell you whether a condition is true or false, and more. Building formulas can become a complex topic, so this chapter starts with the rough mechanics of entering and structuring a formula.

Typing the formula

On its face, typing a formula into a cell works like making any other cell entry: select the cell, type the contents, and press Enter or Tab. However, when you enter a formula, you have to follow structural and mathematical rules for creating the formula correctly so that it can produce the desired result with accuracy.

The first rule: a formula must begin with an = (equal) sign. If you leave off the = (equal) sign, Excel will treat the entry like text or a value instead.

From there, a formula generally includes one or more of these parts:

- **Constants.** These are numbers and text entered in the formula, such as the number 10.

- **Cell or range references.** When you use a reference to a cell or range, Excel uses the contents of that cell or range, usually values, in the formula's calculation. You can type the cell and range references using lowercase letters, if you prefer, and Excel will change the references to uppercase letters.

- **Operators.** These are the symbols that tell Excel what type of calculation to perform, such as + (plus) for addition and - (minus) for subtraction. A later section covers the operators you can use in formulas.

- **Functions.** Functions are essentially shortcuts for building more complex formulas without having to figure out all of the underlying math on your own. Later parts of this chapter cover functions.

After you finish entering a formula, its result rather than the formula itself appears in the cell. If you select a cell holding a formula, the formula appears in the Formula bar. You can edit a formula using any of the same three methods as for other cell entries: double-clicking in the cell, pressing F2, or using the Formula bar.

Cell and range references in formulas

Figure 4.1 shows a few examples of basic formulas using constants, cell references, and operators. Most of us start out creating easy formulas like these and gradually increase the complexity of the formulas we build. You can imagine the endless possibilities.

A16		×	✓	f_x				
◢	A	B	C	D	E	F	G	H
1		Values	Formula Results	Formula Entered in Column C	Calculation Performed by Formula			
2			25	=20+5	Constants 20 and 5 added			
3								
4		5	40	=B4+B6+B8	Values in cells B4, B6, and B8 added			
5		7						
6		12	3.2857143	=B8/B5	Value in cell B8 divided by value in cell B5			
7		19						
8		23	115	=B4*B8	Value in cell B4 multiplied by value in cell B8			
9								

4.1 You can start with creating basic formulas like these with constants, cell references, and operators.

While in many cases it's acceptable to use constants in a formula, as in the example in cell C2 in Figure 4.1, using a cell or range reference ensures that your workbook will be more adaptable. Look again at the examples in Figure 4.1. If you changed the entry in cell B8, the formula results in cells C4, C6, and C8 would change, because the formulas in all three of those cells contain a reference to cell B8. For most users, there might be few instances where it's best to include a constant in a formula.

The examples in Figure 4.1 don't include any range references. That's because when a range reference is used in a basic math formula, it can both create unexpected behavior, where results spill into other cells and generate an error message. Range references come into play when you include functions in formulas, a topic covered later in the chapter.

Genius

You also can create a reference to a cell or range on another sheet, commonly called a *3-D reference*. Include the sheet name followed by an ! (exclamation point) before the reference, as in Sheet2!B18. If the cell or range is in another workbook file, the reference looks like this: '[Product Shipments.xlsx] Sheet2'!B18, with square brackets around the file name and single quotes before the first square bracket and the ! (exclamation point).

Using the mouse to save time

Rather than typing in cell references (or range references when you later start working with functions), you can use the mouse to select a cell (or range) to reference while creating a formula. I tend to prefer using the mouse, because it helps me avoid cell and range reference typos in my formulas.

When you are entering or editing a formula, Excel uses color coding to help you match up each reference on the sheet with the reference in the formula, either in the cell when creating the formula or in the Formula bar when editing the formula. I find this color coding to be particularly helpful when I use my mouse to build a formula, because it gives me a visual confirmation that I'm selecting the correct cell or range.

Let's take a look at an example of using the mouse to create a formula in Figure 4.2. To start, I clicked cell D4 and typed the = (equal) sign. I then clicked cell B4 to enter its cell reference into the formula, typed the - (minus) sign, and clicked cell C4 to enter its cell reference into the formula. As indicated by the callouts in Figure 4.2 (because the color-coding can't appear in the grayscale imagery in this book), cell B4's selection border and shading and its matching cell reference in the formula were color coded blue while I was building the formula. Cell C4's selection border and shading and matching cell reference were color coded red. To finish the formula, I pressed Enter.

C4 color coded red

C4	▼	:	✕	✓	*fx*	=B4-C4	

◢	A	B	C	D	E	F
1	Temperature Tracker					
2						
3	Day	High Degrees F	Low Degrees F	Difference Degrees F	Difference Degrees C	
4	Monday	87	66	=B4-C4		
5	Tuesday	88	67			
6	Wednesday	85	65			
7	Thursday	89	66			
8	Friday	80	67			
9	Saturday	82	63			
10	Sunday	84	65			
11						
12	Average					
13						

B4 color coded blue

4.2 You can click a cell with the mouse to enter the cell reference in the formula.

If you were entering a range reference in a formula (as noted, almost always a formula using a function), you would drag to select the range. If the cell or range to select is on another sheet in the workbook file or in another workbook file altogether, follow these steps to use the mouse to enter the reference in the formula:

1. **If the cell or range to reference is in another workbook file, make sure both files are open.** The file where you want to enter the formula must be the current or active file.

2. **On the desired sheet, click the cell where you want to enter the formula and type the = (equal) sign.**

3. **If needed, enter any initial parts of the formula, such as a function name or open parenthesis.** A later section called "Using parentheses in formulas" details how and when to use parentheses.

4. **When you get to the point where you need to use the mouse to enter the reference, click the tab for the other sheet; or point to the Excel button on the Windows taskbar, click the thumbnail for the other file, and click the desired sheet tab.**

5. **Select the desired cell or range.**

6. **To continue the formula, type the next operator or formula part.**

7. **From there you can type other references and formula parts as needed, or repeat Steps 4 through 6 to continue using the mouse along with the keyboard to build the formula.**

8. **To finish the formula, type any remaining references or parts such as a closing parenthesis, and press Enter.**

You can use the mouse to see some quick calculations without even entering a formula. Just select a range of values and check the status bar area to the left of the view buttons. By default, Excel shows an Average, Count, and Sum of the selected values (see Figure 4.3). I use this feature when I don't need to add a formula but am curious about the result of a particular calculation.

Genius

You can right-click the status bar and use the shortcut menu that appears to customize its offerings, including the calculations it displays for a selected range of values. The calculation choices are grouped near the bottom of the shortcut menu.

4.3 Select a range of values and then check the status bar to see Average, Count, and Sum calculations.

Dealing with minor errors

Even when you use the mouse to increase accuracy when selecting references for a formula, you can still inadvertently click the wrong cell. Or, if you create a formula that generates an error or haven't properly entered the elements of a formula, Excel displays a message box. Figure 4.4 shows an example of the former. I entered a formula with a reference to the cell where I entered it, which is a no-no because a cell can't use its own result in its formula calculation, and so on, and so on, and. . . . The message box in the figure is prompting me to click OK and fix the error myself or to click the Help button to learn more about the error and how to correct it. Other similar message boxes may suggest formula corrections or offer to fix the formula for you.

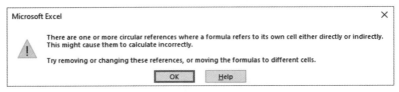

4.4 In some cases, Excel displays a message box prompting you to correct a formula error.

Learning More About Operators and Order of Precedence

The old saying in programming of "garbage in, garbage out" refers to the fact that if program code uses a wrong value or an improper sequence, the program will output inaccurate results, throw an error message, or not run at all. The same applies to Excel formulas. You have to be careful to reference the correct cells and use the correct constants, you have to use the right operators, and you also have to be careful about the sequence and structure of the calculation. Order of precedence is one key to calculation sequence and structure. This section explains the correct use of operators and order of precedence in Excel formulas.

Reviewing operators in Excel

As you learned earlier or maybe already knew, *operators* are the symbols that tell Excel what type of calculation to perform. Excel enables you to use a specific subset of the available universe of mathematical operators and symbols. There are four types or categories of operators in Excel:

- **Arithmetic.** These operators perform the types of basic math you learned in school.

- **Comparison.** These operators compare two values. The result is either TRUE or FALSE, which seems limited, but these operators are typically used as part of a more complex formula.

- **Text (Concatenation).** This operator, normally used with text, enables you to combine entries or contents to display a longer string of text in a cell. You would use a cell reference in the formula to refer to a cell holding text as needed. One trick to keep in mind is that you often have to create spaces manually by including " " (quote space quote) among the parts being concatenated in the formula.

- **Reference.** These operators enable you to build normal and special range references.

Table 4.1 introduces the arithmetic, comparison, and text (concatenation) operators that you can use in Excel, along with a brief example of each. The reference operators require wordier explanations, so I cover them right after the table.

Genius

Entering the four most common operators gives the 10-key keypad another chance to shine. It includes the / (division), * (multiplication), - (subtraction), and + (addition) keys for easier formula entry. If you're a heavy Excel user and your laptop doesn't have a 10-key numeric keypad, you can get a USB version for $20 or so.

The fourth category of operators, reference, holds operators that are generally used with formulas using functions. The reference operators include the following:

- **: (colon).** You've already met this operator, used to indicate a regular range address, as in =SUM(J5:J9).

- **, (comma).** When you need to refer to multiple references, separate them with a , (comma), as in =SUM(C2:C4,F5:F7). The , (comma) is also called the union operator.

Table 4.1 Arithmetic, Comparison, and Text Operators for Excel Formulas

Type	Operator	Action/Meaning/Use	Example	Result
Arithmetic	+	Addition	=20+5	25
Arithmetic	–	Subtraction	=20–5	15
		Negation	=–5	-5
Arithmetic	*	Multiplication	=20*5	100
Arithmetic	/	Division	=20/5	4
Arithmetic	%	Percent	=15%	.15 when used in calculation
Arithmetic	^	Exponentiation	=2^3	8
Comparison	=	Equal to	=D2=C2	TRUE when both cells contain the same value
Comparison	>	Greater than	=D2>C2	TRUE when value in cell D2 is higher
Comparison	<	Less than	=D2<C2	TRUE when value in cell D2 is lower
Comparison	>=	Greater than or equal to	=C10>=D10	TRUE when value in cell C10 is equal or higher
Comparison	<=	Less than or equal to	=C10<=D10	TRUE when value in cell C10 is equal or lower
Comparison	<>	Not equal to	=C10<>D10	TRUE when the values in the cells are not equal
Text	&	Concatenation	="Size"&" "&"L"	Size L

⦿ **(space).** When you need a formula to use the contents of one or more cells located where two ranges overlap, separate the ranges with a (space), as in =SUM(D5:E10 E9:F14). This operator also can be used to generate an array. The (space) is called the intersection operator.

⦿ **# (pound) and @ (at).** These two range operators are not typically ones the user enters. They may be used when Excel generates an array based on a formula or when you're working with an Excel table, as Chapter 8 covers. In addition, you may see the # (pound) sign used in other contexts, as when a cell holding a formula displays an error message, which is in part why I personally don't even think of them as operators.

Note

Excel enables you to insert a complex equation on a sheet for illustration purposes. You might need to do this when reporting on scientific data, for example. To insert a predefined equation, choose Insert ➜ Symbols, and then click the bottom down arrow portion of the Equation button to display the available equations. To build your own equation, choose Insert ➜ Symbols, and then click the top part of the Equation button. Use the Equation tab that appears to create or edit an equation.

Understanding how order of precedence works

Excel generally proceeds from the = (equal) sign to the right in evaluating a formula. For simple formulas such as the ones shown in Figures 4.1 and 4.2, this means that Excel calculates the formula from left to right, as you'd expect. But the different types of operators put a spin on the calculation order.

To determine the order of calculation in a formula, Excel follows the order of precedence, also called the *order of operations*. This means that in a longer formula with different types of operators, Excel calculates the formula in order by operator type. It only goes back to left-to-right order when two operators are at the same level of precedence. Table 4.2 lists the operators by order of precedence, from the first operations performed at the top of the table through the last performed at the bottom of the table.

Table 4.2 Order of Precedence in Excel Formulas

Order of Precedence from First to Last	Operator(s)
Reference operators	: (colon)
	(single space)
	, (comma)
Negation	– (minus), as in -1
Percent	%
Exponentiation	^
Multiplication and division	* and /
Addition and subtraction	+ and –
Concatenation	&
Comparison	=
	< and >
	<=
	>=
	<>

You can see the order of precedence in action by considering a few simple examples with constants:

- **=10+20*5.** If this formula evaluated from left to right, the result would be 150, but because multiplication is performed before addition according to the order of precedence, the formula multiples 20*5 first and then adds 10, for a result of 110.

- **=10^2-5.** This formula calculates a result of 95, because the order of precedence says to handle exponentiation first (10 to the power of 2 is 100) and then subtraction (100-5).

- **=5+20/5-10.** If evaluated from left to right, the result would be -5 (5+20 =25, 25/5=5, 5-10=-5), but under order of precedence, 20/5 is performed first, effectively resulting in 5+4=9, 9-10=-1.

If these simple examples produce such dramatic differences, then you can imagine the massive discrepancies that could result from failure to consider the order of precedence when building a formula. Next, learn about how you can take more control of the order of calculation in a formula.

Using parentheses in formulas

I've never seen the parentheses called math operators in Excel, but I would say that they work along with the other operators to determine the result of a formula's calculation. You can use pairs of parentheses to group calculations within a formula, overriding the order of precedence. For starters, Excel calculates what's inside a pair of parentheses first. (And the parentheses must be used in pairs.) Let's look at one of the examples I listed a moment ago: =10^2-5 calculates to a result of 95. But what if I changed the formula to =10^(2-5)? In the revised formula, Excel performs the 2-5 subtraction first, because it's in the parentheses, and then uses the result of -3 as the exponent. The revised formula calculates a result of .001.

For even more complicated formulas, you may need to nest multiple sets of parentheses within the outer set of parentheses. In that case, Excel works from the innermost set of parentheses out, taking the order of precedence into consideration as needed.

In the example temperature-tracking spreadsheet in Figure 4.5, I couldn't just take the entry from cell D4 in the Difference Degrees F column and use the standard formula to convert it from Fahrenheit to Celsius, because that would give a skewed result. Instead, I had to use the formula for converting from degrees F to degrees C—which is (F-32)*5/9— for the High Degrees F and Low Degrees F entries in cells B4 and C4, respectively, and *then* subtract the low from the high. If you count carefully in the formula shown in the Formula bar in Figure 4.5, you can see that it required six pairs of parentheses and a few layers of nesting.

Formula with nested parentheses

E4		:	×	✓	fx	=((B4-32)*(5/9))-((C4-32)*(5/9))	

◢	A	B	C	D	E	F
1	Temperature Tracker					
2						
3	Day	High Degrees F	Low Degrees F	Difference Degrees F	Difference Degrees C	
4	Monday	87	66	21	11.66666667	
5	Tuesday	88	67			

4.5 Use pairs of parentheses to group calculations and override the order of precedence.

If you leave off a closing parenthesis from any pair, in most cases Excel displays a polite message about it. You can accept a proposed correction, if any, or close the window and make the correction yourself.

Genius

It never hurts to sanity check a formula against another resource to make sure it calculates an accurate result. For example, to verify I entered the formula shown in Figure 4.5 correctly, I used the Temperature Converter in the Windows 10 Calculator app. Google also offers various converters that you can search for and use. Or, examine the formula structure in an Excel template that's similar to your sheet (a great way to learn more about creating formulas in general) or ask a colleague who's an Excel whiz to take a look.

Making a Cell or Range Reference Absolute Rather Than Relative

Notice in Figure 4.5 that the use of the number 32 is truly a constant, representing the difference between the freezing point in Fahrenheit versus the freezing point in Celsius (0), for conversion purposes. You do not want this value to change if you happen to copy or move the formula. Even more, you wouldn't want to put the value 32 in a cell and reference it from the formula, because you wouldn't want another user to be able to change the value.

In other cases, a formula that you intend to copy may need to refer to a particular cell, even when you copy or move the formula, but you may need to be able to change the contents of the referenced cell in the future. Common examples of this include the cell holding the interest rate in a mortgage amortization worksheet or the cell holding a mileage rate on an expense tracking worksheet. In these scenarios, you need to change the reference type in the formula to an absolute reference.

Changing the reference type in a formula

When you just type or use the mouse to select a cell or range reference, Excel treats it as a *relative reference* (or changeable reference) by default. In contrast, an *absolute reference* in a formula cannot change. And there's a third type of reference called a *mixed reference*, where only the column letter or row number is fixed.

You can change the cell reference while entering or editing the formula. After you type or use the mouse to add the reference to the formula, immediately press the F4 key. (When editing the cell or range reference in the formula, click anywhere within the reference and press F4.) This adds a dollar sign with both the column letter and row number in the reference. In the example in Figure 4.6, the $C$3 reference is an absolute reference.

Absolute reference

4.6 Press F4 when entering or editing a formula to change the cell or range reference type.

Continuing to press the F4 key cycles through the rest of the referenced types: mixed with the row fixed (as in C$3), mixed with the column fixed (as in $C3), and back to a plain old relative reference (as in C3). When the reference has been set to the type you need, either continue creating or editing the formula as needed or press Enter to finish.

Absolute range references have been a rare bird in my years of using Excel, but you might have a different experience. Again, use the F4 key when entering or editing a formula to change the reference type for a range reference. An absolute reference for a range includes dollar signs for both column letters and row numbers, as in $B$6:$B$10, and a range reference can be mixed, too.

How referencing works when filling, copying, or moving a formula

The default relative reference type means that if you move, copy, or fill the formula containing the reference, Excel adjusts the cell reference by the corresponding number of rows or columns as needed. For example, say the formula in cell C2 is =B2+5. If you then copy the formula down to cell C3, an increment of one row, Excel adjusts the reference in the formula by one row so the formula now reads =B3+5. That may seem like no big deal, but if you need to fill a formula down a column or across the row and have the formula references change as needed for you, this saves a huge amount of formula entry work.

In Figure 4.7, the formula in cell D4 is =B4-C4. I used the fill handle to fill the formula down through row 10. As the Formula bar in the figure shows, the formula in cell D10 is =B10-C10. Excel adjusted the relative references in the formula accordingly for each row in between 4 and 10, as well.

Relative references incremented to refer to row 10

D10	▼	:	×	✓	fx	=B10-C10		
◢	A	B	C	D	E	F
1	Temperature Tracker					
2						
3	Day	High Degrees F	Low Degrees F	Difference Degrees F	Difference Degrees C	
4	Monday	87	66	21	11.6666667	
5	Tuesday	88	67	21		
6	Wednesday	85	65	20		
7	Thursday	89	66	23		
8	Friday	80	67	13		
9	Saturday	82	63	19		
10	Sunday	84	65	19		
11						
12	Average					

Auto Fill Options button

4.7 Relative references increment when a formula is filled, copied, or moved.

Genius

You also can double-click the fill handle to fill the formula down the column without dragging. Whenever you use the fill handle to perform a fill, the Auto Fill Options button appears. Click it to see variations for completing the fill operation that you can choose. Review the section in Chapter 3 called "Using Auto Fill and Filling Series" for a refresher about using Auto Fill.

Figure 4.8 further illustrates how an absolute reference works. The formula in cell C6 is =B6*$C$3 (refer to Figure 4.6). After that formula gets filled through row 10, the formula in cell C10 is =B10*$C$3, as shown in Figure 4.8. The relative reference in the formula incremented, but the absolute reference to the rate in cell C3 did not.

And, as you might imagine, for a mixed reference, the relative row or column increments, but the fixed row or column does not when the formula is filled, copied, or moved.

C10		▼	:	×	✓	ƒx	=B10*$C$3	

◢	A	B	C	D	E	F	G
1	Expense Tracker						
2							
3	Mileage Rate:		$0.54				
4							
5	Date	Miles	Reimbursement				
6	1-Jun	25	$13.50				
7	4-Jun	35	$18.90				
8	9-Jun	60	$32.40				
9	15-Jun	22	$11.88				
10	19-Jun	40	$21.60				
11							
12							
13							

An absolute reference refers to the
same cell in all rows

4.8 Absolute references do not increment when a formula is filled, copied, or moved.

Understanding and Using Functions

You could spend a lot of time trying to write formulas that use complicated math, but who has extra time on their hands these days? Excel offers hundreds of functions that you can plug in to your formulas to do the math for you. Functions greatly expand what you can do with data, including the ability to look up data or apply a logical test to evaluate data. Earlier in the chapter, I compared formulas to mini programs. Functions in Excel take that concept a step further. Each *function* performs a prebuilt calculation or operation, sometimes eliminating the need to enter any math operators at all. The AVERAGE function is a good example. Instead of entering a lengthy formula such as =(C4+C5+C6+C7+C8+C9+C10)/7, you could boil it down to =AVERAGE(C4:C10). The descriptive function names also make the purpose of the sheet easier to follow.

A formula with a function starts with the = (equal) sign like any other formula and includes a pair of parentheses. The items placed between the parentheses with a function are called *arguments*. Arguments can consist of cell and range references, constants, text strings, and range names. A couple of functions don't require arguments at all, while most require at least one argument. Some have required and optional arguments. And still other functions can have more arguments than you'd think. For example, the SUM and AVERAGE functions can have multiple cell or range reference arguments separated by a comma (which is the union operator covered earlier), as in =SUM(B7:B8,D10:D11).

Caution

Text string arguments must be enclosed with quotation marks. Any comma needed between arguments must be outside the quotation marks. Also note that you do not need to include a space before or after the comma separating two arguments.

For more complex formulas, you can even use a function as one of the arguments for another function, called *nesting* the function. As when a formula includes multiple pairs of parentheses and calculates from the innermost pair out, Excel calculates the nested function(s) first. For example, the formula =IF(SUM(B7:D7)>130000,"Yes","No") first sums the values in the range B7:D7 and then executes the IF function. If the values in B7:D7 total more than 130000 (the logical test), the cell displays Yes (the value if true); for less than or equal to 130000, it displays No (the value if false). IF is one of the logical functions.

Using AutoSum on the Home or Formulas tab

Excel makes commonly used functions available via the AutoSum button, which appears both in the Editing group on the Home tab and in the Function Library group of the Formulas tab. The button has the Greek sigma or sum symbol on it on the Home tab and also includes the word *AutoSum* on the Formulas tab. It's also a split button. If you click the main part of the button, Excel starts a formula with the SUM function by default. If you want to choose another function, click the drop-down list arrow on the right side of the button. (Depending on your screen resolution, the button may be split into top and bottom parts, especially on the Formulas tab, so I'll refer to the main part of the button in either case versus the drop-down list arrow.) The functions available via the AutoSum drop-down list are as follows:

- **SUM.** Sums or adds up the total of the values in the specified range.

- **AVERAGE.** Sums the values in the range and then divides by the number of values to calculate the average.

- **COUNT.** Called Count Numbers on the drop-down list, this function counts the number of value entries in the specified range. You could use it to find the number of samples collected for a scientific study, for example.

- **MAX.** Finds the highest value in the specified range. You might use this function to find the month with the highest sales.

- **MIN.** Finds the lowest value in the specified range. This function could be used to find the lowest expense amount in a sheet.

In most cases, you would specify a single range with each of these functions. That said, when you're creating the formula, you also can use the comma between one or more additional cell or range references in between the parentheses. Follow these steps to create a formula with a common function using the AutoSum button:

1. **Click the cell to the right of or below the range that you want to use as the argument.** Excel will automatically suggest the range as the argument for the formula.

2. **Do one of the following:**

   ● **Choose Home → Editing → AutoSum (main part of button) or Formulas → Function Library → AutoSum (main part of button).**

   ● **Choose Home → Editing → AutoSum (drop-down list arrow) or Formulas → Function Library → AutoSum (drop-down list arrow), and then click the desired function.** Figure 4.9 shows AutoSum on the Formulas tab.

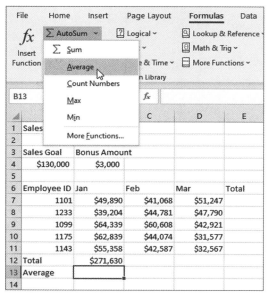

4.9 AutoSum provides a quick way to enter common functions in a formula.

3. **Drag a handle to adjust the selected range as needed or simply drag over the range to select.** For example, in Figure 4.10, I needed to drag a bottom handle up to eliminate the total calculated by another formula in cell B12 from the suggested range. As an option, at this point you could work within the parentheses to add cell and range references, as shown in the ScreenTip that appears below the cell with the new formula.

B13	▼	:	✕ ✓ ƒx	=AVERAGE(B7:B11)	
◢	A	B	C	D	E
1	Sales and Bonus Calculations				
2					
3	Sales Goal	Bonus Amount			
4	$130,000	$3,000			
5					
6	Employee ID	Jan	Feb	Mar	Total
7	1101	$49,890	$41,068	$51,247	
8	1233	$39,204	$44,781	$47,790	
9	1099	$64,339	$60,608	$42,921	
10	1175	$62,839	$44,074	$31,577	
11	1143	$55,358	$42,587	$32,567	
12	Total	$271,630			
13	Average	=AVERAGE(B7:B11)			
14		AVERAGE(number1, [number2], ...)			
15					

Drag a handle to adjust the suggested range

4.10 You can keep or adjust the range suggested as the argument or simply drag over the range you want to select.

4. **Press Enter or Tab to finish entering the formula.** Excel automatically enters the closing parenthesis in the formula for you. Less typing!

Genius

Sometimes Excel flags a formula when there's no error. For example, if your range argument skips a cell or two immediately above or to the left of the formula entry, the error button may appear to the left of the cell. To tell Excel to stop flagging that error for that cell, click the error button and then choose Ignore Error. Or, you can simply ignore the buttons and green error indicator triangles, as I've done in some figures in this chapter.

Typing a function in a formula

The earlier description of function arguments may have made you wonder how you're supposed to know which arguments a function requires. Fortunately, as shown in the ScreenTip in Figure 4.11, Excel provides helpful argument prompts when you're using any of the various methods for creating a formula. The prompts show you which arguments to use and in what order they need to be entered for the function to calculate correctly.

If you think you know the exact name of the function that you need and have a rough idea of what arguments it uses, you can simply type the formula in the desired cell or click the cell and then work in the Formula bar. If you're less sure of the formula name and its arguments, you can type the formula anyway. A feature called Formula AutoComplete provides the help you need to finish the formula. Here's how it works:

1. **Click in the cell where you want to enter the formula, or click the cell and click in the Formula bar.**

2. **Type = (equal) plus the first letter or two (or three) of the function name.** As shown in Figure 4.11, a drop-down list with matching functions appears.

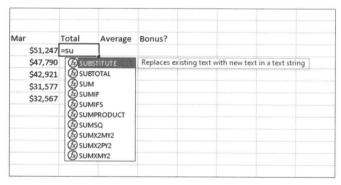

4.11 Formula AutoComplete lists matching functions.

Note   As when entering cell and range references, you do not have to type the function name in ALL CAPS when you enter it into the formula. Excel will convert the function name to all caps for you when you finish entering the formula.

3. **Double-click the function to use in the drop-down list.** Optionally, you also can press the down arrow key to select the function in the drop-down list, and then press the Tab key to enter it in the function. Once the function is entered in the formula, the ScreenTip below the formula changes to display the required arguments.

4. **Use the mouse or keyboard to enter the specified arguments.** For some functions that require a type of argument that exists either in the program or in the workbook file (such as another function or a range name), AutoComplete displays a list of choices, as shown in the example in Figure 4.12. Double-click the choice to use in the list.

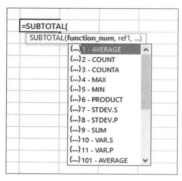

4.12 The SUBTOTAL function's first argument calls for another function, which you can double-click in the list of allowable choices.

5. **Enter or specify additional arguments as prompted by the ScreenTip, including a comma after each argument except the last one.**

Genius

As you add arguments, the ScreenTip shows the next argument to enter in bold to guide you about what to enter next. Optional arguments have [ ] (square brackets) around them.

6. **Enter the) (closing parenthesis) if needed, and then press Enter or Tab to finish the formula.** In many cases, Excel will let you skip entering the closing parenthesis, but if you get an error message, you may need to go back and add it at the end of the formula.

Note

The #VALUE! error is one of the most common and general errors in Excel and can often happen when a formula performs subtraction or other common math operations but the referenced cells hold text. It also can happen if you enter a date in a format that Excel doesn't recognize—causing Excel to treat it as text rather than as a date entry—and then create a formula that references that cell.

Using the Formulas tab to insert a function

The Function Library group of the Formulas tab on the ribbon provides access to all of Excel's functions. Depending on what online resource you consult, the number of available Excel functions is north of 450 and likely approaching 500. It seems unlikely that even the most avid Excel user has them all committed to memory.

That being the case, the Formulas tab can jump-start you in finding the function you need. You can either browse to find more frequently used functions of a particular type or search for a function if you're not quite sure which function performs the calculation you want.

Choosing from the Function Library

Your local public library helpfully catalogs books by genre for you with signs at the end of the stacks. The signage shows you where to find fiction, nonfiction, reference titles, and books for young adults and children, and some libraries even break it down further from there, with subgroups such as mystery and science fiction. I suspect the Function Library group on the Formulas tab received its name due to its similar organizational structure.

In addition to hosting the AutoSum button you learned about earlier, the Function Library group organizes functions into categories such as Financial, Logical, Text, Date & Time, and more. The Recently Used category includes functions that you've used recently, so it's a go-to category for many users. If you choose More Functions in the group, as shown in Figure 4.13, a menu with additional function categories appears. You can move the mouse pointer over a category in the menu to see the functions in that category.

Before you choose a function, first click the cell where you want to insert the formula. Then start looking for a function in the Function Library group of the Formulas tab by choosing the category you think the function is in. If the category has a scrolling list, you may need to scroll down to look for the function you need. To see a ScreenTip describing what a function does, move the mouse pointer over it, as shown in Figure 4.14. Checking out the description gives you a better shot of finding the function you need, rather than just going by memory of what a particular function does.

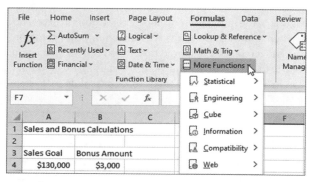

4.13 The Function Library organizes common functions into several categories.

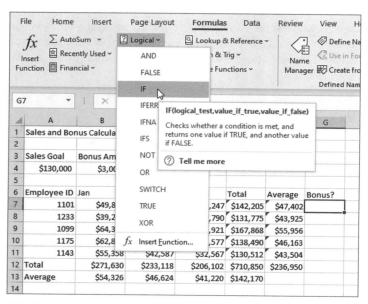

4.14 Each category presents a list of functions.

If you do not find the function you need in the first category you view, no worries. Excel doesn't insert a function until you click it in the category list. So just choose another category and continue until you find the function you want. When you do click a function to choose it, the Function Arguments dialog box shown in Figure 4.15 opens. It lists the arguments for the function and sometimes fills in a suggestion for the first argument for you. If not, you can view the description for the argument lower in the dialog box and enter the required information for the argument. As in similar dialog boxes in Excel, you can type the argument yourself in its text box, or you can use the mouse to specify a cell or range reference. If the cell or range you want is visible, just select it in the sheet. If you can't see the cell or range, click the collapse button at the right end of the argument text box to collapse the dialog box, make the selection, and then click the expand button.

Collapse/expand button

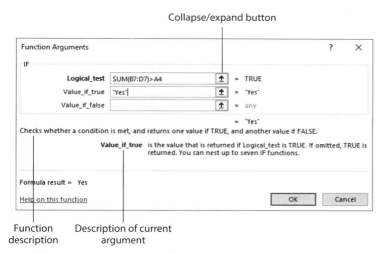

Function description

Description of current argument

4.15 The Function Arguments dialog box appears after you insert a function from one of the categories.

Genius

To nest a function in the Function Arguments dialog box, you have to type it as shown for the top argument in Figure 4.15. To verify that nested function arguments or any other arguments are calculating correctly, look at the = expression to the right of the argument text box. For the Logical_test argument shown in the figure, =TRUE to the right is the correct result and an indication that the nested function and its arguments are entered correctly.

When you finish entering one argument, press Tab or click to move to the next argument, checking the description if needed. The name of each required argument appears in bold beside its text box. The other arguments with nonbold names are optional. When you finish entering all the arguments, click OK to finish inserting the formula.

Using Insert Function to find a function

If you'd rather not browse for a function and want to take a more direct route, you can search for a function using the Insert Function dialog box. You don't even have to know the function's name, as the dialog box enables you to search using a description of the calculation or other action you want to perform. Follow these steps to search for a function:

1. **Click the cell where you want to insert the formula with a function.**

2. **Choose Formulas → Function Library → Insert Function or press Shift+F3.** The Insert Function dialog box opens.

Genius

No matter which ribbon tab is currently selected, you can use the Insert Function button on the Formula bar next to the Formula bar text box to open the Insert Function dialog box. The Insert Function button on the Formula bar has the same symbol as the Insert Function button on the Formulas tab.

3. **Type part of the function name or a description in the Search for a Function text box at the top of the dialog box.**

4. **Click the Go button.** As shown in the example in Figure 4.16, the Insert Function dialog box displays possible matches in the Select a Function list.

Search description

Possible matches

4.16 Use the Insert Function dialog box to search for a function.

5. **Double-click the desired function in the Select a Function list or click the function and click OK.** The Function Arguments dialog box opens.

6. **Use the Function Arguments dialog box as described in the previous section to specify arguments and finish entering the formula.**

Genius

Earlier in the chapter, I explained how to tell Excel to ignore an error in a cell. If you've done that but suspect that an ignored error is now creating calculation problems, choose File → Options, choose Formulas at the left side of the Excel Options dialog box, click the Reset Ignored Errors button under Error Checking, and click OK. You also can clear the check box beside Enable Background Error Checking under Error Checking to turn off error indicators altogether.

Using Range Names in Formulas

You can use a range name as an argument for many different types of functions. This enhances the accuracy of your formulas. Not to mention that a formula such as =SUM(NorthOffice) seems more descriptive of the formula's purpose than =SUM(B7:B11). Excel treats range names in formulas as absolute references, so keep that in mind when moving or copying any formula with a range name as an argument. After you create range names in your workbook, you can enter them when creating a formula using any of the main methods discussed in this chapter, as follows:

- **Using AutoSum.** After you choose the function you want using the AutoSum button or list, type the range name between the parentheses and press Enter. Sometimes Excel suggests a range name when you use AutoSum, and if the suggested range name is correct, you can just press Enter to accept it and finish the formula.

- **Typing with Formula AutoComplete.** As you type the formula, when you get to the point where you want to enter the range name as an argument, type the first letter or two. The list of possible matches that Formula AutoComplete displays includes range names, as shown in Figure 4.17. Range names are indicated with a small sheet or grid icon with two blue-shaded cells to the left of the range name. Use the down arrow key to select the range name, and then press Tab to enter it into the formula. Finish the formula from there.

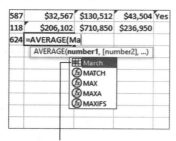

Range name icon

4.17 Formula AutoComplete lists matching range names (among other matches) after you type the first few letters of the name.

 Using the Function Arguments dialog box. Type a range name in an argument text box, repeat as needed, and finish creating the formula with the dialog box. For some functions, it might be useful to assign a range name to even a single cell to make it easier to understand the nature of the calculation. For example, for some financial functions, you might create a range name for a cell holding an interest rate or one holding the number of periods in the loan.

Note

The #NAME? error displays in a cell when a formula refers to a range name that doesn't exist, or perhaps when the range name has been entered incorrectly. Check and correct any range names used in the formula to clear up this error.

How Do I Create a PowerPoint Presentation?

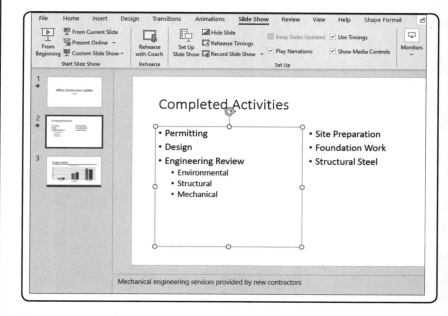

1 **2** **3** **4** **5** **6** **7** **8** **9** **10** **11**

It's tough to connect with an audience when it's just you standing up and speaking. Adding reinforcing bullet points and visuals on-screen behind you involves your audience members and engages their minds. Whether you're giving a project status update or presenting a pitch deck to raise money for your business, you can use Power-Point to create a presentation that enhances your message and your confidence as a speaker. Learn how to build and run through a presentation in this chapter, from choosing a slide layout and adding and rearranging slides, all the way to preparing and presenting the show.

Understanding Slide Layouts

Chapter 1 explained that each slide in a PowerPoint presentation uses a slide layout with predefined placeholders. The available slide layouts and the formatting and arrangement of the placeholders on each layout depend on the theme applied to the presentation file or whether you created the file using a template. (Chapter 6 covers themes.) Slide layouts make it easier to create slides that are consistent in appearance and formatting, which in turn enhances the professionalism of your presentation, especially if you play it on-screen as a slide show as described later in the chapter.

The default Office Theme offers Title Slide, Title and Content, Section Header, Two Content, Comparison, Title Only, Blank, Content with Caption, and Picture with Caption slide layouts. Some templates may offer fewer or additional layouts. As you learned in Chapter 1, you click a text placeholder and type the text. The slide layout positions and formats the text according to the size and formatting already set up for the placeholder. Later sections in this chapter explain how to add other types of placeholder content.

To change the layout applied to a slide, click the thumbnail for the slide in the Thumbnails pane at the left side of Normal view, choose Home ➔ Slides ➔ Slide Layout, and then click the thumbnail for the desired layout in the gallery that appears. PowerPoint automatically rearranges the slide's contents to the new slide layout.

Note

When you perform certain activities in PowerPoint, such as changing the slide layout for a slide, the Design Ideas pane opens at the right. You can explore ideas and select one from the pane if desired. Click the pane Close (X) button when you're finished.

Change to Slide Master view to edit or create slide layouts. Any changes you make to an individual layout will be applied to all slides in the presentation file that use that slide layout. Choose View ➔ Master Views ➔ Slide Master to change to that view. Select a layout to edit at the left (see Figure 5.1) or choose Slide Master ➔ Edit Master ➔ Insert Layout to create a new layout. (To make formatting changes that apply to all of the slide layouts, scroll all the way up in the left pane and select the Slide Master thumbnail at the top.) Make the desired changes using the choices on the Slide Master and Home tabs. (Chapter 6 provides more coverage of using the Home tab to change formatting.) For example, you could use the Slide Master ➔ Master Layout ➔ Insert Placeholder menu to select a placeholder to add to the current layout, and then drag on the layout in the main Slide pane to create the placeholder. Or, you can click an existing placeholder to select it and then drag a white selection handle to resize it. Choose Slide Master ➔ Close ➔ Close Master View to finish editing layouts.

Slide Master tab   Slide Master thumbnail

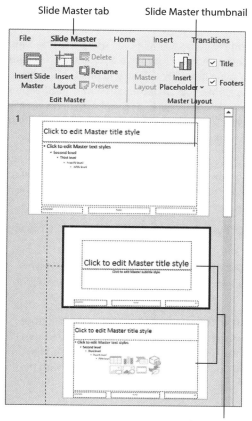

Slide layouts
with various
placeholders

5.1 Work in Slide Master view to make changes to slide layouts.

Caution

It's not a best practice to edit slide placeholders on the slide itself in Normal view, especially to change text formatting. This can make it more difficult to make global formatting updates later. If you've made these kinds of changes and need to revert the selected slide to the original slide layout formatting, choose Home → Slides → Reset.

113

Adding Slides

When you create a new blank presentation file, it has a single slide using the Title Slide layout. Presentation files created from other templates may have additional slides with suggested content. PowerPoint gives you some flexibility in how you build your presentation from there. You can do it one slide at a time, you can reuse slides from another presentation file, and you can even import an outline you've already developed in Word. Let's look at these three methods—using the New Slide button, reusing slides, and importing an outline—so you can decide which one works best with your content creation style.

PowerPoint inserts any new slide(s) that you add below (after) the slide that's currently selected in the Thumbnails pane at the left side of Normal view. That means the first step for adding slides is to click one of the slide thumbnails in that pane, no matter which method you use.

The New Slide button in the Slides group of the Home tab is a split button, so you can use it in two different ways:

- **Adding a slide with a different layout than the selected slide.** Click the down arrow portion of the New Slide button, and then choose the slide layout to use for the new slide in the gallery (Figure 5.2).

- **Adding a slide with the same layout as the selected slide.** Click the main (top) part of the New Slide button or press Ctrl+M. The only time this technique doesn't work is when the selected slide uses the Title Slide slide layout; in this case, New Slide inserts a slide using the Title and Content slide layout after the one with the Title Slide layout.

Genius

There are differing opinions about the optimal number of slides for a presentation. Some experts recommend limiting briefer presentations, such as business pitches and team updates, to 10–15 slides. But many talks, such as scientific presentations, may last 30 minutes to an hour. For a longer presentation like that, you may need one to two slides per minute.

If you've already developed a presentation that has the content you need for a new presentation, you can reuse slides from the other presentation. Choose Home ➔ Slides ➔ Reuse Slides or choose the Reuse Slides command from the bottom of the New Slide gallery. (Sometimes it takes a few moments after you create or open a PowerPoint file for the Reuse Slides button to appear.) The Reuse Slides pane opens at the right and shows presentation files that you've worked with recently. Use it to display the slides in another presentation file and then insert them into the presentation.

Reuse Slides button

New Slide button
down arrow

Slide Layout button

Reset button

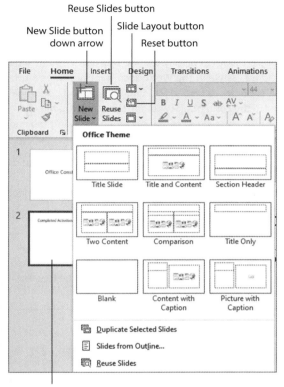

Selected slide in Thumbnails pane

5.2 Choose a slide layout to use for a new slide after clicking the New Slide button down arrow.

Note

You also can reuse a slide within the current presentation file by duplicating it. Right-click the slide in the Thumbnails pane in Normal view, and then choose Duplicate Slide from the shortcut menu. You also can select multiple slides in the pane using Shift+click or Ctrl+click and then choose Home → Slides → New Slide (down arrow) → Duplicate Selected Slides.

If you've already developed an outline in Word, you can use that outline as the basis for new slides in a presentation. The trick is you have to use the heading styles in Word, as described in Chapter 2 in the section entitled "Using Outlining to Organize Your Thoughts." For example, let's say you've written a lengthy research report and now you need to give a

115

presentation about your findings. You could create a copy of the Word document, delete the body text leaving only the headings, save your changes to the file, and import that version of the file into PowerPoint.

When you use this process, the imported slides generally use the Title and Content slide layout. Each heading using the Heading 1 style in the Word document becomes a title for a separate slide, and the headings below using the Heading 2 style (and additional numbered heading styles) are placed in the content placeholder. Note that you may have to adjust the bullet levels for the imported text in the content placeholder using Tab and Shift+Tab, as revisited shortly in this chapter.

After you create a new presentation so that there's a first slide with the Title Slide layout or otherwise have selected a slide after which you want to insert the imported slides, choose Home → Slides → New Slide (down arrow) → Slides from Outline. Navigate to and select the file to use in the Insert Outline dialog box, and then click Open.

Note

You also can divide a presentation into sections that you can collapse and expand as you work. To add a section, choose Home → Slides → Section → Add Section. Enter a name in the Section Name text box of the Rename Section dialog box, and then click the Rename button.

Rearranging and Deleting Slides

Whether you've built your presentation one slide at a time or have imported a previously created outline, you may find the need to change the order of slides or even remove a slide from the presentation from time to time. You can rearrange slides by dragging slide thumbnails in these three views, displayed via the Presentation Views group of the View tab:

- **Normal view.** Select the thumbnail for the slide to move in the Thumbnails pane, and then drag the thumbnail to the desired new position. The thumbnails rearrange to the new order immediately. The downside is that this view shows a more limited number of slides in the Thumbnails pane.

- **Slide Sorter view.** Because this view shows only slide thumbnails, it typically can show more thumbnails than Normal view, making moving slides around a little easier. Select and drag slide thumbnails to new locations as needed.

- **Outline view.** This view shows slide contents and a smaller icon for each slide. Move the mouse pointer over the icon for the slide to move. When the pointer changes to a four-headed arrow, drag. As shown in Figure 5.3, a gray line appears to indicate the new location the slide will take after you release the mouse button.

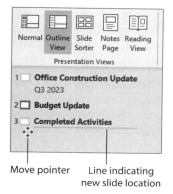

1 □ **Office Construction Update**
    Q3 2023

2 □ **Budget Update**

3 □ **Completed Activities**

Move pointer   Line indicating
               new slide location

5.3 You can move slides by dragging them in Outline view (shown here), Normal view, and Slide Sorter view.

You also can delete a slide in any of these views by right-clicking its thumbnail or icon and then choosing Delete Slide. This command removes the slide without warning, so if you realize you deleted the slide by mistake, press Ctrl+Z or click the Undo button on the QAT.

Genius

You can hide a slide if you only have it in the presentation for reference or if you want it to not appear as part of your on-screen show. In either Normal or Slide Sorter view, select one or more slide thumbnails, right-click the selection, and choose Hide Slide in the shortcut menu. The thumbnail contents will appear grayed out for any hidden slide. Right-click a thumbnail and choose Hide Slide to unhide the slide.

Working with Content Placeholders

You've already learned that adding text to a basic text placeholder such as a title only requires clicking in the placeholder, typing the contents you want, and then clicking outside the placeholder. Content placeholders enable you to do much more, adding different types of content within the placeholder's designated area. This section provides an overview of how content placeholders work, while later chapters provide more detail about adding certain types of contents, such as charts and tables.

Regular content

Presentations have long relied on a classic bulleted list structure rather than paragraphs for presenting text. In my opinion, the reason for this is twofold. First, a presentation serves more as a summary document and guide for the speaker, so it shouldn't have as

117

much text as a detailed description document. Second, when you're displaying the presentation as a show before an audience, the audience can take in only so much on-screen information at a time. It's too much to expect an audience to pay attention to what you're saying and read paragraphs on-screen.

As a result, a content placeholder on a slide layout is set up by default to treat text in the placeholder as a bulleted list. (Though you can add other types of content, too.) Click in the placeholder on the current slide in the Slide pane, type the first bullet, and press Enter to move to the next bullet in the list. Figure 5.4 shows a basic bulleted list entered in a content placeholder.

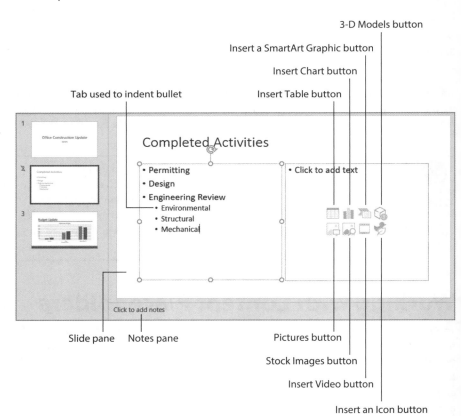

5.4 Content placeholders are set up for bulleted lists and other types of content.

PowerPoint bulleted lists work just like the ones in Word, which I described in the Chapter 2 section "Creating Bulleted and Numbered Lists." You can press Tab to indent a bullet, and subsequent bullets use the same indent. Press Shift+Tab to outdent back to a higher level. The corresponding (and somewhat confusingly named) ribbon commands are Home ➔ Paragraph ➔ Increase List Level and Home ➔ Paragraph ➔ Decrease List Level. You also can change a selected bulleted list to a numbered list with the Home ➔ Paragraph ➔ Numbering button.

Genius

Each slide should focus on one topic or idea. From there, opinions vary about the appropriate amount of content. According to the "5x5 Rule," each slide should only have five bullets with five words per bullet. But proponents of the "6x6 Rule" or "7x7 Rule" are open to more text. For me, it boils down to an audience's reading and attention levels. I'd likely make a presentation geared for an audience of high school students much more content light than a presentation for a group of engineers.

For the right content placeholder in Figure 5.4, I've added callouts identifying the buttons for inserting other types of content in a content placeholder. (The Picture with Caption slide layout only allows you to insert pictures in its content placeholder.) Chapters 7–9 will explain how to add pictures, icons, SmartArt graphics, tables, and charts, so you can skip ahead to the relevant sections in those chapters if you're eager to add those items to a presentation.

Note

You can create a special type of presentation called a photo album using the Insert ➔ Images ➔ Photo Album choice. Use the Photo Album dialog box to select the photos to include in the album, choose Picture Options and Album Layout settings, and reorder and correct photos as needed. Then click Create to generate the photo album presentation.

Speaker notes

Picking up on the points I made about keeping the text on slides brief, the more detailed description of your slide contents can be placed in the speaker notes. The speaker notes can consist of more details that you intend to share when delivering the presentation before an audience, including anecdotes and jokes that you may use to enhance the story.

I also like to document sources that I've used for facts or details within the speaker notes. As with moving slides, you can enter and edit your speaker notes in a few different views:

- **Normal view and Outline view.** Both of these views have a Notes pane below the current slide in the Slide pane (see Figure 5.4). You can click in that pane and type your notes as needed. You can format the text there as you would other text, including pasting copied information such as source website URLs. When you need to see more of the Notes pane, you can drag the divider between it and the Slide pane to make it larger.

- **Notes Page view.** This view displays how Notes pages will look when printed, with a single slide at the top of the page and a larger notes area for that slide below. This enables you to have a larger view of the notes area, making it easier to add lengthier notes. Chapter 11 explains how to print a presentation, and you can choose to print Notes pages to use when you deliver your presentation before an audience.

Editing Slide Content

I bet you can guess what I'm going to say, and you'd be correct. Editing slide content in PowerPoint works much as described for Word in Chapter 2. You can use many of the same mouse and keyboard methods for selecting and editing text, such as double-clicking to select a word and then typing its replacement. You can click to position the insertion point, and then use the arrow keys to move it around. The Backspace and Delete keys work the same, too.

Like Word, PowerPoint also gives you the ability to set tab stops in a text or content placeholder, and the process works much as it does in Word, as well. Click the Home ➜ Paragraph group dialog box launcher, click the Tabs button in the Paragraph dialog box, and then continue as described in the Chapter 2 section "Working with Tabs and Indent Settings." The only difference is that you can't create leaders with tabs in PowerPoint.

As for most Microsoft 365 apps, PowerPoint enables you to include and respond to comments when collaborating with other users on presentation contents. You can select the text to comment on, choose Review ➜ Comments ➜ New Comment, type the comment text (see the example in Figure 5.5), and click the Close (X) button in the Comments pane. To read and respond to a comment, click in the content placeholder and then click the comment marker or indicator to open the Comments pane. You also can use the buttons in the Comments group of the Review tab to work with comments.

Comments group

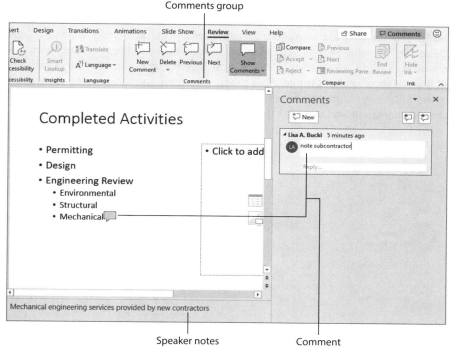

Speaker notes   Comment

5.5 You can discuss additions, corrections, and changes using the comments feature.

Changing Slide Size or Background

By default, the themes in PowerPoint use a Widescreen (16:9) slide size. This ensures that when you play the presentation as an on-screen show, it fills the wider orientation used by most modern computer screens and projectors. That said, you may come across an older presentation file or template that uses the Standard (4:3) size and want to change it to the wider orientation. To change between orientations, use the Design → Customize → Slide Size choices shown at the left in Figure 5.6.

Generally speaking, you don't have to worry about slide size if you need to print the presentation (a subject covered in the final chapter of this book). PowerPoint automatically scales each slide to fit one page for the selected printer and paper size, usually 8.5" x 11",

121

even for a presentation using the Widescreen (16:9) slide size. However, if you're using PowerPoint to create a more special-purpose document, such as a banner or infographic poster, you may need to change both the paper size and the orientation. To do so, choose Design → Customize → Slide Size → Custom Slide Size to open the Slide Size dialog box shown at the right in Figure 5.6. Open the Slide Sized For drop-down list and choose any of the presets or choose Custom. After choosing Custom, enter the desired dimensions in the Width and Height text boxes. Under Slides in the Orientation section, choose the desired orientation, and then click OK.

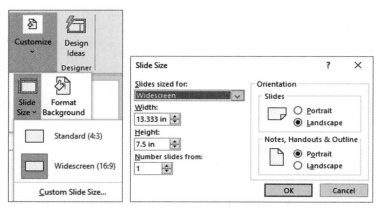

5.6 Change the slide size to reflect the screen size to be used for on-screen playback and special printouts.

Caution

When creating printouts for a nonstandard paper size, you may also need to change the paper size in your printer's Properties settings.

Preparing and Playing the Slide Show

Sure, you can print handouts of a presentation to communicate with an audience. But using your presentation file to present an on-screen slide show while you deliver your remarks to your audience provides a boost to your messaging and audience engagement. You can enhance that engagement even more by adding transitions between slides and animation to objects. This section covers those finishing touches, as well as how to play the big show.

122

Adding transitions

A *transition* is a motion effect that occurs when you advance from one slide to the next in an on-screen slide show. PowerPoint includes dozens of transition effects, and you can add a sound, specify how long the transition lasts, and choose how to advance to the next slide. You apply transition settings using the Transitions ribbon tab, shown in Figure 5.7.

5.7 Set up transitions between slides using this ribbon tab.

Working in Normal, Outline, or Slide Sorter view, follow these steps to apply a transition to one or more slides:

1. **Select the thumbnail(s) or icon(s) for the slide(s) to which you want to apply a transition.** You can use Shift+click or Ctrl+click to select multiple slides if needed.

2. **Choose Transitions, and then click the More down arrow button at the bottom-right corner of the Transitions gallery in the Transition to This Slide group.** If the transition you want already is visible, you don't have to open the gallery.

3. **Click the desired transition in the gallery.** The gallery groups the available transitions under Subtle, Exciting, and Dynamic Content. You may want to experiment with a few choices to make sure you're pleased with the effect. Immediately after you choose the transition, a preview of the selected transition plays on the slide or thumbnail. A star appears with the slide thumbnail to indicate the slide has a transition applied.

4. **Choose settings in the Timing group as needed to enhance the transition.** For example, you can choose a sound from the Sound drop-down list, change the Duration setting for the transition, or set an automatic timing for the slide to remain on-screen by checking After and entering the desired display time in the accompanying text box.

5. **(Optional) Choose Transitions → Timing → Apply To All to apply the specified transition and settings to all slides in the presentation.**

123

Genius

Recent versions of PowerPoint offer the Morph transition, which provides an easier way to create animation for slide objects. Just apply the Morph transition to a slide, duplicate the slide, and then move objects to new positions on the duplicated slide. The duplicated slide must remain immediately after the original for this to work. Easy peasy.

Adding animations

Similar to a transition, an *animation* is a motion effect that applies to an individual slide object. You apply animations using the Animations tab.

Caution

When it comes to transitions and animations, less can be more. If all the transitions you apply in a show are from the Exciting grouping and you likewise animate every slide object, then the animations lose their punch. Consider saving the bold transitions for only the most important slide or two and the big animations for objects presenting key presentation takeaways.

Applying an animation works similarly to the process just described for applying a transition. On the slide, click the object to animate. Display the Animations tab (Figure 5.8), choose an animation from the Animation gallery, and then choose other settings such as Timing group choices. On the slide, boxed numbers appear to show you the order in which the animations will play. If you want to review how that looks, click the Preview button in the Preview group.

By default, if you apply animation to a placeholder containing a bulleted list, PowerPoint animates the bullets to come in one at a time, with sub-bullets animating along with the "parent" bullet above. You can click a sub-bullet in the placeholder and then choose Animations ➔ Timing ➔ Start ➔ On Click (yes, reapply the setting even though it appears to be already applied) to fix this. That's just one of the many adjustments you can make to applied animations using the Animations tab.

You also can choose Animations ➔ Advanced Animation ➔ Animation Pane to open the Animation Pane pane, which lists all the animations applied in the current slide. Right-click an animation there to display a shortcut menu with additional commands for customizing the animation. Click the pane's Close (X) button when you're finished.

Boxed numbers indicate animation order

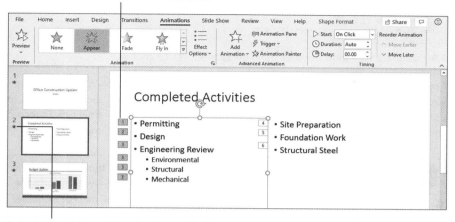

Indicates transition and/or animation applied

5.8 Animations apply motion to individual slide objects.

Playing the show

You should always, always, always review your presentation as an on-screen slide show carefully before going live. Pressing the F5 key starts the show from the beginning. Depending on how you set up your transitions and animations, you can either press the Spacebar or click with the mouse to advance through the slides and animations, or use a presentation remote controller. (Ideally, you'd run through the show at your presentation venue before the audience enters the room to make sure all your equipment works.) Press F1 at any time to see additional shortcut keys, such as pressing B to toggle between a black screen and the current slide. Press Esc at any time to stop the playback. I also frequently use the Shift+F5 keyboard shortcut to start the show from the current slide so that I can check the transition and animations.

You also can use the settings on the Slide Show tab shown in Figure 5.9 to perform other setup and sharing tasks, such as presenting the show online, setting up for multiple monitors or displays, or creating a custom version of the slide show that might have fewer slides than the full presentation.

125

5.9 Customize slide show playback using the Slide Show tab's choices.

Choosing Set Up Slide Show in the Set Up group opens the Set Up Show dialog box, where you can choose settings for both presented and automated shows, such as whether to use slide timings, loop continuously, or play without narrations and animations. To record show narration, use the Slide Show → Set Up → Record Slide Show command.

Genius

When you've set up a presentation to include automated (timed) transitions and animations—as well as any audio you might record—you can use the File → Export command to create a video or animated GIF file. For example, I've exported a presentation as a video that I included in an online course. For some Microsoft 365 subscriptions, you also can publish the presentation to the Microsoft Stream secure video sharing service for your organization.

How Do I Use Formatting to Enhance My Documents?

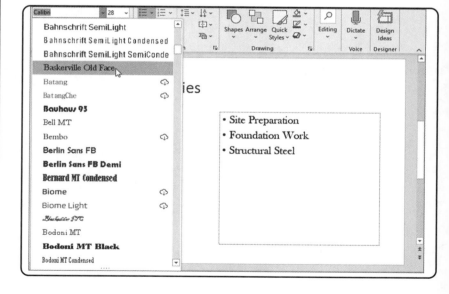

There's no reason to stick with plain, boring Word pages, Excel worksheets, and PowerPoint slides using the default formatting. In contrast, upping your document formatting game gives you the opportunity to highlight important content, make the document easier for your readers to understand, and even sprinkle in some organizational branding. This chapter shows you how to apply formatting for document function and flair. The chapter coverage begins with the must-know skill of applying number and date formats in Excel. The chapter then reviews key formatting techniques, including working with text formatting, borders, styles, and themes, as well as clearing formatting.

Changing the Number or Date Format in Excel

In a couple of earlier spots in the book, such as in the "Number formatting on the fly" section of Chapter 1, I touched on the fact that Excel offers special formats for some types of cell entries, especially numeric and date values. By applying a number format to include a particular symbol and number of decimal places with a cell entry, for example, you can communicate to your readers whether the cell entry is a currency value or a percentage. When you do not format on the fly when typing in cell entries, you later might need to apply a number format to the cell. The number format indicates more specifically what type of value the cell holds, whether to display a currency or percentage symbol, whether to use the comma thousands separator, and how many decimal places to display.

Excel in most cases applies the default General format to plain cell entries that you make, even for text entries. (One notable exception is that Excel immediately uses the Date or Time number format for recognized dates and times.) You can use the tools in the Number group of the Home tab to change the number format in one of three different ways. First, you can click one of the buttons identified in Figure 6.1 to make an immediate formatting change.

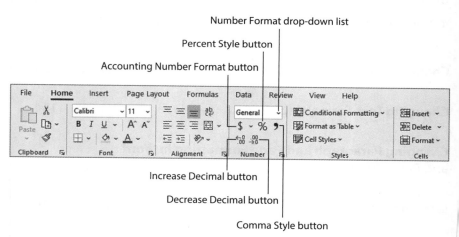

6.1 Use the Number group of the Home tab to change the number format applied to a selected cell or range in Excel.

Genius

The Increase Decimal button displays another decimal place each time you click it, while Decrease Decimal does the opposite. These buttons are the fastest way to adjust the in-cell decimal places displayed with the most common number formats. If you reduce the number of displayed decimal places for a calculated formula result or number, Excel rounds the displayed decimal value up or down as needed.

As shown in Figure 6.1, the Number Format drop-down list displays the name of the currently applied number format, which is the default General format for the selected cell. You can open the drop-down list to apply even more common number formats, as shown in Figure 6.2. One of the nice features of this method is that the list previews each format as it would appear when applied to the current cell. If you look at the left side of Figure 6.2, you can see that the Accounting format's preview looks about right, but the Short Date example of 9/6/3851 clearly looks out of whack!

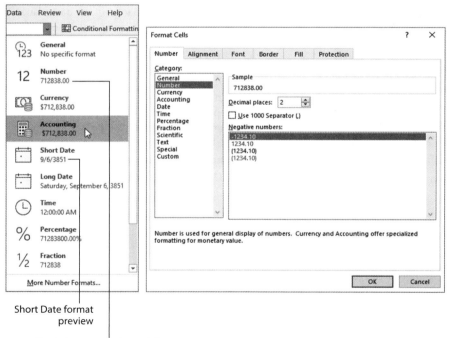

Short Date format preview

Check the preview for each format

6.2 The Number Format drop-down list and Number tab of the Format Cells dialog box preview various formats for a selected cell.

Finally, you can use the Number tab in the Format Cells dialog box to apply a different number format or to tweak a format, which gives you the most control over how values appear. To open the dialog box, choose More Number Formats from the bottom of the Number Format drop-down list, click the dialog box launcher in the lower-right corner of the Number group of the Home tab, or right-click the selection and choose Format Cells. Choose the approximate type of format you want in the Category list at the left, and then work with the settings that appear to adjust the format as desired. The right side of Figure 6.2 shows the available settings for the Number category, which includes choosing whether to include the comma thousands separator and choosing an appearance for negative values in the Negative Numbers list. The Sample area also offers a preview of the current cell's contents. Click OK when you finish choosing a format and its options.

Using number formats

Now that you know how to apply a number format, it's worthwhile to review when and how to use the various formats. I'll start with the most common formats for numbers:

- **Number.** Having a Number number format seems redundant, but the basic flavor of this format displays a number with two decimal places, no thousands separator, and no symbol of any type. (Refer to Figure 6.2.) You might use the Number format for statistical data, but it also can be used in business sheets to reduce the number of currency symbols.

- **Accounting.** The Accounting number format by default adds two decimal places to the number, displays a currency symbol aligned at the far-left side of the cell, and includes the comma thousands separator if applicable. For users in the United States, the $ currency symbol is used. Clicking the main part of the Accounting Number Format button in the Number group applies the format directly. To display another currency symbol, choose it from the button's drop-down list or use the Format Cells dialog box.

- **Currency.** This format is similar to the Accounting format, but it displays the currency symbol just to the left of the number rather than at the left edge of the cell. This format also gives you additional control over how negative numbers display via the Number tab of the Format Cells dialog box. This format displays zero values as $0.00, while the Accounting format displays zero values as $ - (a currency symbol and a dash). Finally, this format aligns the values all the way to the right side of the cell, while the Accounting format leaves a little space between the right end of the cell entry and the right cell border. Figure 6.3 shows the Currency format used with the Number format to show some financial values.

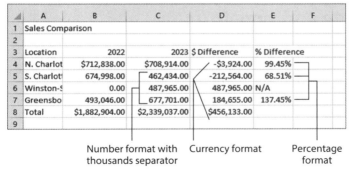

	A	B	C	D	E	F
1	Sales Comparison					
2						
3	Location	2022	2023	$ Difference	% Difference	
4	N. Charlot	$712,838.00	$708,914.00	-$3,924.00	99.45%	
5	S. Charlot	674,998.00	462,434.00	-212,564.00	68.51%	
6	Winston-S	0.00	487,965.00	487,965.00	N/A	
7	Greensbo	493,046.00	677,701.00	184,655.00	137.45%	
8	Total	$1,882,904.00	$2,339,037.00	$456,133.00		
9						

Number format with   Currency format   Percentage
thousands separator   format

6.3 Use number formats to control the display of financial values.

Genius

In some cases, when you apply the Accounting or Currency number format, the added decimal places increase the column width. To avoid the column width change and apply either of these number formats without decimal places, you have to use the Number tab of the Format Cells dialog box. Just select the desired format from the Category list, change the Decimal Places entry to 0, and click OK.

● **Percentage.** When you use the Percent Style button in the Number group of the Home tab, it simply adds the % (percent) sign to the number. If you apply the Percentage number format using the Number Format drop-down list, it adds the % (percent) sign plus two decimal places, as illustrated in Figure 6.3. Since 1 equals 100% mathematically, make sure you enter the number as a decimal value (.10 for 10 percent) before applying the number format. Or, if the number format changes the number unexpectedly, edit the value after applying the number format.

Caution

Chapter 1 explained that you can type the % (percent) symbol right after a number to format it as a percentage. Excel then treats the number as a decimal (25% is .25) in calculations and applies the Percentage number format. However, when you apply the Percentage number format to a cell holding a whole number with the General number format, Excel treats the entry as a multiple of 100%, so 25 becomes 2500.00%. Clicking the Percent Style button in the Number group does the same, so 25 becomes 2500%.

Using date and time formats

Once Excel correctly recognizes a cell entry as a date or time, you can apply a new format to change the date or time's appearance. If you check back with Figure 6.2, you can see that the Number Format drop-down list offers two number formats using common styles for communicating dates:

- **Short Date.** Displays the date in the 8/1/2023 style.
- **Long Date.** Displays the date in the Tuesday, August 1, 2023 style.

However, you might want to display the date in an even more abbreviated way, such as 1-Aug, or choose a longer format that includes the time, or maybe even use 24-hour military time. Excel offers numerous other number formats in the Date and Time categories of the Number tab of the Format Cells dialog box. The Date category offers several different formats you can select from the Type list, and of course, you'd choose Time in the Category list to see the formats for times.

Note

You can use the choices in the Scientific, Text, and Special categories on the Number tab in the Format Cells dialog box to format a selection as scientific notation, store a numeric entry as text, or apply formatting to special numbers such as ZIP codes.

Changing Text Formatting

Every new Word document file, Excel workbook file, or Outlook message uses default formatting for basic text or cell entries: 11 pt. Calibri font. Yawn. (PowerPoint slide layouts have more variety.) When everything looks the same, it's not only boring, but it's also a problem, because your intended audience can't tell which information is most important. Ask yourself, do they want to review each and every individual sentence or number, or do they want to jump right to the bottom-line conclusions or calculations? Formatting can help provide a road map through the content you lay out.

This section of the chapter introduces you to what's sometimes called *direct* or *manual* formatting in Microsoft 365 apps, where you pick and choose the specific combination of formatting settings that you want and apply them one at a time. I'll cover one group of settings here and then cover a few more settings in the later section, "Working with Borders and Shading."

You can use choices in the Font group of the ribbon's Home tab (Format Text tab in an Outlook Message window) to apply a setting; click the dialog box launcher in the Font group to open the Font or Format Cells dialog box to the Font tab; or right-click a selection, choose Font or Format Cells, and go to the Font tab in the dialog box. Also, in some cases, when you make a selection, the Mini Toolbar appears and offers some of the font and other formatting choices.

Genius

Keep in mind that less can be more when it comes to any type of document formatting. Good design sometimes means editing *yourself* and keeping your formatting choices sleek and simple, using formatting selectively for emphasis. Emphasizing everything means that nothing is emphasized. Some design experts recommend emphasizing 10 percent or less of the text in any document.

Applying font formatting

The Home tab of the ribbon presents most of the direct formatting choices in the Font group, Paragraph group (Word and PowerPoint), and Alignment group (Excel). (In Outlook, it's the Font and Paragraph groups of the Format Text tab in the Message window. From here on out, I'll assume you can find settings as needed in Outlook.) Figure 6.4 identifies some of the key choices in Word's Font group that you can apply to the selection. The Font group in the other apps have these choices in common, but may offer slightly different choices, too. Recall from the Chapter 1 section called "Selecting content in PowerPoint" that you can generally select a text or content placeholder itself to change all the placeholder's text, but you have to select text within a placeholder to format only that text. I'll just cover the highlights of font formatting here.

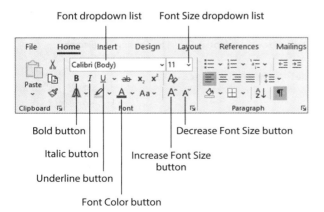

6.4 The Font group holds choices for adjusting the appearance of selected text.

135

The font refers to the overall style of the letters and numbers in the text or cell contents. As its name suggests, you use the Font drop-down list to choose the font that you want to apply to a selected cell or range. When you open the Font drop-down list and move the mouse pointer over a font, the app displays a Live Preview of how the font would look if you applied it to the selection, as shown in the example in Figure 6.5. You could then click the font to apply it to the selection. Newer versions of the Microsoft 365 apps also offer a feature called *cloud fonts*. These fonts don't initially install with the apps and have a cloud icon beside them in the Font drop-down list. Clicking one of these fonts downloads and installs it on your computer, making it available for use in the Microsoft 365 applications.

Mouse pointer over the font to preview

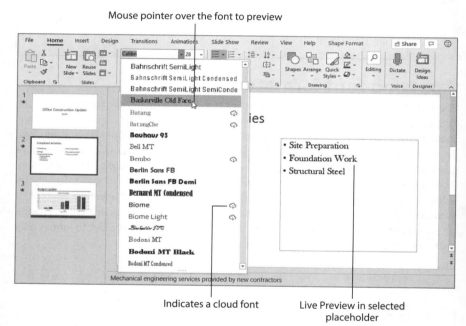

Indicates a cloud font

Live Preview in selected placeholder

6.5 Check the Live Preview of the font choice in the text.

What Do I Need to Know About Font Types?

Generally speaking, there are two different types of fonts: serif (which have small strokes at the end of the letters) and sans serif. (Some fonts with really crazy serifs can be considered a different class of font, referred to as a *decorative font*.) The default Calibri font is an example of a sans serif font. Serif fonts are generally considered to be more readable because the serifs guide the eye between characters. They are also thought of as more formal, and some in the design community pooh-pooh them as being too old school. Don't let that prevent you from using serif fonts when appropriate. When you want your text to look more formal or have a packed document that you want to ensure is readable, try a serif font or two before just going with a sans serif font. Design experts also advise using only two different fonts overall—one for headings and one for other content. If you must use a third font, use it sparingly.

The other formatting choices shown in Figure 6.4 are fairly self-explanatory. Use the Font Size drop-down list to change the size of the entry in pt. (points, with 72 points per inch). Either you can open the list and click a size or you can change the entry in the Font Size text box and press Enter. In Word, and to some degree in PowerPoint, there's a general rule of thumb that the wider the column of text, the larger the font size should be for readability. Some also argue that for a PowerPoint presentation that will be delivered as an in-person slide show, bullet points should be 24 pt. size or larger. The Bold, Italic, and Underline buttons apply (or remove) the specified type of formatting to the selection. The keyboard shortcuts for these three buttons are Ctrl+B, Ctrl+I, and Ctrl+U, respectively. The Underline button also includes a drop-down list that you can use to change between regular single Underline and Double Underline. In accounting documents, it's typical to use single underline formatting for subtotals and double underline formatting for grand totals. Use bold, italics, and underlining sparingly to emphasize content such as headings, as overuse of these types of formatting can make a sheet look cluttered.

Genius

With a 3-D selection in Excel (a selection spanning multiple sheets as explained in Chapter 1), any formatting changes you make apply to all the sheets. Say you are creating a workbook to track sales information from three stores. You want each store's sales to be on a separate sheet, but you also want the sheets to have identical layout and formatting. After you add the sheets, you could use 3-D selections when you make entries and apply formatting to save time and get consistent content, appearance, and branding.

137

You can click the Increase Font Size or Decrease Font Size button to adjust text size. Each click increases or decreases the size to the next size listed on the Font Size drop-down list. Contents with a larger font size tend to stand out more. As with other types of formatting, limiting the number of font sizes used in each document will avoid a cluttered or overdesigned appearance.

Note

PowerPoint's AutoFit feature automatically sizes text within a placeholder based on how much text you add. To turn this feature off so you can have more control over font size, right-click the placeholder and then choose Format Shape. In the Format Shape pane at the right, click the Text Options button at the top, and then click the Textbox button just below it. Click Text Box to expand the settings if needed, and then click the Do Not AutoFit option button. Close the pane by clicking its Close (X) button.

Font Color is another split button. The left side of the button displays a font color, and clicking that part of the button applies the color to the selection immediately. To choose another color, click the drop-down list arrow on the right side of the button. A gallery or palette of colors appears, as shown in Figure 6.6. As for the Font drop-down list, moving the mouse pointer over a color in the gallery displays a Live Preview of the color in the contents of the selected cell or range. Click a color to apply it.

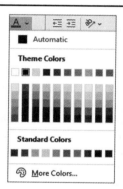

6.6 You can choose another font color for the selected cell or range.

Note

Chapter 11 covers how to add headers and footers that will appear on every page when you print a document. The preset header and footer options don't include any special formatting. You can format the header and footer contents to a limited degree, with the available choices in the Font group of the Home tab.

Excel does offer strikethrough, superscript, and subscript formatting via the Font tab of the Format Cells dialog box. To open the dialog box, click the dialog box launcher in the lower-right corner of the Font group on the Home tab, or use one of the methods described earlier. In the Effects area at lower left, use the Strikethrough, Superscript, and Subscript check boxes as needed, and then click OK. Word and PowerPoint similarly offer some additional options on the Font tab of the Font dialog box that appears when you click the dialog box launcher in the Font group of the Home tab. These extra options under Effects include Small Caps, All Caps, and Hidden (to create hidden text).

Applying alignment formatting

Figure 6.7 shows the Paragraph group of the Home tab in Word at left and the Alignment group of the Home tab in Excel at right. (PowerPoint also has a Paragraph group on the Home tab and Outlook's Format Text tab in a Message window has a Paragraph group.) These groups offer various tools for changing the horizontal and vertical alignment of a selection. First, take a look at the buttons that are common in the apps:

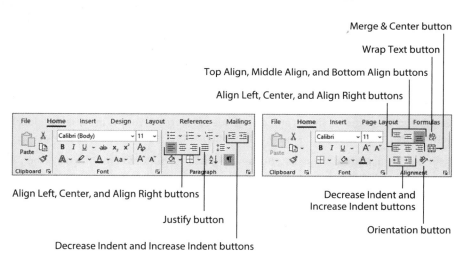

6.7 You can change the alignment, indention, and some other aspects of the selection.

- ◉ **Align Left, Center, and Align Right.** These buttons align text relative to the left and right margins in Word, and the cell or placeholder boundaries in Excel and PowerPoint. In Excel and PowerPoint, changing the alignment has the most impact when the column or placeholder is wider than its contents.

- ◉ **Justify.** Word, PowerPoint, and Outlook also have this paragraph alignment choice, which adjusts the spacing between words on a line so that all the lines of the formatted paragraph or placeholder align at both the left and the right to the margins, column width (when the text is formatted in columns), or placeholder. Be advised that this can result in gaps or *loose lines* in lines of text with fewer words. That said, multicolumn publications such as newspapers, newsletters, and scholarly journals frequently use this alignment.

● **Decrease Indent and Increase Indent.** When you want just a little space between the left margin or left cell or placeholder boundary and the contents, choose one of these buttons. In PowerPoint, these buttons are called Decrease List Level and Increase List Level and don't become active until you've selected the text *within* a placeholder, specifically one holding a bulleted list; using the buttons changes both the amount of indention and the outline level of the selected text.

Note

All of the Paragraph group alignment choices in Word and Outlook apply to the entire paragraph that holds the insertion point or all selected paragraphs. In PowerPoint, the alignment choice applies to all the text in a selected placeholder. If you've clicked a bullet item in a placeholder, the alignment choice applies to it. Likewise, if you've selected more text in the placeholder, the alignment choice applies to the whole selection.

Excel's Alignment group, shown at the right side of Figure 6.7, throws in some additional settings that are crucial in working with the alignments of the selected cell or range:

● **Top Align, Middle Align, and Bottom Align.** These buttons come into play when the row height has been changed, so you want to choose how the contents should align relative to the top and bottom boundaries of the cell. For example, Middle Align can be a nice choice if you want white space both above and below the cell contents and if you want to offset the cell contents from the cells above or below.

● **Wrap Text.** This causes the text to wrap to two or more lines within the cell, based on the column width. To create manual line breaks as you enter text, press Alt+Enter.

● **Merge & Center.** Select a range of cells to merge and then click this button to both merge the cells and center the contents of the leftmost or upper-left cell within the merged area. Merging and centering a title above the range of detailed data gives the sheet a polished look. Clicking the drop-down list arrow for this button displays a menu of additional commands, including Unmerge Cells for returning to a normal range of separate cells.

Orientation. Clicking this button also opens a menu of preset choices for rotating text. If you click Format Cell Alignment at the bottom of the menu, the Format Cells dialog box opens with the Alignment tab displayed. In addition to using this tab to apply any of the alignment formatting already discussed, you can use the controls in the Orientation area at the upper right to set a custom rotation for a selection. PowerPoint has a similar Text Direction button for rotating text in a placeholder. It offers Horizontal, Rotate All Text 90°, Rotate All Text 270°, and Stacked choices.

Genius

You can use the Format Painter to copy various formatting from one selection to another. Select the text, cells, or placeholder with the formatting to copy, choose Home ➔ Clipboard ➔ Format Painter, and then drag over the other text, cells, or placeholder to format. You also can double-click the Format Painter button to lock it on, click or drag to copy the formatting to multiple other locations, and then press Esc or click the button again to turn off Format Painter.

Figure 6.8 shows a number of formatting selections from the Font and Alignment groups of the Home tab applied in an example Excel worksheet, for a sense of the possibilities. Some of the changes are obvious, such as the fact that I applied a different font to the title and labels in the sheet and increased the font size for the title. I changed the font color for all the total values to green and all the average values to blue. I wrapped some titles, used a preset to rotate others, and applied both vertical and horizontal centering to offset some labels from the values below them. Finally, the left-aligned text entries for the Bonus? column looked too crowded next to the right-aligned values in the Average column, so I used the Increase Indent button to add just enough space to make the Bonus? column more clean and readable.

141

Wrapped labels   A1:G1 merged and centered

	A	B	C	D	E	F	G
1	**Sales and Bonus Calculations**						
2							
3	**Sales Goal**	**Bonus Amount**					
4	$130,000	$3,000					
5							
6	**Employee ID**	Jan	Feb	Mar	**Total**	**Average**	**Bonus?**
7	1101	$49,890	$41,068	$51,247	$142,205	$47,402	Yes
8	1233	$39,204	$44,781	$47,790	$131,775	$43,925	Yes
9	1099	$64,339	$60,608	$42,921	$167,868	$55,956	No
10	1175	$62,839	$44,074	$31,577	$138,490	$46,163	Yes
11	1143	$55,358	$42,587	$32,567	$130,512	$43,504	Yes
12	**Total**	$271,630	$233,118	$206,102	$710,850	$236,950	
13	**Average**	$54,326	$46,624	$41,220			
14							

Angle Counterclockwise preset applied   Indented

Middle Align and Center applied

6.8 I've applied various formatting settings to enhance this example worksheet.

Changing Paragraph and Page Formatting in Word and PowerPoint

In Word and PowerPoint, *line spacing* (the space between lines in a paragraph) and *paragraph spacing* (the space between paragraphs) present additional formatting considerations. (You can change line and paragraph spacing in Outlook, too, but in my experience, that's a rare thing to do.) This section explains how to change these two crucial settings.

Note

How line and paragraph settings—as well as other design settings—impact document appearance also depends on some of the page setup settings, such as margins, orientation, and paper size. To learn how to change those settings, consult the "Changing Page Settings" section in Chapter 11.

Changing overall line spacing

The default Normal style in Word's Normal.dotm template has a quirky line spacing setting of 1.08 lines, which is just a tad more than single spacing. On the other hand, in a blank PowerPoint presentation file, the default line spacing setting is 0.9, a little less than single spacing. Other themes, templates, and styles may have differing line spacing settings. There may be times when you want to change the line spacing to adjust the document's appearance or need to change the line spacing to comply with a document formatting standard. For example, style guides for student reports typically require double line spacing.

You can change the line spacing to one of several preset settings or choose a custom setting. As for alignment settings, changes to the line spacing in Word and Outlook apply to the entire paragraph that holds the insertion point or all selected paragraphs. In PowerPoint, the line spacing choice applies to all the text in a selected placeholder. If you've clicked a bullet item in a placeholder, the line spacing choice applies to it. Likewise, if you've selected more text in the placeholder, the line spacing choice applies to the whole selection.

Choose Home ➜ Paragraph ➜ Line and Paragraph Spacing (Word) or Home ➜ Paragraph ➜ Line Spacing (PowerPoint) to display the preset line spacing choices. (In Outlook, the command in the Message window is Format Text ➜ Paragraph ➜ Line and Paragraph Spacing.) Point to a preset to see a Live Preview of that spacing in the text, as in the example in Word shown in Figure 6.9.

To apply a custom line spacing, choose Line Spacing Options below the preset Line and Paragraph Spacing (Word) or Line Spacing (PowerPoint) choices. The Paragraph dialog box appears, with the Indents and Spacing tab displayed. (You also could open the dialog box by clicking the Paragraph group dialog box launcher.) Open the Line Spacing drop-down list under Spacing and choose At Least (not available in PowerPoint), Exactly, or Multiple. Enter the desired amount of spacing (in lines) in the At text box, and then click OK.

Changing spacing before and after paragraphs

Adding a bit of "cushion" white space between the elements in a document or presentation can help make text easier to read and follow. In Word's default Normal.dotm template, the heading styles all are set up to include a little extra white space before any paragraph using the style. For example, the Heading 1 style is set to use 12 pt. of extra space before (above) the heading. The Normal style for text includes 8 pt. of space after the paragraph by default. This is why you don't have to press Enter twice after each paragraph in Word. The right amount of visual separation between the headings and text is already built in to the styles. (This is not true for the Normal style in an Outlook message.) PowerPoint similarly has a bit of space built in before each bullet item.

Line and Paragraph Spacing button

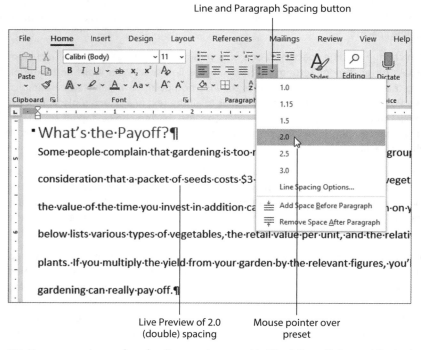

Live Preview of 2.0   Mouse pointer over
(double) spacing   preset

6.9 You can preview and apply a line spacing preset in Word, PowerPoint, and Outlook.

You can add and remove line spacing in Word (and Outlook) using the choices below Line Spacing options as shown in Figure 6.9. The available choices depend on whether there is added space before or after the paragraph. To specify a specific amount of text between paragraphs, follow these steps:

1. **Choose Home → Paragraph → Line and Paragraph Spacing → Line Spacing Options (Word) or Home → Paragraph → Line Spacing → Line Spacing Options (PowerPoint).** In Outlook, the command is Format Text → Paragraph → Line and

Paragraph Spacing ➜ Line Spacing Options. You also can click the Paragraph group dialog box launcher. The Paragraph dialog box opens, with the Indents and Spacing tab selected. Word's Paragraph dialog box appears in Figure 6.10. PowerPoint's dialog box is more simplified, with fewer settings and no Preview area.

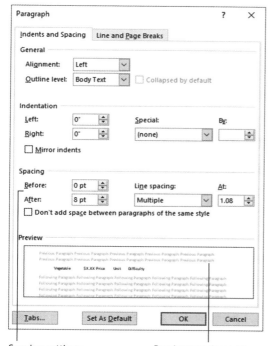

Spacing settings   Preview spacing settings

6.10 Specify custom paragraph and line spacing in Word, PowerPoint, and Outlook using the Paragraph dialog box.

2. **Under Spacing, enter the desired amount of spacing in points in the Before and After text boxes as needed.** You also can use the increment arrows for each text box to change the values.

3. **Click OK.**

Genius

In Word, you can change the paragraph spacing of the entire document by choosing an option from the Design ➜ Document Formatting ➜ Paragraph Spacing gallery.

Working with Borders and Shading

The additional direct formatting choices covered in this section apply to the page or cell itself, rather than the text on the page or within the cell or placeholder. You can think of this as formatting the container or background for the document information. This section shows you the design possibilities of using borders and shading to highlight information.

Using borders and shading in Word

Borders and shading are great design tools for calling attention to important information on a page or on-screen. For example, you can use a border below the information at the top of a newsletter to anchor it and make it stand out, or you can use shading to call attention to a particular paragraph or quotation. Keep your audience in mind when applying shading in particular. Applying dark shading to dark text or light shading to light text reduces contrast and can make text unreadable.

After you select the paragraph(s) to which you want to add borders or shading, use the Shading button and Borders button (which initially displays a grid with a bottom under-line on it) in the Paragraph group of the Home tab to apply a choice that you like based on the Live Preview. By default, clicking the main part of the Borders button without making another selection applies a bottom border to the selected paragraph (but not the individual lines in the paragraph). Some of the Border presets, such as Inside Borders, don't have any impact in a Word paragraph and work better for Excel, as described later. I often use Outside Borders, which places a border around the entire paragraph, and Bottom Border, which places a border below the paragraph. No Border removes any previously applied border. Changing border settings or creating custom borders in Word works much like the process for applying a custom border in Excel, described in the upcoming section, "Changing cell borders and shading in Excel."

Note

PowerPoint treats each placeholder as a shape. This means you use choices in the Quick Styles gallery in the Drawing group of the Home tab or the Shape Styles group choices on the Shape Format tab to change the fill and outline for the entire placeholder. You can apply a highlight color to selected text in a slide placeholder by choosing the Home → Font → Text Highlight Color down arrow and then clicking the color to use.

Adding a page border in Word

Adding borders to the pages in a Word document can make the document seem more formal and complete. You can apply the page border to the whole document or the current section. Choose Design ➔ Page Background ➔ Page Borders. The Borders and Shading dialog box opens with the Page Border tab displayed. Under Setting, click a thumbnail for a preset type of border. Figure 6.11 shows the available border types. I used Box in this example.

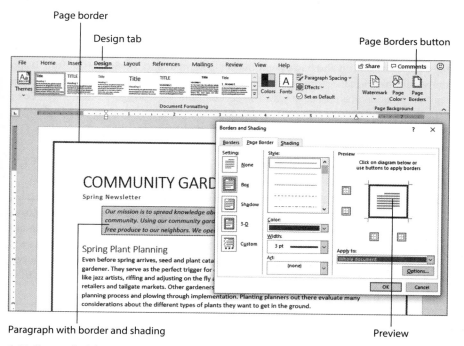

Page border

Design tab

Page Borders button

Paragraph with border and shading

Preview

6.11 I've applied the Page Border settings shown here in the Borders and Shading dialog box to the example document.

Make choices for the Style, Color, and Width settings. Make a choice from the Apply To drop-down list to determine on which pages the border will appear. Whole Document adds the page border to all the pages, while the other choices enable you to apply the border to all or part of the current section. Click OK.

Genius

Use the Design → Page Background → Page Color gallery to apply a background color to the pages in a Word document, but be aware that the background color doesn't print, even if you save the document in one of the web page formats. In PowerPoint, choose Design → Customize → Format Background to open a pane where you can choose a color, gradient, picture, texture, or pattern fill for the selected slides. PowerPoint slide backgrounds *do* print.

Changing cell borders and shading in Excel

In Excel, the Font group of the Home tab includes the Fill Color button (which is next to the Font Color button and has a paint bucket icon on it) and the Borders button. Using these buttons, you can create dimension and contrast between cells on the sheet or highlight information in a particular way. The Fill Color button works just like the Font Color button, except that it applies a fill or background color (also called *cell shading*) to the selected cell or range. You can click the left or main part of the button to apply the currently displayed color. To apply another color, click the drop-down list arrow on the right side of the button, move the mouse pointer over various colors to see a Live Preview of the color on the selection, and then click the color you ultimately want.

Genius

If you click the Select All button where the row numbers and column letters meet, you can apply a background fill color to all the cells in the sheet. A fill created in this way does print, but only within the selected print area and margins. Chapter 11 covers printing. You also can select a page background image using the Page Layout → Page Setup → Background choice, but this type of background only appears on-screen and does not print.

You can apply any of a number of different border presets by clicking the drop-down list arrow for the Borders button and then choosing a preset style to use, as in Word. The borders applied by the various choices generally surround the outside boundaries of the selected range, with the exception of the All Borders choice. Other choices include Outside Borders (a box around the outside of the selected range), Top and Bottom Border, Top and Thick Bottom Border, and of course, No Border, which removes any previously applied border. Use the Line Color and Line Style submenu choices to make the border less plain. (Word doesn't give you these options.) Choosing More Borders from the bottom of the Borders button menu opens the Format Cells dialog box with the Border tab displayed, as shown in Figure 6.12. (Choose Borders and Shading to open the Borders and Shading dialog box with the Borders tab displayed in Word. Word also has a border Width choice in addition to the choices described here.)

148

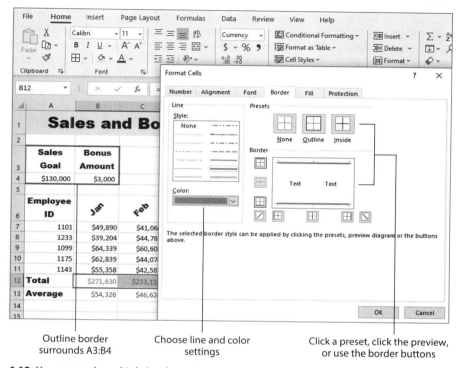

Outline border
surrounds A3:B4

Choose line and color
settings

Click a preset, click the preview,
or use the border buttons

6.12 You can apply multiple border settings at once using the Border tab.

Use the Border tab to choose multiple settings to apply at once in the selected range. In the Line box, choose from the Style list, and then use the Color drop-down list to choose a line color. Then, you can apply the line in one of three ways. You can click one of the three buttons under Presets. You can click directly on the preview to apply a border to the desired location. Or, you can click one of the Border buttons surrounding the preview to choose the border position. Click OK to apply your final choices.

Using Styles

You may not want to spend time overthinking what combination of formatting and borders to apply in a Word document or Excel worksheet. (As noted earlier, in PowerPoint you can only apply shape style formatting overall to a placeholder.) And you may not want to spend your time applying each and every combination of formatting to paragraphs and ranges throughout the file. Styles simplify the job for you, making it easy to apply consistent, complementary text formatting throughout the file.

In Chapter 2 I touched on Word styles with regard to building a document outline. The outlining process relies on the numbered Heading 1 through Heading 9 styles. Word's Normal.dotm template includes dozens of other styles, including the trusty Normal style, along with Title, Subtitle, Strong, Quote, and more. To apply a style, first click to position the insertion point in a paragraph or select multiple paragraphs. Choose Home ➔ Styles ➔ Styles to open the Styles gallery. (If you can already see part of the Styles gallery, click the More down arrow button at lower right to open the gallery and display more styles.) Move the mouse pointer over a style to see the Live Preview, and then click the style to apply. To see even more styles, click the Styles group dialog box launcher to open a moveable Styles pane. It includes a scrolling list of even more styles to apply, and if you want to see *even more*, click the Options button, open the Select Styles to Show drop-down list in the Style Pane Options dialog box, choose All Styles, and then click OK.

I consider Excel cell styles a woefully overlooked feature. To apply a cell style to the selected cell or range, choose Home ➔ Styles ➔ Cell Styles to open the Cell Styles gallery shown in Figure 6.13. Move the mouse pointer over a style to see a Live Preview in the selected cell or range, and then click the style you want to use. In the example in the figure, I've applied the Title style to the contents of cell A1, the Input Style to B3:B5, and 40% shaded accent colors to A3:A5 and A7. I'm in the process of applying the Output style to cell B7.

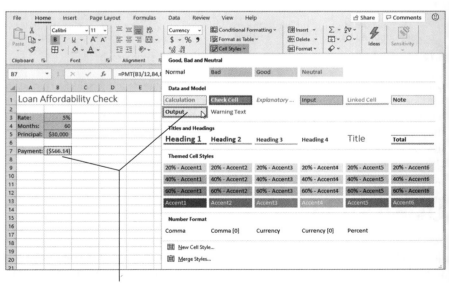

Output style being applied

6.13 Find predefined formatting in Excel's Cell Styles gallery.

Using cell styles provides the same advantages of using styles in a word processing document. They are already designed for you, so you don't have to try endless combinations of font, size, color, fill, and borders. If you stick with using the cell styles for the majority of your worksheets—especially the ones that identify specific actions such as Input, Calculation, Note, or Warning Text—you'll produce sheets that are more attractive, usable, and consistent.

Genius

Conditional formatting applies different formatting to Excel cell values based on rules and comparisons. You can find top and bottom values, show how values compare with color scales, and explore dozens more choices. There are two ways to apply conditional formatting to a selected range in Excel. Choose Home → Styles → Conditional Formatting, and then work from there. Or, move the mouse pointer over the selection, click the Quick Analysis button (Ctrl+Q) that appears at the lower-right corner, and work from there.

Even better, if you apply a different theme to the file, any styled text in a Word document or cells formatted using the choices under Themed Cell Styles in Excel update automatically to reflect the style formatting in the new theme. (I cover themes shortly.) If you give styles a try, I predict you'll stick with them.

Caution

Any direct formatting that you apply from the Font, Paragraph, or Alignment groups on the Home tab overrides the applicable style formatting, such as the style's font size, cell fill color, or paragraph formatting. Reapply the style to remove the direct formatting.

While in Excel, you can create a new style using the New Cell Style choice at the bottom of the Cell Styles gallery, although it's much more common to edit and create styles in Word. In my opinion, that's because Word documents tend to be more visual media, while the emphasis is on the data in Excel. In Word, choose Home → Styles → Styles → Create a Style to start the process of creating a new style.

Clearing Formatting

Sometimes it's harder to back up than to go forward. You may have changed various formatting settings applied to a selection, and now you can't remember exactly what you did. In this situation, the ability to clear formatting from text or a cell or range saves the day. Select the Word document text, Excel cell or range, or PowerPoint placeholder or text with the formatting to clear. Choose Home ➜ Font ➜ Clear All Formatting (Word and PowerPoint) or Home ➜ Editing ➜ Clear ➜ Clear Formats (Excel). This leaves the cell contents in place while removing the formatting, including the number format. The Clear menu in Excel includes other choices, such as Clear All, which removes both the cell contents and the formatting.

Understanding Themes

A theme is a collection of colors, fonts, and effects settings that you can apply to a Microsoft 365 file. Each new blank file you create in Word, Excel, or PowerPoint (as well as Outlook messages) uses the Office Theme by default. When you change from one theme to another, the app applies the new theme's colors, fonts, and effects throughout the file. Using the same theme for all your business documents also can help build a recognizable brand in the minds of your customers and colleagues, so it's worth the time to learn more about this perhaps under-used formatting feature in Microsoft 365.

Reviewing elements of a theme

Each theme offers a specific collection selected to work well together and lend a consistent, attractive design. The combination of design choices in each theme also suggests, well, a theme or mood for the content. For example, if you work in the finance or banking field, you might use the Dividend theme. Those in science or aviation might try the Celestial or Vapor Trail theme. There are more than 30 themes that install with Microsoft 365.

Each theme consists of the following three design elements:

- **Theme colors.** Each theme has a palette of 12 colors, some of which are used in specific instances or used along with cell styles. The first four are dark and light variations for text and backgrounds. Then there are six accent colors. The final two are colors for hyperlink cell entries and followed hyperlinks.

- **Theme fonts.** The theme fonts specify the heading font and body font. The heading font is used with the heading cell styles, while the body font is used for cell entries that don't have a heading style applied.

- **Theme effects.** The theme effects provide formatting for objects such as shapes and SmartArt, which are covered in Chapter 7. The effects include fills, shadows, border styles, and shading that change the look of graphics.

Changing themes

In Word and PowerPoint, the Design tab includes the Themes gallery and some other overall design settings. The Themes gallery is in the Document Formatting group in Word and the Themes group in PowerPoint. The Page Layout tab in Excel likewise includes many of the settings that affect overall sheet or workbook design, including the Themes gallery in the Themes group. (Find themes in the Options → Themes group in an Outlook message window.) If you move the mouse pointer over the Themes button in Word, Excel, and Outlook or over the first theme thumbnail in PowerPoint, a ScreenTip showing the name of the currently applied theme appears. Follow these steps to change the theme used by the file:

1. **Open the Themes gallery using the method for the app you're working in:**

   - **Word:** Design → Document Formatting → Themes

   - **Excel:** Page Layout → Themes → Themes

   - **PowerPoint:** Design → Themes → More button for gallery

   - **Outlook:** Options → Themes → Themes

2. **Scroll down if needed, and then move the mouse pointer over a theme to display a Live Preview.** See Figure 6.14.

3. **Click the theme you want to apply.**

4. **If you're using PowerPoint, you can click one of the choices in the Variants group to adjust the theme's colors.**

Theme variants (PowerPoint only)

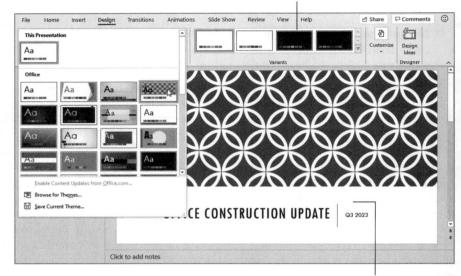

Theme Live Preview

6.14 Change the theme in the Themes gallery.

The apps usually adjust necessary formatting changes for you, but you should still check all the pages, sheets, or slides in the file to see if you need to make any formatting adjustments after changing the theme.

Genius

I've often advised that the theme you select for a PowerPoint presentation should be based on whether you intend to distribute it in print form or display it as a slide show. As a general rule, dark text on a light background works best for print, while light text on a darker background works best for a show, especially when it will be played back in a darkened room.

154

How Do I Use Graphics?

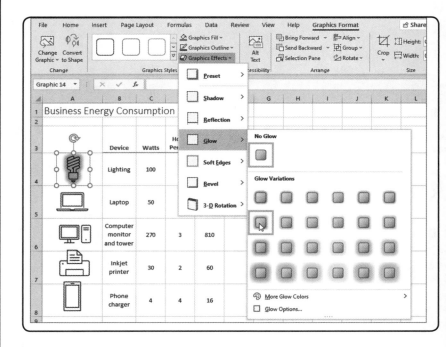

1 2 3 4 5 6 7 8 9 10 11

Infographics combine text, graphics, and charts to simplify or summarize an idea or concept. What does that have to do with Microsoft 365, you ask? Many infographics include data and statistics—you know, the type of information you may be developing in your Word pages, Excel worksheets, and PowerPoint slides. You can include graphics to add your organization's logo, highlight important values or takeaways, show a product image, or even illustrate a process. This chapter shows you how to insert and edit various types of graphics to make the info in your documents more memorable.

Inserting Simple Graphics

The main Microsoft 365 apps offer many types of graphics that you can add to a document. Unsurprisingly, you can find the choices for inserting various types of graphics in the Illustrations group of the Insert tab in Word and Excel and an Outlook message window. PowerPoint divides the graphics choices between the Illustrations and Images groups. While all the apps have roughly the same tools, they are arranged slightly differently on the ribbon in the various apps. Figure 7.1 shows the Illustrations group in Word as an example. In Excel, at lower screen resolutions, the group collapses down

7.1 Use the Illustrations group of the Insert tab to add graphics.

to a button that you have to click to display the group's choices. The rest of this section shows you how to add the various types of graphics and provides examples of when you might use each type. You'll learn a little later in the chapter how to move, size, and otherwise format graphics after you've inserted them.

Shapes

Choosing the Shapes button in the Illustrations group of the Insert tab opens the drop-down gallery, as shown in Excel in Figure 7.2. The gallery groups the shapes by type, and you can scroll down if needed to view additional shapes. You can pause the mouse pointer over a shape to see a ScreenTip with the shape's name.

To add a shape, in most cases you click the shape you want in the Shapes gallery and then drag on the page, worksheet, slide, or Outlook message body to create a shape that's the size you need. That said, a few tips or exceptions come to mind:

● **Inserting a shape at the default size.** To insert a shape at the default size, which is usually 1" x 1", just click once in the document after choosing the shape from the gallery. This works well when you want to insert multiple shapes that are exactly the same size.

● **Inserting a perfect circle or square.** If you choose the Oval or Rectangle shapes, you can press and hold Shift while dragging to create a perfect circle or square.

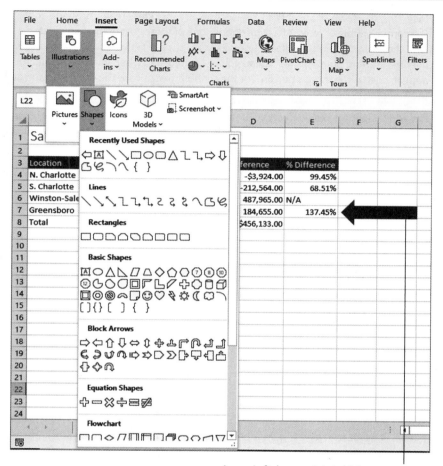

Arrow: Left shape points to highest percentage

7.2 Shapes are grouped by type in the Shapes gallery.

● **Inserting a curve.** The Curve choice in the Lines section of the Shapes gallery creates a special type of curve called a Bézier curve, which bends around a series of points. After you choose this tool, click to place the first point, click to place additional points, and then double-click the final point.

159

● **Inserting freeform shapes.** The Lines section also includes Freeform: Shape and Freeform: Scribble choices. After you choose one of these, just drag as you please with the mouse. To finish a filled freeform shape, just move the mouse pointer back over the starting point for the outline you've created, and when you see the fill appear, release the mouse button. For the scribble, just release the mouse button at the end of the scribble.

You can add shapes for purely decorative purposes, but it's even more powerful to use them to highlight important information or add new information that can't be conveyed by a simple label. For example, the arrow in Figure 7.2 points to the highest calculated % Difference. The Equation Shapes are mathematical operators that could be used to illustrate a calculation. There are Flowchart shapes that could be used along with some of the line and connector shapes in the Lines section of the Shapes gallery to create a process flowchart diagram like the ones traditionally used in the engineering and programming fields, among others.

The gallery also has sections with Stars and Banners and Callouts. A *callout* is a bubble or box with short descriptive text and a line or pointer to what the callout describes. A later section in this chapter, "Adding text to shapes," explains how to add text to shapes, including rectangles and other basic shapes, block arrows, callouts, and others.

Pictures

In the past, you could only insert picture or graphic files from your computer in a document. That was adequate if the goal was limited to inserting a company logo or product image. Now Microsoft has incorporated more ways to find and insert graphic files, although you can still insert a file from your computer.

The newest addition is the availability of *stock images*—images that you can use in your documents without the need to hire a photographer or graphic designer. Stock image providers usually charge a fee or royalty, but Microsoft offers its collection of stock images for royalty-free use to its Microsoft 365 subscribers. The stock images fall into five categories: Images, Icons (which I'll cover separately a little later), Cutout People, Stickers, and Illustrations. Here's how to insert a stock image, which requires that your computer be connected to the Internet:

1. **Choose Insert → Illustrations → Pictures → Stock Images.** In PowerPoint, you also can click the Stock Images button in a content placeholder, and the Pictures → Stock Images command is in the Images group. A window that you can use to search for stock images appears, as shown in Figure 7.3. The Images category is selected by default. The pictures you see and the search terms below the Search box vary each time you open the window, so your screen will differ accordingly from Figure 7.3.

Search box   Categories   Search terms

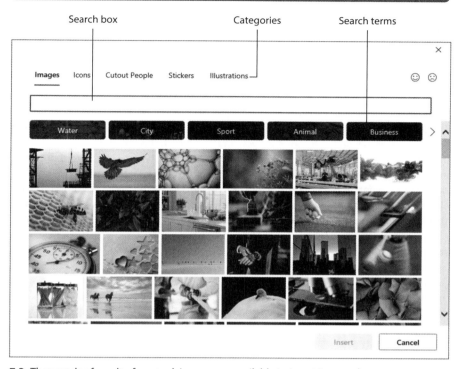

7.3 Thousands of royalty-free stock images are available to insert in your documents.

2. If needed, click one of the other categories at the top of the window.

3. Browse or search for images, as follows:

- Scroll the search terms below the Search box to the right or left using the arrows, and then click a term. Pause until matching images appear.

- Click in the Search box, type a search term or phrase, and either press Enter or pause until matching images appear.

4. Scroll down through the pictures if needed, and then click the thumbnail for the picture to insert so that a check circle appears in its upper-right corner. Optionally, you can select multiple images. The Insert button shows the number of selected images in parentheses, as in (2).

5. Click the Insert button. The selected image downloads and appears in the document.

Genius

Other sources of stock imagery include iStock (www.istockphoto.com) and Shutterstock (www.shutterstock.com). These two services in particular offer some images that are royalty-free after you pay a fee or purchase a subscription. There are many other sources for free graphics; just make sure you choose a reputable source and scan downloaded files for viruses.

The Insert → Illustrations → Pictures → Online Pictures choice uses a search engine to find other pictures on the Internet for you. In PowerPoint, this command is found in the Images group. In the Online Pictures window that appears, type a search word or phrase in the Search box and press Enter. Figure 7.4 shows the Online Pictures window and identifies a few key features. Perhaps the most important one is the Creative Commons Only check box. I recommend you leave the Creative Commons Only check box checked so that you know you won't be violating the image creator's copyright.

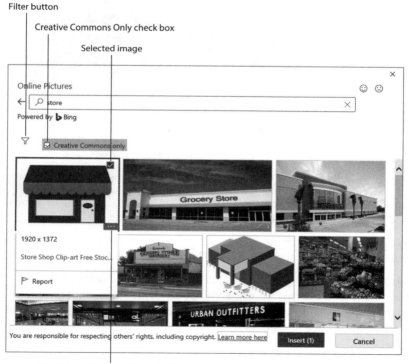

7.4 Online Pictures uses a search engine to search the Internet for matching images.

Note

Creative Commons (CC) is an organization and framework for licensing copyright protected works for free. The six main license levels, all of which require that attribution be given to the image's creator, are described at creativecommons.org/about/cclicenses. Some creators choose to release content under less restrictive public domain licenses. Sometimes a caption with the required attribution appears automatically with the downloaded image. In other cases, you can right-click the image and click View Source to identify the license and any required attribution.

If you move the mouse over any image thumbnail, the More Information and Actions button (with three dots on it) appears in the lower-right corner of the thumbnail. Click it to see more information about the image, such as the image size or sometimes a link to the source image online. Clicking the Filter button opens a scrolling list of categories by which you can filter the matches, including Size, Type, Layout, and Color. Just make the choices you need in each category, such as choosing Small under Size, which requires clicking the Filter button again for each filter to apply. Or, choose Clear All Filters at the bottom of the list to remove previously applied filters.

To select an image to download, click its thumbnail so that a check box appears in its upper-right corner. Then click Insert to download the image and place it in the document.

Finally, inserting a graphic file stored on your computer, an external network drive, or USB flash drive works much like opening a workbook file. Choose Insert ➜ Illustrations ➜ Pictures ➜ This Device, navigate to the location holding the image file in the Insert Picture dialog box that appears, select the picture, and click Insert. In PowerPoint, the command for inserting pictures is in the Images group, or you can click the Pictures button in a content placeholder. You can insert pictures from many common graphics file formats, including JPEG, PNG, TIFF, and more. Only files using one of the allowable formats appear in the Insert Picture dialog box. You would use this technique to insert your company logo or a digital photo you've taken of a product.

Note

You can add a background image that appears on every page, sheet, or slide, such as an organization logo, but you have to do that as part of a header or footer. Chapter 11 covers this technique, which is another way to add a graphic and bolster brand identity in a document, in the section called "Creating Headers and Footers."

Icons

If you really want to add an infographic feel to a worksheet, try adding icons. Icons are part of the royalty-free stock imagery now offered to Microsoft 365 subscribers. Choose Insert ➔ Illustrations ➔ Icons to open the stock image window with the Icons category selected at the top, as shown in Figure 7.5. (Note that the graphics available in the Illustrations category also have a clean, infographic look like the icons.) As you saw earlier for stock images, you can either enter a search term or scroll through the search terms below the box and click one. (The icons and search terms you see will vary.) Scroll down if needed, and then click the thumbnail for the icon to insert so that a check circle appears in its upper-right corner. Then click Insert.

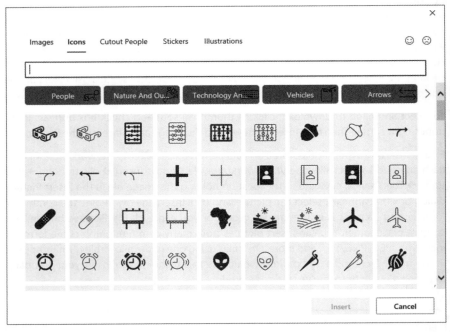

7.5 You can search for an icon to add in this window.

The icons you insert can be edited like other graphics, and not just the icon size. You can change other settings such as fill and line colors, too. See the later section called "Changing styles" to learn more.

164

Selecting and Formatting Graphics

In most cases, you can simply click an inserted graphic of any type to select it. You can Shift+click or Ctrl+click when you need to select multiple graphics, such as when you need to align them or want to apply similar formatting.

When a graphic is selected, a tab with formatting settings—sometimes called a *contextual tab* or a *context-sensitive tab*—appears on the ribbon, usually to the far right. The name of this contextual tab varies depending on the type of graphic that's selected:

- **Shape Format.** Appears when a shape is selected.
- **Picture Format.** Appears when a picture is selected.
- **Graphics Format.** Appears when an icon is selected.

You also can right-click a graphic and then choose its "Format" command (again, the name varies) at the bottom of the shortcut menu to open a pane with various formatting choices to the right of the document. The formatting choices are so numerous that I can't cover them all, so this section touches on the basics.

To deselect one or more selected graphics, click away from the selection on a blank area.

Adding text to shapes

A shape on its own can look a little nondescript and may not communicate everything you need to communicate to your audience. For greater clarity, you can add text to a shape by following these steps:

1. **Double-click the shape or right-click it and choose Add Text (Word and Outlook) or Edit Text (Excel and PowerPoint).** The blinking insertion point appears within the shape. For callout shapes, the insertion point appears in the shape automatically when you add it to the sheet.

2. **Type the text.** You can press Enter if you need to break the text into multiple lines after specific words; otherwise, the app will wrap the text within the shape as needed.

3. **While you're adding the text, you can select it within the shape and use the choices in the Font group of the Home tab to change formatting.** I usually find that it's easier to use Shift plus the arrow keys to select text while working in a shape.

4. **Click outside the shape to finish.** In Figure 7.6, the banner shape on the PowerPoint slide has descriptive text added.

COMPLETED ACTIVITIES

- PERMITTING
- DESIGN
- ENGINEERING REVIEW
  - ENVIRONMENTAL
  - STRUCTURAL
  - MECHANICAL

- SITE PREPARATION
- FOUNDATION WORK
- STRUCTURAL STEEL

All Subcontractors Are Licensed
and Bonded

7.6 Shapes become more explanatory with added text.

If you need to edit the shape's text, you can repeat Step 1 or click within the text in the shape. Make changes using the editing techniques you've already learned about elsewhere in the book and then click outside the shape to finish.

Changing styles

The choices on the Shape Format, Picture Format, and Graphics Format tabs and the various formatting panes vary a bit, but generally they offer the ability to apply preset styles from the current theme. For shapes and icons, the Shape Styles and Graphics Styles groups hold a gallery of preset styles you can apply and fill, outline, and effects menus. As with other types of formatting, you can point to a choice in the gallery or menu to see a Live Preview, as in the example in Figure 7.7, and then click a choice to apply it to the selected object.

Genius

The Change Graphic button in the Change group at the far left in Figure 7.7 enables you to swap out one graphic for another. This works great if you've already formatted the graphic, because the new graphic will use the same formatting you applied to the previous one.

The concept of "styles" works a bit differently on the Picture Format tab. The Picture Styles group holds a Quick Styles gallery, and its style choices are presets that change the picture "frame" or outline, as well as including other effects such as rotation and shadows. The Picture Styles group also has Picture Border and Picture Effects choices. What you may think of as "styles" for pictures are collected in the Adjust group, in four galleries of presets:

Change Graphic button   Styles gallery   Graphics Format tab

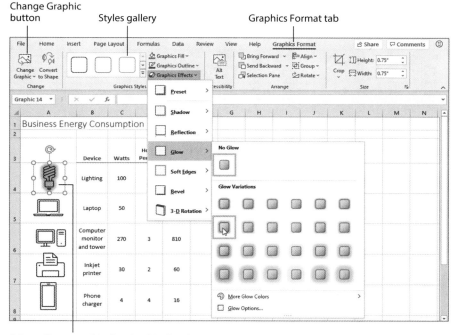

Selected icon graphic showing Live Preview

7.7 It's easy to apply a preset style to a shape or icon, as well as to change the fill, outline, and effects.

- **Corrections.** Enables you to experiment with Sharpen/Soften and Brightness/Contrast variations.

- **Color.** Offers Color Saturation, Color Tone, and Recolor choices.

- **Artistic Effects.** Includes effects you can use to add interest to the picture, such as Paint Strokes and Crisscross Etching.

- **Transparency.** Holds presets for adjusting how see-through the image is.

Figure 7.8 shows the Picture Format tab where you can find all these choices. The figure also includes the Format Picture pane, with the Picture Color tools displayed. To get to those settings in the pane, you right-click a picture and choose Format Picture. Then click the Picture button at the top of the pane, and click Picture Color to expand its settings. You can leave the pane open as long as needed to move between and change settings and then click the pane Close (X) button to finish.

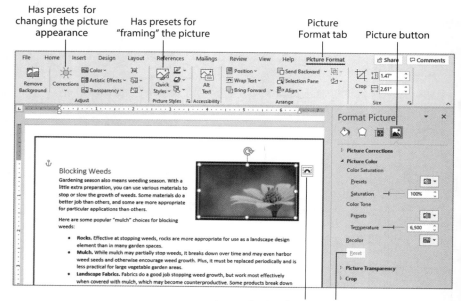

Has presets for changing the picture appearance

Has presets for "framing" the picture

Picture Format tab

Picture button

Layout Options button

Format Picture pane

7.8 The Picture Format tab offers numerous types of presets.

Genius

If you've gone a little bit off the rails with too many picture format choices, select the picture and choose Picture Format → Adjust → Reset Picture.

Changing sizing and position

The fix for a misplaced graphic is pretty simple. Select it, and then use the mouse to drag it to another location.

Genius

To move a graphic to a location that's not visible on-screen, you may prefer to cut and paste rather than dragging with the mouse. Cut the graphic (Ctrl+X), move to the approximate location where you want the graphic to appear, click there, and then paste (Ctrl+V). Of course, you have to cut and paste to move a graphic from one document page, workbook sheet, slide, or file to another.

When it comes to resizing graphics, a few more subtleties come into play, and you can choose from a few different techniques:

- **Drag a handle.** White selection handles appear around the shape when it's selected. Move the mouse pointer over one of these handles until the pointer changes to a two-headed white arrow (see Figure 7.9), and then drag to the desired size and dimensions. If you want to maintain the same proportions in both dimensions (or aspect ratio), press and hold the Shift key while dragging a corner handle.

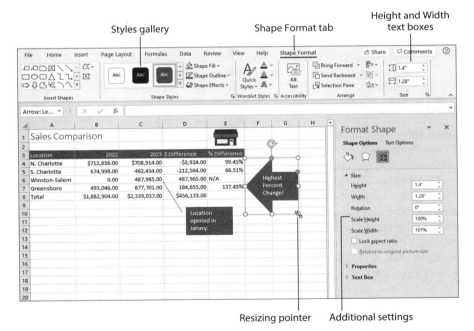

7.9 You can drag a resizing handle or use other methods to resize a graphic.

● **Use the Height and Width text boxes.** Each of the three Format tabs has Height and Width text boxes that you can use to adjust the graphic's size. Just select the entry in one of the text boxes, type a new entry, and press Enter. Or click the increment arrows at the right end of each text box to change the size incrementally.

● **Use the "Format" pane or Layout dialog box.** If you click the dialog box launcher in the lower-right corner of the Size group, the "Format" pane (Format Shape in the case of Figure 7.9) opens in Excel and PowerPoint and displays the Size settings. In Word and an Outlook message window, the Layout dialog box opens with the Size tab displayed. Not only can you adjust the Height and Width, but you can also use the Scale Height or Scale Width choices to change the image size by a percentage. The Lock Aspect Ratio check box controls whether the graphic resizes proportionally in both dimensions. You can use the Reset button to return the picture to its original size. Close the pane or dialog box when you've finished choosing resizing settings.

Caution

When using the Height and Width text boxes, keep in mind that the aspect ratio may or may not be locked, depending on the type of graphic. For example, the aspect ratio for shapes is generally not locked, so if you change the height, the width does not adjust, and this may distort the graphic. Pictures and icons, on the other hand, generally have a locked aspect ratio by default.

When you see a Crop button in the Size group of one of the "Format" tabs (usually the Picture Format tab), it means you can crop out or eliminate part of the graphic that you don't want to show. Click that button, move the mouse pointer over the black border that appears until you see a black crop pointer, and then drag toward the middle of the graphic. Click outside the graphic or click the Crop button again to apply the crop. Cropping doesn't remove the cropped contents; it just hides them, so you can reset the picture or icon to redisplay the cropped portion by clicking the Reset button under Size & Properties and then Size in the "Format" pane (Excel and PowerPoint). In Word and an Outlook message, choose Picture Format → Adjust → Reset Picture down arrow, and then click Reset Picture & Size to remove the crop.

Working with layering, alignment, and rotation

There may be times when your design calls for multiple graphics, such as if you're combining multiple graphics to create something new or if you're using multiple icons to pump up your document. Each of the "Format" tabs has an Arrange group, which offers the tools for positioning multiple graphics relative to one another in these two situations:

- **Layering.** Do you want the left half of the blue circle to be in front of or behind the right half of the red square where they overlap? You could select the blue circle and click the Bring Forward or Send Backward button. Each of those buttons also has a drop-down list arrow at the right that you can click so you can choose the Bring to Front or Send to Back command from the respective choices.

- **Aligning.** In cases where you want to align objects with more precision, select all the objects to align, and then click Align Objects in the Arrange group of the displayed "Format" tab. A menu of choices for aligning the objects horizontally or vertically relative to one another appears. For example, in Figure 7.10, I selected five inserted icons and then used Align Center to make sure they line up in a nice column. The commands in the menu are grouped. The first three control the horizontal alignment of the selected shapes, and the next three control the vertical alignment. The Distribute Horizontally command spaces graphics evenly between the far-left and far-right selected graphics, and Distribute Vertically spaces graphics evenly between the top and bottom selected graphics.

Rotation handle

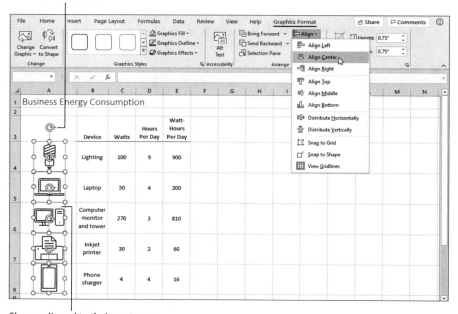

Shapes aligned to their centers

7.10 Aligning objects relative to one another creates a neater layout.

171

Genius

I use the Align Center and Align Middle choices a lot, because they create a uniform look even when the selected graphics have different sizes. And it's often the case that for a vertical arrangement of graphics like the one in Figure 7.10, I'll use Align Center and then Distribute Vertically for optimal alignment in both directions.

You also can change the rotation of a graphic either to add interest or to fix a flaw. For example, if you inserted a digital photo that you took with your phone, it might look like it's "lying on its side" and needs to be rotated 90 degrees. Changing the rotation is another instance where you can use various methods, depending on the degree of precision you need:

- **Use the rotation handle.** Figure 7.10 has a callout to a little doohickey called the *rotation handle*. When you move the mouse pointer over it, the pointer changes to a black version of the handle's circular arrow. At that point you can drag to the left or right to apply mild rotation, or you can drag diagonally for greater rotation. Yup, this is the least precise method.

- **Use the Rotate Objects presets.** The Arrange group of the applicable "Format" tab holds the Rotate Objects button. It has four presets for rotating a graphic: Rotate Right 90°, Rotate Left 90°, Flip Vertical, and Flip Horizontal. The first two are the go-to fixes for badly rotated camera pictures, and the latter two are essentially 180-degree rotations. Each of these is a precise, easy rotation to apply.

- **Use the "Format" pane.** The last choice on the Rotate Objects menu is More Rotation Options. Choosing it in Excel and PowerPoint opens the applicable "Format" pane to the Size settings shown in Figure 7.9. You can change the value in the Rotation text box to a precise rotation between 0 and 360 degrees. In Word or an Outlook message window, choosing More Rotation Options opens the Layout dialog box with the Size tab displayed. Change the setting in the Rotation text box (under Rotate) as needed. Close the pane or dialog box after changing the setting. This, obviously, enables the most control over the rotation applied.

Note

In reality, 0 and 360 degrees are the same position, so if you still want a tiny amount of rotation, use a value less than 360 in the Rotation text box of the applicable "Format" pane. Also note that this text box allows you to enter values greater than 360, which then creates the question, "How many degrees of rotation have I really applied?" It seems easier to just stick with 0 to 359 as Rotation text box entries.

Working with wrapping in Word

If you refer back to Figure 7.8, you'll notice that the picture appears beside the text. That wasn't accomplished by creating columns. Instead, I changed the text wrapping and position settings for the image after selecting it. *Text wrapping* controls how text flows beside, around, or through a graphic. *Position* refers to a preset location on the current page to which you can move the graphic. The Wrap Text and Position choices are found in the Arrange group of the applicable "Format" tab. There are numerous Wrap Text and Position choices that you can choose from. To achieve the look shown in Figure 7.8, I selected the graphic and then chose Picture Format → Arrange → Position → Position in Top Right with Square Text Wrapping. I could have chosen Picture Format → Arrange → Wrap Text → Square and then dragged the picture to that corner, too. Note that you also can use the Layout Options button identified in Figure 7.8 to change wrapping and related settings.

Creating and Working with SmartArt

As if the preceding array of graphics types wasn't enough, Microsoft 365 apps enable you to create a special type of diagram called *SmartArt*. SmartArt automatically adds a predesigned shape to illustrate each text item you add, so you don't have to draw individual shapes, insert text, line up the shapes, and so on, to create a comprehensive graphic. You can create a SmartArt graphic to diagram a list, process, cycle, hierarchy or org chart, and many other types of relationships. Some SmartArt formats even enable you to insert pictures. The possibilities are endless, so this section covers the essentials with a simple example or two in the figures.

Adding a SmartArt graphic

The initial steps for adding a SmartArt graphic are fairly consistent. To insert SmartArt in the current document, follow these steps:

1. **Choose Insert → Illustrations → SmartArt.** In PowerPoint, you also can click the Insert a SmartArt Graphic button in a content placeholder. The Choose a SmartArt Graphic dialog box appears.

2. **Choose a category in the list at the left, and then click a thumbnail in the middle section.** A preview and description of the selected diagram type appears at the right, as shown in Figure 7.11. You can continue browsing the formats by changing categories and thumbnails until you find a format you think will work.

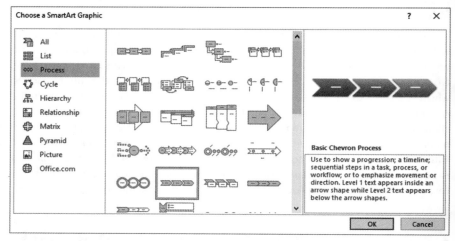

7.11 Preview the SmartArt diagram type before inserting the graphic.

3. **With the desired category and thumbnail selected, click OK.** The initial shape appears with placeholder text. By default, a Text pane with *Type Your Text Here* at the top appears beside the graphic.

Note

The SmartArt Design ➔ Create Graphic ➔ Text Pane button toggles Text pane display on and off, so choose that button if you don't see the pane. The pane also disappears when the SmartArt graphic isn't selected, and clicking back in a shape with the [Text] prompt reselects the SmartArt.

4. **Type the text for each shape on a separate bullet line in the Text pane.** You can use the down arrow key to move down from one line to the next for the initial three bullets. After that, you can press Enter to add more bullets (and individual shapes in the graphic). Figure 7.12 shows the first two items in a list of data entered for a SmartArt graphic and the resulting shapes. (Most SmartArt graphics list more items. I chose to show an "in-process" list so the text in the shapes would be legible in the figure. You can see that the third bullet line in the Text pane has a [Text] placeholder for the third shape, awaiting the next entry.) Some SmartArt formats have indented sub-bullets below the main level bullets. Press Tab to indent a bullet and convert it to a sub-bullet. Optionally, you can click a shape in the diagram and type its contents.

SmartArt Design tab   Format tab

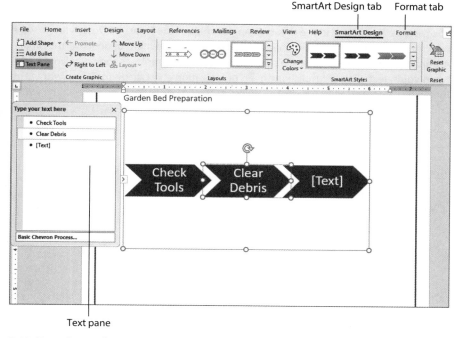

Text pane

7.12 Enter the text for each SmartArt shape in the Text pane.

5. **Drag the graphic to a new location and resize it as needed.** For example, you could drag the graphic to the left side of an empty document and drag a corner selection handle to enlarge it so that the text is more readable.

6. **Click outside the graphic to finish.**

Caution

SmartArt graphics can be pretty big, so sometimes it makes sense to place one on a page, sheet, or slide by itself (or along with a title). Next, create, size, and position it as desired. Finally, add any supporting data next to the graphic.

Some types of SmartArt graphics have an additional step to complete before Step 5: adding the pictures. For layouts requiring pictures, the Text pane and/or shapes include a button you can click to insert a picture. The Insert Pictures dialog box that appears enables you to choose whether to insert a file, stock image, online picture, or icon.

175

Editing and rearranging shapes

You can use the choices in the Create Graphic group of the SmartArt Design tab to work with the shapes in the graphic. The choices that are active there depend on the Smart-Art graphic type and the currently selected shape. For example, as shown in Figure 7.13, when you select a lower-level shape in an organization chart diagram (found within the Hierarchy category), nearly all of the choices in the Create Graphic group become active and available.

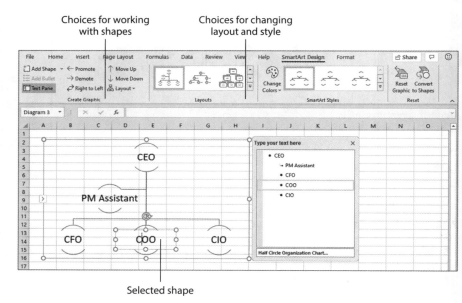

7.13 The Create Graphic group holds the choices for working with the shapes in a SmartArt graphic.

Again, covering all the possibilities of how every choice works in every graphic type and shape position would involve more pages than we're able to spend together, so experiment at your leisure. Here, I'll just point out the Add Shape choice, which you can use to add a shape into the diagram if you're not comfortable doing it via the Text pane, and the Layout button, which you can use to change the arrangement of the shapes for some SmartArt diagrams.

Genius

You often don't need the assistant shape that's just below and to the left of the top level of an organization chart graphic, as in the example in Figure 7.13. Here's the trick for deleting it. Select the SmartArt graphic, click the assistant shape in the graphic, and then click the selection border *again* to make sure that the shape is really selected. Then press the Delete key.

Changing the graphic type and formatting

To change the overall layout and style for a selected SmartArt graphic, you can use the SmartArt Styles and Layouts galleries in the groups of those names on the SmartArt Design tab, as shown in Figure 7.13. Changing the applied style can really change the look of the graphic, as SmartArt Styles often are more three-dimensional than styles for other types of graphics such as shapes. The SmartArt Styles group also includes the Change Colors button, which opens to a gallery of alternate color combinations, based on the theme applied to the document, that you can apply to the graphic.

The name of the Layouts gallery is a little misleading, because the choices here basically change to another overall SmartArt design. You can even click More Layouts at the bottom of the gallery to go all the way back to the Choose a SmartArt Graphic dialog box.

The Format tab (refer to Figure 7.12) offers choices more tailored to formatting an individual shape that you've selected by clicking it within the overall SmartArt graphic. The Change Shape choice in the Shapes group enables you to change the shape of the selected item, while the Shape Styles group holds the choices for restyling the selected shape.

Deleting Graphics

To delete a graphic of any type, click it so that selection handles appear around it, and then press the Delete key. Use caution when you do this, however, because the apps don't give you any warning before zapping away your lovely graphic. If you need the graphic back, press Ctrl+Z or click the Undo button on the QAT immediately to undo the deletion.

You can keep graphics you've created handy for later use by collecting them in a separate file in Word, on a separate sheet in an Excel workbook file, or on the gray area surrounding the current slide in the Normal view in PowerPoint. Create a new blank Word file or Excel sheet, and then name it something like Graphics or Scrap. Then, when you no longer want a graphic, cut it and paste it to the Graphics or Scrap location. In PowerPoint, you may have to zoom out in order to drag an object off the slide onto the gray area.

Genius

Each of the Format tabs also has a Selection Pane button in the Arrange group. Clicking this button opens the Selection pane, where you can select a graphic by clicking its name. The more useful feature of this pane is that you can click the eye icon to the right of any listed graphic to toggle display of the graphic on and off. If you think you might want to use a graphic later, you can hide it rather than deleting it.

How Do I Manage Lists of Information?

	A	B	C	D	E	F	G	H
1	Dinnerware Stock							
2								
3	ID ▼	Item ▼	Pattern ▼	Size (in.) ▼	Cost ▼	Retail Price ▼	# in Stock ▼	Inventory Cost ▼
4	1	Cup	Lily	3	2.50	5.00	73	182.50
5	2	Cereal Bowl	Rose	6	6.00	10.00	112	672.00
6	3	Saucer	Rose	6	1.50	3.00	88	132.00
7	4	Dinner Plate	Sunflower	10.5	10.00	20.00	51	510.00
8	5	Saucer	Sunflower	6	1.50	3.00	69	103.50
9	6	Soup Bowl	Lily	8	10.00	20.00	37	370.00
10	7	Salad Plate	Rose	8	4.25	8.50	115	488.75
11	8	Cup	Rose	3	2.50	5.00	144	360.00
12	9	Cereal Bowl	Lily	6	6.00	10.00	30	180.00
13	10	Saucer	Lily	6	1.50	3.00	133	199.50
14	11	Salad Plate	Sunflower	8	4.25	8.50	151	641.75
15	12	Soup Bowl	Sunflower	8	None		88	880.00
16	13	Soup Bowl	Rose	8	Average	20.00	91	910.00
17	14	Cereal Bowl	Sunflower	6	Count / Count Number	10.00	58	348.00
18	15	Salad Plate	Lily	8	Max / Min	8.50	131	556.75
19	16	Dinner Plate	Rose	10.5	Sum	20.00	111	1110.00
20	17	Cup	Sunflower	3	StdDev / Var	5.00	103	257.50
21	18	Dinner Plate	Lily	10.5	More Function	20.00	100	1000.00
22	Total				▼			8902.25
23								

Many organizations and individuals live and die by their lists. Lists of products. Lists of employees. Home inventory insurance lists. To-do lists. The Microsoft 365 apps excel at helping users track lists in neat rows and columns. You can organize list information in a basic way or create a table to hold a list. You can sort and filter list contents with ease and apply attractive styles to tables. If you no longer need the fancy features, convert the table back to a regular list. This chapter shares all of these list skills so you can run your lists like a boss.

Adding a Table in Word or PowerPoint

A *table* is a grid of rows and columns used to organize information in a Word document or on a PowerPoint slide. Unlike a much larger Excel worksheet, each Word or PowerPoint table typically has a much more limited number of rows and columns in order to fit within page margins or a slide placeholder. This section helps you get a handle on creating tables in these two Microsoft 365 apps. Well, really three Microsoft 365 apps, because tables in an Outlook message work largely the same as tables in Word.

Adding the table and making entries

You can add a table at the insertion point in a Word document or into the body of an Outlook message. Or, you can add a table in a content placeholder in a PowerPoint slide. While there are alternative ways to insert a table, such as using the Insert Table dialog box or drawing the table, follow these steps to take the easiest route:

1. **Choose Insert → Tables → Table to display the choices for creating tables, including the Insert Table grid.**

2. **Move the mouse pointer diagonally on the grid to specify how many rows and columns you want the table to have, and when you reach the right dimensions, click the lower-right highlighted square.** As you move the mouse pointer over the grid, a Live Preview of the table appears on the page, in the message, or in the slide content placeholder.

3. **Type each table cell entry, pressing Tab to move to the next cell.** If an entry is too long to fit in the cell, the entry automatically wraps to a second line. If you want to create a new line manually within a table cell, press Enter. If you reach the end of the table and need another row, just press Tab. Presto, the new row appears!

4. **Click outside the table when you finish to deselect it.**

Genius

> If you want a PowerPoint slide to have only a table on it, apply the Blank slide layout to the slide and then use the Insert → Tables → Table command to add the table. If you use the Title Slide or Title Only layout to insert the table, it will appear on top of the title text placeholder rather than on the main area of the slide.

In PowerPoint, if you click the Insert Table button in a content placeholder, the Insert Table dialog box appears. Adjust the values in the Number of Columns and Number of Rows text boxes as desired, and then click OK.

If you need to make changes to table cell contents, just click the cell (which also reselects the table) and make the desired changes using editing techniques you've learned about previously. You can click or press Tab or Shift+Tab to move between the cells as needed.

Adding and deleting rows or columns

Working with table rows and columns is similar to working with the rows and columns in an Excel sheet. If you want to select a row, move the mouse pointer to the left of it until the white mouse pointer tilts right (Word) or a black right arrow pointer appears (PowerPoint), and then click. To select a column, move the mouse pointer above it so a black down arrow pointer appears, and then click. Of course, when the right mouse pointer appears, you can drag to select multiple rows or columns. You also can move the mouse pointer over a row or column boundary so that a split pointer appears and then drag to resize the row or column.

Genius

I've often needed to work with more precise row height and column width measurements, especially when I wanted multiple tables in a document to have consistent row and column sizes. Select a cell in the row or column to resize, and then use the choices in the Cell Size group of the Layout tab to make adjustments. The Alignment group of the Layout tab likewise helps you work with the alignment of table cell contents, including the vertical alignment of cell contents and rotation.

Word makes it easiest to insert a row or column, in my opinion. Just move the mouse pointer to the left of the row border or above the column border at the location where you'd like to make the insertion, and then click the + (plus) button, as in the example shown in Figure 8.1. Word and the other apps also offer the Rows & Columns group on the Layout tab (see Figure 8.1). You can use its choices to insert a row above or below the row with the selected cell (the cell holding the insertion point) or to insert a column to the left or right of the column with the selected cell. Clicking the Delete button in the group opens a menu with choices for deleting cells (Word only), columns, rows, or the entire table.

Click to select entire table   Rows & Columns group   Layout tab

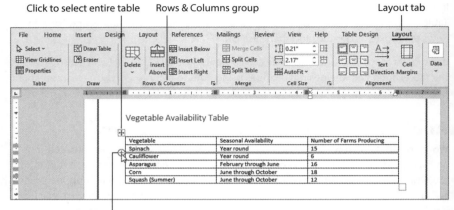

| File | Home | Insert | Design | Layout | References | Mailings | Review | View | Help | Table Design | Layout |

Vegetable Availability Table

Vegetable	Seasonal Availability	Number of Farms Producing
Spinach	Year round	15
Cauliflower	Year round	6
Asparagus	February through June	16
Corn	June through October	18
Squash (Summer)	June through October	12

Plus for inserting row or column

8.1 Point and click to insert a new row or column in a Word table.

Note

Figure 8.1 also identifies the button with the four-headed arrow that appears at the upper-left corner of a selected table in Word and Outlook. It's called the table move handle, but is also sometimes called the table select handle. When you move the mouse pointer over the handle, the pointer changes to a four-headed arrow. At that point, you can use it to drag the table to a new location in the document or message or click it to select the entire table.

Arranging a List in Excel

Excel can function as a simple database, enabling you to use the Data tab to perform common but powerful business tasks such as sorting and filtering the list. There's a catch, as usual. You have to arrange the data correctly so that Excel's data management tools can recognize the list. Good list setup requires following just a few straightforward rules:

- **The list should be in a contiguous range.** Any blank column or row would essentially split the table, though it's usually okay to have a few blank cells here and there within a list.

- **There should be at least one blank row above the table and one blank column to the right.** This is essentially the opposite of the first rule. It's important because if you do sort or filter the table, that could also change the location or position of any cell touching the list whether you want that or not.

- **There generally should be a row at the top of the table with the label for each column of information.** In database lingo, these are called *field names*, where each column holds a separate field or type of information. Various dialog boxes in Excel also call these *headers*, or a *header row*, which are separate from the sheet headers with row numbers and column letters.

- **Each column should hold a single type of information.** A column should hold all text entries, all currency, all dates, and so on.

- **Each column should hold a discrete piece of data to facilitate sorting and filtering.** The classic example of flubbing this rule is putting both a first name and a last name in the same field or column. The first name should be one column and the last name another column; otherwise, you wouldn't be able to sort the list by last name. Similarly, you wouldn't want to include a product's size or color in the same cell with the product name. When in doubt, break it out (to its own field).

- **Each complete list entry should occupy a single row.** One person's contact information should be in a single row, the details about one product should be in a single row, and so on. Database folks call each row entry a *record*.

Some of the figures in earlier chapters showed simple lists of data, so I developed a more robust example for Figure 8.2.

Excel includes some special shortcut key combinations for moving within the contiguous table range and making selections within the table range. These can be especially important to know if you have a long list of data, such as data you've imported from a database or other source. Give these shortcut key combos a try in your lists:

- **Ctrl+up arrow or Ctrl+down arrow.** Pressing one of these keyboard shortcuts moves to the top or bottom row of the table, within the current column. When the active cell is in a column outside a table, these shortcuts move to the top or bottom row of the sheet instead. (Though if you're working below the table, the first time you press Ctrl+up arrow, it moves to the bottom row of the table.)

- **Ctrl+left arrow or Ctrl+right arrow.** Pressing one of these keyboard shortcuts moves to the far-left or far-right column of the table, within the current row. When the active cell is in a row below or above the table, these shortcuts move to the far-left or far-right column of the sheet. (If you're working to the right of the table, the first time you press Ctrl+left arrow, it moves to the far-right column of the table.)

- **Ctrl+Shift+arrow.** This keyboard combination makes a selection in the direction of the arrow key that you press, starting from the active cell and stopping at the edge of the table. Outside of a table, Ctrl+Shift+right arrow selects the row from the active cell through the rightmost column of the sheet, while Ctrl+Shift+down arrow selects the column from the active cell down to the last row in the sheet.

- **Ctrl+Shift+* (asterisk).** This keyboard combo selects the entire table as well as any other contiguous range.

Headers for each column of data in the list in row 3

Blank row above list

List in range A3:F21

	A	B	C	D	E	F	G
1	Dinnerware Stock						
2							
3	Item	Pattern	Size (in.)	Cost	Retail Price	# in Stock	
4	Cup	Lily	3	2.50	5.00	73	
5	Cereal Bowl	Rose	6	6.00	10.00	112	
6	Saucer	Rose	6	1.50	3.00	88	
7	Dinner Plate	Sunflower	10.5	10.00	20.00	51	
8	Saucer	Sunflower	6	1.50	3.00	69	
9	Soup Bowl	Lily	8	10.00	20.00	37	
10	Salad Plate	Rose	8	4.25	8.50	115	
11	Cup	Rose	3	2.50	5.00	144	
12	Cereal Bowl	Lily	6	6.00	10.00	30	
13	Saucer	Lily	6	1.50	3.00	133	
14	Salad Plate	Sunflower	8	4.25	8.50	151	
15	Soup Bowl	Sunflower	8	10.00	20.00	88	
16	Soup Bowl	Rose	8	10.00	20.00	91	
17	Cereal Bowl	Sunflower	6	6.00	10.00	58	
18	Salad Plate	Lily	8	4.25	8.50	131	
19	Dinner Plate	Rose	10.5	10.00	20.00	111	
20	Cup	Sunflower	3	2.50	5.00	103	
21	Dinner Plate	Lily	10.5	10.00	20.00	100	
22							
23							

Complete entry in each row

Blank column to the right of list

8.2 A list of data occupies a contiguous range in Excel.

Genius

You can use data validation to prevent entries of the wrong type in an Excel list or table column. Select a column range, and then choose Data → Data Tools → Data Validation (main part of button). Use the Allow drop-down list to specify a type of validation to apply, such as Whole Number or Date. Specify other settings (choices vary depending on the validation type), and click OK. The range will then only accept entries that match the validation criteria.

The Data Tools group of the Data tab includes numerous tools you can use to help build and clean up lists, including Flash Fill, Remove Duplicates, and Text to Columns, which enables you to divide the entries in one column into multiple columns.

Understanding Excel's Table Feature

Allow me to further satisfy your inner list maniac by introducing Excel's table capabilities. When you convert a regular range of data to a table, it becomes a named object with expanded capabilities to help with data management, analysis, and design. Read on to discover how you can upgrade from a plain old list to a table.

Converting a range to a table

You can create as many tables as needed on a single worksheet, because each table functions as an independent unit. That said, each range that you want to convert to a table should follow the same rules as when arranging a list. In particular, you want to make sure that there's a header row with labels for each column, and no blank rows or columns within the range. And, you want to make sure that blank columns and rows surround the table so that Excel can properly separate the table from any other data or tables on the sheet.

Genius

As part of prepping a range to convert to a table, you also should clear any cell styles that you've applied to cells in the range with Home ➔ Editing ➔ Clear ➔ Clear Formats. (However, you may not want to clear formatting from cells with number formats applied.) Otherwise, the cell styles will fully or partially override the table style formatting, creating an inconsistent or perhaps even unreadable appearance in the affected cells.

Follow these steps to create a table with the default table style from the workbook theme:

1. **Click any cell in the range.**

2. **Choose Insert ➔ Tables ➔ Table or press Ctrl+T.** Excel selects the range to convert, which is why it's important to follow the layout rules. The Create Table dialog box also appears.

3. **Verify the settings in the Create Table dialog box.** You want to make sure that the whole table range is specified in the Where Is the Data for Your Table? text box and that the My Table Has Headers check box is checked.

4. **Click OK.** The conversion happens immediately, and the range is now a table.

5. **Click outside the table to deselect it.** You can now see the table formatting, as for the example shown in Figure 8.3.

	A	B	C	D	E	F	G
1	Dinnerware Stock						
2							
3	ID ▼	Item ▼	Pattern ▼	Size (in.) ▼	Cost ▼	Retail Price ▼	# in Stock ▼
4	1	Cup	Lily	3	2.50	5.00	73
5	2	Cereal Bowl	Rose	6	6.00	10.00	112
6	3	Saucer	Rose	6	1.50	3.00	88
7	4	Dinner Plate	Sunflower	10.5	10.00	20.00	51
8	5	Saucer	Sunflower	6	1.50	3.00	69
9	6	Soup Bowl	Lily	8	10.00	20.00	37
10	7	Salad Plate	Rose	8	4.25	8.50	115
11	8	Cup	Rose	3	2.50	5.00	144
12	9	Cereal Bowl	Lily	6	6.00	10.00	30
13	10	Saucer	Lily	6	1.50	3.00	133
14	11	Salad Plate	Sunflower	8	4.25	8.50	151
15	12	Soup Bowl	Sunflower	8	10.00	20.00	88
16	13	Soup Bowl	Rose	8	10.00	20.00	91
17	14	Cereal Bowl	Sunflower	6	6.00	10.00	58
18	15	Salad Plate	Lily	8	4.25	8.50	131
19	16	Dinner Plate	Rose	10.5	10.00	20.00	111
20	17	Cup	Sunflower	3	2.50	5.00	103
21	18	Dinner Plate	Lily	10.5	10.00	20.00	100
22							
23							

8.3 Tables have their own styles and added features.

Genius

There are two more ways to create a table with the default table style. Press Ctrl+Shift+* to select the list range, click the Quick Analysis button that appears at the lower-right corner, click Tables at the top of the pop-up that appears, and then click Table to instantly convert the range. The absolute fastest method is to click a cell in the table, press Ctrl+T, and just press Enter to accept the settings in the Create Table dialog box.

If you're interested in exploring the available table styles while converting a range to a table, the steps are slightly different:

1. **Click any cell in the range.**

2. **Choose Home → Styles → Format as Table.** The gallery of table styles appears. Move the mouse pointer over a style to see a descriptive ScreenTip. You may need to scroll down the gallery to view additional styles.

3. **Click the style to apply.** Excel selects the range to convert and opens the Format As Table dialog box.

4. **Verify the settings in the Format As Table dialog box.** You want to make sure that the whole table range is specified in the Where Is the Data for Your Table? text box and that the My Table Has Headers check box is checked.

5. **Click OK.** The conversion happens immediately, and the range is now a table.

6. **Click outside the table to deselect it.** The converted table has the style you selected in Step 3.

Note

Ctrl+Shift+* selects the entire table after you've clicked a table cell. To select an entire column within the table, click a cell in the desired column and press Ctrl+Spacebar. To select an entire row within the table, press Shift+Spacebar. The latter two shortcuts work outside of tables, too, and select the entire sheet column or row.

Importing or connecting to a list of data

If a list of data already exists in another type of file and you want to use that data in Excel, you can import the data into a new workbook file. Excel can readily import various types of files, so long as the data is properly structured. File types that Excel can import include delimited TXT and CSV files; various types of database files including Microsoft Access, HTML and XML files; and more.

Choose File → Open → Browse, open the file type drop-down list, and choose the type of file to import. Then navigate to the location holding the file, click the file, and click Open. Some files, such as TXT and CSV files, open directly as a new workbook file. If the file is delimited and the Text Import Wizard dialog box appears, follow its prompts to finish importing the file. Then, all you need to do is choose File → Save As.

For other file types, you may first see a Microsoft Excel Security Notice message, saying data connections have been blocked. Click Enable. Then, a dialog box like the Import Data dialog box shown in Figure 8.4 appears. In this case, when importing from an Access database file, the dialog box suggests importing the data as a table by default. Make your choices in the dialog box, and then click OK. If you see additional prompts or choices, respond to them as needed to import the data. Then save the file as needed.

Figure 8.4 also includes an Only Create Connection option. What the heck does that mean, you ask? It means that the imported Access list, by default, has a data connection between the Excel workbook where you imported the data and the original Access file. Why would that be needed?

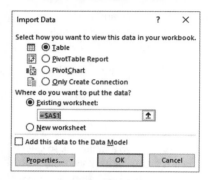

8.4 Excel may prompt you for some details when you import data.

While Excel offers simple data functions, many organizations use full-blown relational databases or other comprehensive database management systems, some of which may be cloud-based. We're talking about thousands of rows (records) of data at a time, in many cases. This is not the sort of situation where it's easy to retype or even copy the data, for obvious reasons. Even worse, the data in your workbook would become out of date relative to the original source almost instantly, given the ongoing changes typically made to database information in large corporations.

The data connection enables Excel to retrieve updated data from the data source. It also enables you to query the data, if you have data query skills and want to give it a try. Sometimes the data connection itself is a query. The Get Data button in the Get & Transform Data group on the Data tab enables you to both import data and establish a connection to the data source. As shown in Figure 8.5, you can move the mouse pointer over any of the items in the Get Data menu to see the specific choices within that overall type of data source. (The menu's data source types can vary depending on the type of Microsoft 365 subscription you have and other factors, so your choices may differ from the ones in Figure 8.5.) The available choices enable you to connect both with data stored on a network and with data stored using various cloud services and tools such as Azure and Salesforce.

After you choose a data source type, the process for connecting to it varies. You may be prompted to specify a URL for a data source, a server location, or a mailbox address, for example. Your organization's database administration pros can give you the information you need to connect with the data source. In the case of a file such as a database file on a network, the Import Data dialog box opens so that you can navigate to the file, click it, and click Import. Depending on the file type, from there you will see a window where you can preview the data or select which database object to import. Click Load to load the data as a table on a new sheet in the workbook. Click the main part of the Refresh

All button any time you want to update the table with fresh data from the connected data source.

Genius

The Stocks and Geography buttons in the Data tab's Data Types group create updatable data. Type a stock ticker or place (such as a state) into a cell, reselect the cell, and click either Stocks or Geography. If prompted, make a choice in the Data Selector pane. To view data, click the stock or geography cell, click the Insert Data button that appears to the right, and choose the type of data to display. The requested statistic appears in the cell to the right.

Get Data button   Refresh All button   Data types

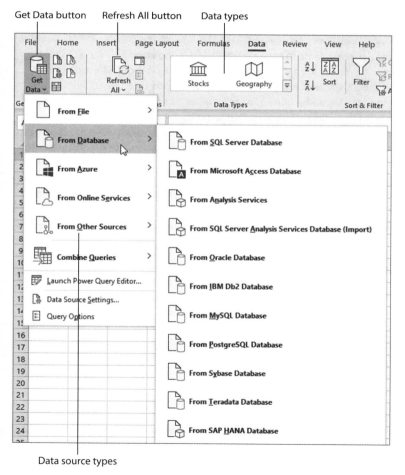

Data source types

8.5 Get Data both imports data as a table and creates a data connection.

Resizing a table

When you add new information in a row below a table or a column to the right of a table, the table automatically expands to encompass the new information. Excel automatically applies the appropriate table style to the additional information. This convenient feature means you don't have to spend your time manually applying formatting.

You also can resize a table before entering new data in it. The bottom-right corner of the bottom-right cell in a table has a little blue triangle that is the sizing handle for the table. You can drag it to increase or decrease the number of columns or rows in the table. This sizing handle doesn't let you drag diagonally.

Renaming a Table

Excel assigns a generic name to each table you add to the workbook file, as in Table1, Table2, and so on. You can rename the table by clicking a table cell, selecting the contents of the Table Design ➔ Properties ➔ Table Name text box, typing a new name, and pressing Enter. The same general rules for what a range name can include apply to table names. For a refresher about those, jump back to "Creating Range Names" in Chapter 3. Why bother changing the table name? Two reasons come to mind immediately. If you have multiple tables on the current sheet, you can use the Name box to select a particular table. Having more descriptive table names applied will make that navigation trick easier. Plus, table names on the current sheet appear in the Go To dialog box that appears when you press Ctrl+G or F5, and the more explanatory table names will make it clearer where you want to go.

Adding a total row

Displaying a total row below a table falls right into that bucket labeled "Work Smarter, not Harder." The total row enables you to select a function to perform a calculation on the data in the column above. It takes only a few steps:

1. **Click a cell in the table.**

2. **Choose Table Design ➔ Table Style Options ➔ Total Row.** You are clicking the Total Row check box to check it in this case. To hide the total row later, you would clear the check box.

3. **Click the total row cell below the column to calculate, click the arrow button, and then click the function to apply.** As shown in Figure 8.6, several of the usual suspect functions appear on the list, or you can choose More Functions to select another function.

	A	B	C	D	E	F	G	H
1	Dinnerware Stock							
2								
3	ID ▾	Item ▾	Pattern ▾	Size (in.) ▾	Cost ▾	Retail Price ▾	# in Stock ▾	Inventory Cost ▾
4	1	Cup	Lily	3	2.50	5.00	73	182.50
5	2	Cereal Bowl	Rose	6	6.00	10.00	112	672.00
6	3	Saucer	Rose	6	1.50	3.00	88	132.00
7	4	Dinner Plate	Sunflower	10.5	10.00	20.00	51	510.00
8	5	Saucer	Sunflower	6	1.50	3.00	69	103.50
9	6	Soup Bowl	Lily	8	10.00	20.00	37	370.00
10	7	Salad Plate	Rose	8	4.25	8.50	115	488.75
11	8	Cup	Rose	3	2.50	5.00	144	360.00
12	9	Cereal Bowl	Lily	6	6.00	10.00	30	180.00
13	10	Saucer	Lily	6	1.50	3.00	133	199.50
14	11	Salad Plate	Sunflower	8	4.25	8.50	151	641.75
15	12	Soup Bowl	Sunflower	8	None	20.00	88	880.00
16	13	Soup Bowl	Rose	8	Average	20.00	91	910.00
17	14	Cereal Bowl	Sunflower	6	Count / Count Number	10.00	58	348.00
18	15	Salad Plate	Lily	8	Max / Min	8.50	131	556.75
19	16	Dinner Plate	Rose	10.5	Sum	20.00	111	1110.00
20	17	Cup	Sunflower	3	StdDev / Var	5.00	103	257.50
21	18	Dinner Plate	Lily	10.5	More Function	20.00	100	1000.00
22	Total				▾			8902.25
23								

8.6 Choose the function to use to calculate a column in a total row cell.

4. Repeat Step 3 to choose functions in other total row cells as desired. Excel automatically inserts the SUM function for the far-right column, so you should change or remove that function (None is one of the function choices) as dictated by your data.

Note You also can add a calculated column to an Excel table. The formulas in a table's calculated column use a special kind of reference called a structured reference. To add the column, enter a name for the column in the header row to the right of the last column in the table, click the cell below, type an = (equal sign), and then use the mouse and operators to build the formula.

Sorting and Filtering Lists and Tables

Breaking your lists and tables into discrete fields of information makes the data more useable, because it means you can sort and filter the list. These two forms of basic data analysis help you find more meaning in the list. You can arrange the list contents in a more meaningful way, such as sorting by customer or order number. Or, you can limit the list to just the items that are relevant for a particular purpose. These processes work better when you include a header row with column names in Word and Outlook tables and Excel lists, so make sure you've included a header row.

You can sort a list or table in Word, Outlook, and Excel. As the name says, sorting rearranges the entries (rows) in a list into a new order. Placing entries in alphabetical order (A to Z or Z to A) always comes to mind, but Excel also can sort by number and date.

Note

If you want a sorted table in PowerPoint, you can copy the table to Word, sort it there, copy it again, and paste it back on the PowerPoint slide. You might have to fix the table formatting after doing so, however.

The quickest way to sort according to the contents of a single column in Excel is to click a cell in the column and then choose either Data ➔ Sort & Filter ➔ Sort A to Z or Data ➔ Sort & Filter ➔ Sort Z to A.

Note

In the olden days, when you sorted any list in Excel, the entire worksheet rows moved. This was a problem if you had other ranges of data to the right of the list or table. Now, Excel only changes the order of the rows in the list or table. This is why you need to leave one or more blank columns to the right of the list or table. If you don't, nonlist data touching the list gets sorted, too.

Follow these steps to sort data in a Word or Outlook table by one or more columns or an Excel list or table by two or more columns, sometimes called a multilevel sort:

1. **Click in the list or table you want to sort, preferably in the first column to sort by in a table.** In Word and Outlook, you also can select a "list" of contiguous paragraphs if you want to sort the paragraphs by the first word in the paragraph.

2. **Choose the appropriate sort command, as listed here.** The Sort dialog box appears. Word and Outlook select the table or the entire document if you have not previously selected a list of paragraphs, and Excel selects the list or table on the sheet.

   ● **Sorting selected paragraphs in Word:** Home ➔ Paragraph ➔ Sort

   ● **Sorting selected paragraphs in Outlook:** Format Text ➔ Paragraph ➔Sort

● **Sorting a table in Word or Outlook:** Layout ➜ Data ➜ Sort (When a table is selected in Word, two Layout tabs appear. Choose the command from the far right Layout tab. You also can choose the Home ➜ Paragraph ➜ Sort command in Word.)

● **Sorting a list or table in Excel:** Data ➜ Sort & Filter ➜ Sort

3. **In the first Sort By row in Excel, choose the column to sort by from the Sort By drop-down list; in Word and Outlook, the correct choice should be selected under Sort By.** In Word and Outlook, Paragraphs will be selected under Sort By when you're sorting a selected list of paragraphs, while the name of the column holding the insertion point will be selected if you are sorting a table.

4. **Choose the sort order by choosing Ascending or Descending in Word or Out-look or by using the Order drop-down list in Excel.** You optionally can use the Type list in Word and Outlook to choose a sort type (Text, Number, or Date) or use the Sort On list in Excel to choose to sort according to certain formatting settings rather than the cell values.

5. **To add a sort level, use the Then By drop-down list in the Word or Outlook Sort dialog box or click the Add Level button in the Excel Sort dialog box.** The latter adds a Then By level below the Sort By level in Excel.

6. **Repeat the techniques presented in Steps 3 and 4 to specify sort settings for the Then By row.** From here, you could optionally repeat the previous step and this one to add sort levels.

7. **Make sure that Header Row is selected under My List Has in the Word or Outlook Sort dialog box or My Data Has Headers is checked in the Excel Sort dialog box if that is true of your list or table.** As noted earlier, using a header row facilitates the sort, because you know the name of the column(s) you're sorting by.

8. **Click OK.**

Figure 8.7 shows Excel's Sort dialog box with settings for two sort levels applied, as well as the resulting sort in the table. I sorted first by the Pattern column in A to Z order and second by Cost from Largest to Smallest. Press Ctrl+Z to undo the sort before saving the file.

Genius

In the sheet shown in Figure 8.7, I added a column with numbers at the far left to number the items in their original order. You can do this in a list that you might sort a lot but need to be able to return it to its original order. Even if you hide that column from view, you can still sort by it.

Data sorted first by Pattern   Sort buttons   Filter buttons

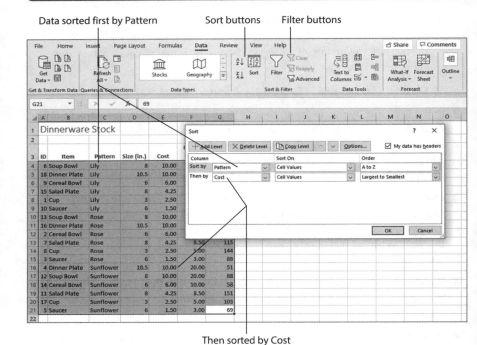

Then sorted by Cost

8.7 Use the Sort dialog box to sort by multiple columns.

Excel's filtering feature doesn't change the list or table order. (Sorry, no filtering is available in the other apps.) Filtering just temporarily hides some of the rows so you can focus on relevant information. Filtering is just as easy as sorting. By default a filter button appears on each header row cell in a table so that you don't have to display them manually. Clicking a filter button displays choices for sorting and filtering. To turn on filter arrows for a list, choose Data ➜ Sort & Filter ➜ Filter. Click the filter arrow for a column to filter by, and in the menu/dialog box that appears (refer to the left side of Figure 8.8), click the (Select All) check box to clear it. Click to place a check in the check box for each entry in that column that you want to display in the filtered data, and then click OK. Repeat the process for other columns to further filter and narrow the list of matches. Figure 8.8 shows a list filtered to only show rows with Lily in the Pattern column. Notice that the filter arrow for a filtered column changes to include a little filter icon. The row numbers for the filtered rows also change to blue.

Filter arrow

Indicates a filtered column

Filtered for rows with Lily

Filtered for rows with Lily

8.8 Filtering displays only matching rows.

To remove a filter from a column, you can click its filter arrow, click the (Select All) check box to recheck it, and then click OK. To clear filters from all columns, choose Data ➔ Sort & Filter ➔ Clear. You can then choose Data ➔ Sort & Filter ➔ Filter to toggle off the filter arrows.

Genius

In Excel, the Table Design ➔ Table Style Options ➔ Filter Button check box enables you to toggle the table header filter buttons on and off, as does the Data ➔ Sort & Filter ➔ Filter button. You might want to turn them off to discourage other users from filtering the table, for example.

Changing Table Styles

If the default table style or a style you selected when creating the table no longer suits your needs, it's easy to change it. When you click a cell in the table, the Table Design tab becomes available. In Word, Outlook, and PowerPoint, click the Table Design tab, and then click the More (down arrow) button in the lower-right corner of the Table Styles gallery in the Table Styles group to open the gallery of styles. In Excel, click the Table Design tab, and then click the Quick Styles button in the Table Styles group to open the gallery. Use the mouse to Live Preview a new design on your table (see the example from PowerPoint in Figure 8.9), and then click the winning style to apply it.

Table Style Options   Table Design tab

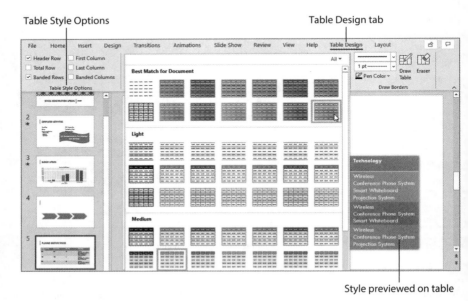

Style previewed on table

8.9 A new table style quickly updates a table's appearance.

To the left of the Table Styles group of the Table Design tab, several choices for controlling specific aspects of the table style appear in the Table Style Options group. Click to check or uncheck those check boxes to choose whether to display special formatting for items such as banded rows or banded columns.

Converting a Table Back to Regular Content

Converting a table back to regular text in Word or PowerPoint or back to a regular range in Excel will be the one of the easiest things we've done in the chapter, so it's a nice way to wrap up our discussion. One cool thing about converting an Excel table back to a range is that the range retains the formatting from the table style. It looks just as attractive as the table, but it lacks the table functionality. You may need to convert a table back if the table formatting or functionality creates a problem with copying the table's contents to another application. To convert a table back to regular contents, use one of these procedures:

- **Word and Outlook.** Click any cell in the table. Choose Layout ➔ Data ➔ Convert to Text. Click a delimiter option under Separate Text With, and then click OK.

- **PowerPoint.** There's no direct way to convert a table back to text in PowerPoint. However, you can copy a table to a Word document, convert it to text there, and copy and paste it back to a PowerPoint slide.

- **Excel.** Click a cell in the table. Choose Table Design ➔ Tools ➔ Convert to Range. Click Yes when prompted to confirm the conversion.

How Do I Present My Data in Charts?

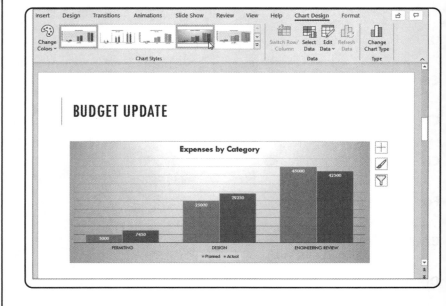

You've probably heard the buzzy term *data visualization* thrown around a lot lately. Charts you can create in the Microsoft 365 apps are one form of data visualization. You can create numerous types of charts to present data in accessible visual formats. Because the apps' charting tools are so flexible, you can deploy charts in a variety of ways in a file and apply different layouts and formatting. This chapter mentors you in data visualization skills, including creating, formatting, and changing charts.

Using Different Chart Types

A *chart* presents a graphical or visual representation of a selected set of data. In Chapter 7, I compared the graphics you can work with in Microsoft 365 documents to elements of many infographics, which present a narrative through text, data, graphics, and charts. A chart you create in an app can be used as part of an infographic approach or can stand alone as a data visualization.

Word, Excel, PowerPoint, and Outlook include dozens of chart types you can use to illustrate data. That said, you need to use the right chart type for your data; otherwise, your chart will provide visual misinformation. Table 9.1 provides a general overview of the chart types. In Excel, each category includes multiple subtypes, or the specific variants of the main chart type that you can apply when you create a chart. For example, some chart types have 2-D and 3-D subtypes. Word, PowerPoint, and Outlook organize charts slightly differently, with some of the subtypes from Excel presented among the overall chart types. Table 9.1 also mentions a subtype or two within each Excel category.

Table 9.1 Overall Chart Types in the Microsoft 365 Apps

Name	Description and Excel Subtype Examples
Column or Bar	Compares discrete values from a few categories. Subtypes include Clustered Column and 3-D Stacked Bar.
Line or Area	Compares many points of data to illustrate trends, usually over time. Subtypes include Line with Markers and 3-D Area.
Pie or Doughnut	Identifies proportions of a whole, with the whole assumed to be 100%. Choose a Pie subtype to chart a single series, and choose Doughnut for multiple series. Subtypes include Pie of Pie and 3-D Pie.
Hierarchy	Identifies proportions of a whole, when the data is organized in a hierarchy of categories. Subtypes include Treemap and Sunburst.
Statistic	Evaluates and presents the data in common statistical analysis charts. Subtypes include Pareto and Box and Whisker.
Scatter (X,Y) or Bubble	Illustrates the relationship between multiple sets of values. Subtypes include Scatter with Smooth Lines and Markers and Scatter with Straight Lines.

Name	Description and Excel Subtype Examples
Waterfall, Funnel, Stock, Surface or Radar	Catchall category with special-purpose charts listed in the category name. Subtypes include Wireframe 3-D Surface and Radar with Markers.
Combo	Compares mixed values or values that vary greatly in scale along two axes using two chart types. Subtypes include Clustered Column - Line on Secondary Axis and Stacked Area - Clustered Column.

Creating a Chart in Excel

The first step in creating any chart in Excel is to select the data to be charted. The Charts group of the Insert tab on Excel's ribbon, shown in Figure 9.1, has a button for each general chart type listed in Table 9.1. As for other galleries or lists of choices shown earlier in the book, you can click a chart type button and then move the mouse pointer over one of the choices to see a descriptive ScreenTip and a preview of how the chart would look if applied to the selected data. Often you'll be able to see right away if a particular chart depicts the data in a misleading or nonmeaningful way.

You can't just select any old data. Excel must be able to identify each *series* and *category* of data in the selected range. Usually, each series is contained in a single row or single column, with each item in the series being called a single *data point* that's charted with a column, pie wedge, or other data marker, depending on the chart type. Categories group similar data points in some chart types.

Caution You generally do not want to select any total row or column along with other data when creating a chart, because that would skew the appearance of the charted data. In charts where you want to show the total data on its own, you might *only* select the total data.

For Figure 9.1, I selected the range A3:C15. Excel correctly identified that the Shipments entries in column B formed one series, and the Total Value entries in column C formed a second series. And yes, it's a good idea to include row and column labels in the selection so that Excel can use them to label parts of the chart. Because the series varied widely in scale, the combo chart being previewed looked good. I could have just clicked to apply that subtype to the chart. Note that other chart types, such as High-Low-Close, require the data series to be arranged in a more particular order.

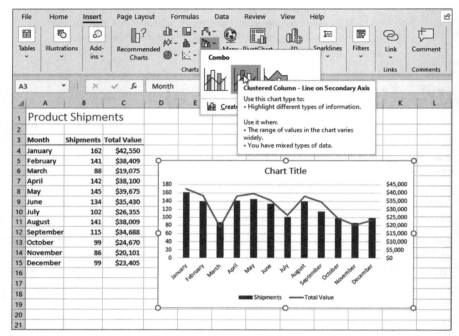

9.1 Use the chart type buttons in the Charts group of the Insert tab in Excel to explore the available charts.

Caution

If you select multiple series and create a pie chart, Excel charts only the first series of data, because pie charts show only one series. Each data point in the series becomes a slice in the pie. What if the labels for your data points are one or more rows or columns away from the series itself, such as having the labels in column A and the series in column D? Select the labels, Ctrl+drag to select the series, and then create the pie chart.

Selecting the data to chart and then using the Insert → Charts choices to create a chart is one way to create a chart, but there are numerous others. Excel now has built-in intelligence to analyze the chart data and recommend appropriate chart types, a feature called

Recommended Charts. You can choose your own chart type or a recommended one in these additional ways to create a chart after you've selected the data to chart:

- **Insert Chart dialog box.** Click the Charts group dialog box launcher on the Insert tab to open this dialog box. On the Recommended Charts tab (see Figure 9.2), you can click a thumbnail from the suggestions at the left to see a larger preview and description and then click OK to choose that chart type. Alternatively, you can click the All Charts tab and click choices at the left and the top to preview various chart types and subtypes; then click OK to create the desired chart.

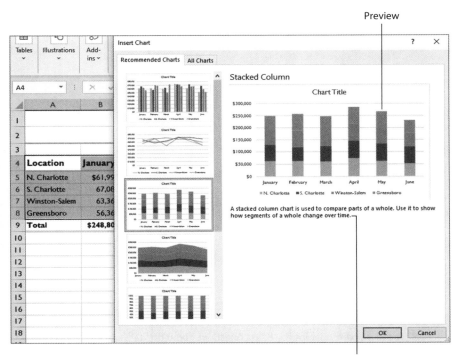

9.2 The Insert Chart dialog box offers Recommended Charts.

- **Quick Analysis.** After you select the range to chart, click the Quick Analysis button that appears at the lower-right corner or press Ctrl+Q. Click Charts at the top of the pop-up, move the mouse pointer over a button for a Recommended Charts suggestion to see a preview, and then click the chart type to create.

● **Ideas Pane.** Choose Home ➔ Ideas ➔ Ideas (or Home ➔ Analysis ➔ Analyze Data in some versions) to open the Ideas pane, which analyzes the data, displays suggested charts, and enables you to ask questions about the data, as shown in the example in Figure 9.3. Point to the right side of the pane to display a scroll bar that you can use to see additional results and options. Click Insert Chart within a chart thumbnail to create a chart as shown in the preview, and then close the pane.

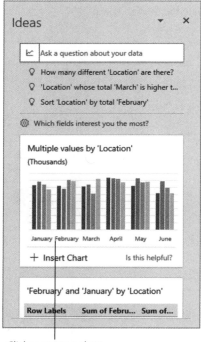

Click to create a chart

9.3 The Ideas pane enables you to ask questions about the data and create a chart.

Genius

If you're incorporating numerous charts in a workbook file or on a dashboard sheet, sticking with similar chart types will make the design much more cohesive. For example, you probably don't want to mix 2-D and 3-D chart types. Some designers prefer not to use 3-D charts at all, arguing that they can distort the relative appearance of the data, especially for 3-D pie charts.

The final step to creating a chart is moving it into the position you want and resizing it if needed. As for other graphics that you learned about in Chapter 7, you can click a chart to select it. Then you can drag it into the desired position on the sheet or press and hold the Shift key while dragging a corner handle to resize the chart proportionally. You also can cut, copy, and paste the selected chart. Click outside the chart to deselect it.

Note

You can select a range of data to chart and then press F11 to create a new chart on its own separate sheet, called a *chart sheet*. You also can choose Chart Design → Location → Move Chart to open the Move Chart dialog box. Click the New Sheet option button, edit the name if needed, and then click OK. From there, you can select the chart on the chart sheet to change the chart type and formatting as needed.

Creating a Chart in Word or PowerPoint

When you create a chart in Word or PowerPoint, a little surprise happens: an Excel window opens for you to enter the chart data. Follow these steps to call on your Excel skillset as you create a chart in Word or PowerPoint:

1. **Select the location where you want the chart to appear.** In Word, this means moving the insertion point. In PowerPoint, this usually means selecting a slide with a content placeholder or creating or selecting a slide using the Blank or Title Only slide layout.

2. **Choose Insert → Illustrations → Chart.** You also can click the Insert Chart button in a PowerPoint content placeholder. The Insert Chart dialog box opens. The All Charts tab (which is the only tab in the dialog box) lists the chart types down the left. In PowerPoint, a Design Ideas pane also might appear.

3. **Click a chart type at the left.** The subtypes for that chart type appear along the top of the tab.

4. **Click a subtype.** A preview of the subtype appears in the dialog box.

5. **Click OK.** This is the point where the Excel window for creating the chart data appears, displaying example data to guide your entries.

6. **Enter the chart data.** For most chart types, you'll enter category names down column A and series names across row 1 starting in cell B1, and the rest of the entries in the range in the blue selection box.

7. **To change the charted cells, drag the bottom-right selection handle of the blue selection box.** For example, in Figure 9.4 I dragged the blue selection handle to the left so that the chart included only one column of data.

Sizing handle to drag to change charted data

Excel window for entering chart data in Word

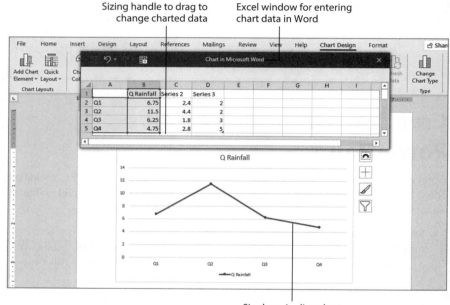

Single series line chart

9.4 When entering data for a Word or PowerPoint chart, you can drag in the Excel window to change how much data is charted.

8. **Click the Excel window Close (X) button to finish entering the data.**

Note

The process for inserting a chart in an Outlook message body is the same as in Word or PowerPoint, starting with choosing Insert → Illustrations → Chart. Even though the capability is available, I've never used it. Practically speaking, when I've had to share charts with others, it's in the context of a much more robust Word, Excel, or PowerPoint file that I attach to the message. Chapter 10 covers message attachments.

In Word, you can resize the chart as needed after clicking it to select it, and you can change the text wrapping settings as needed so that you can drag the chart to another position. In PowerPoint, you generally don't want to resize a chart that's in a content placeholder, but may do so as needed on a slide using the Blank or Title Only slide layouts.

Changing the Chart Type and Layout

After you create a chart, elements of the chart, including the chart type, aren't set in stone. When you select a chart by clicking it, the Chart Design and Format contextual tabs appear with settings for changing or refining the chart's appearance. If you choose Chart Design ➔ Type ➔ Change Chart Type, the Change Chart Type dialog box opens. It looks and works just like the Insert Chart dialog box you used to create the chart. You can use the choices on either the Recommended Charts or All Charts tab in Excel or the All Charts tab in Word and PowerPoint to select another chart type. Click OK to apply the change.

Note

In Excel, you also can use the Insert ➔ Charts group choices to preview and change the chart type for the selected chart.

Beyond changing the overall chart type, a chart has many different elements that you can edit or reformat, as shown in the example in Figure 9.5. Obviously, you would want to change the Chart Title placeholder contents to a more descriptive title, and the next section covers making those kinds of changes. The plot area is where the data is plotted, usually along two axes for most chart types: the horizontal (category) axis and the vertical (value) axis. In the example in Figure 9.5, you can see that the months appear as the categories along the horizontal (category) axis, and the values for the first series, Shipments, appear beside the vertical (value) axis at left. The Shipments series is plotted as a column chart. (If multiple series of monthly data had been plotted as the column chart, each month category would include a column for each series.) Because the example is a combination chart with a line chart used to show the values for the Total Value series, a secondary vertical (value) axis appears to the right of the plot area to show the values for the line chart. A legend at the bottom of the chart shows the name, color, and shape or appearance for each series of data in the chart.

Note

The horizontal (category) axis is also called the *x-axis*, and the vertical (value) axis is also called the *y-axis*, as in traditional mathematics.

Charted data with color coding   Chart title   Chart Design tab   Format tab

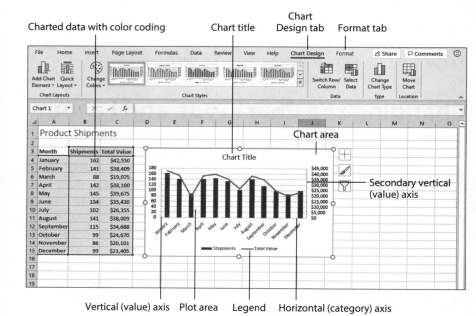

Vertical (value) axis   Plot area   Legend   Horizontal (category) axis

9.5 The position of chart elements depends on the layout.

If you want to change the overall arrangements of the elements in the chart, you can do so quickly by changing the layout. The layout determines which chart elements appear and where, and in some cases, the layout also modifies the sizing or spacing for elements such as column chart data points (columns). To preview and change the layout for the selected chart, choose Chart Design → Chart Layouts → Quick Layout. Move the mouse pointer over a layout in the gallery to view a Live Preview on the chart and see a ScreenTip listing the elements included in the layout. Figure 9.6 shows the same chart as Figure 9.5 with a preview of a different layout. The previewed layout doesn't include a chart title, adds horizontal (category) and vertical (value) axis titles, changes the angle of the category labels, moves the legend from below the chart to the right of the chart, and uses a different background for the plot area. To apply one of the layouts, click it in the gallery.

Genius

Too many data points can overload some chart types. Some data visualization experts recommend that a pie chart have no more than five or six data point slices. In a line chart with markers, the data points can become indistinguishable and nonmeaningful when crammed together on a small chart. To fix the situation, examine your data and consider whether you can group or categorize it, or perhaps use the Chart Filters button (see Figure 9.6) to limit the displayed data.

Change Chart Type button

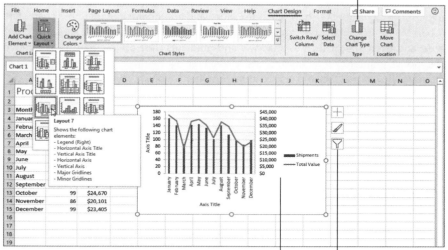

Live Preview of Layout 7   Chart Filters button

9.6 Use the Quick Layout gallery to preview and apply a new layout.

Formatting Chart Elements

You can edit and format chart elements individually as needed to meet your design and communications objectives. For example, you would obviously want to replace the place-holder text for the chart title or an axis title. To do so, select the chart, and then click the title or axis element on the chart area so that a selection box with blue handles appears around it. Type the text to add, which appears in the Formula bar as you type (Excel only), and then click outside the element selection box. While a box for a text element is selected, you also can use the choices in the Font group of the Home tab and the Shape Styles and WordArt Styles groups of the Format tab. These formatting choices work as described earlier in the book.

Genius

To use text contained in an Excel worksheet cell as the chart title or an axis title, select the title box on the chart, click in the Formula bar, type the = (equal) sign, click the cell that holds the title text, and then press Enter. If you later update the cell contents, the title updates automatically in the chart.

211

As for other graphics, the default formatting for charts comes via the theme applied to the file. The Chart Styles group of the Chart Design tab offers two galleries: one for changing just the colors for the chart (Change Colors) and another for changing the chart style (Chart Styles). The chart style controls fonts; fill for the data markers, plot area, and chart area; and even effects such as shadows and gradients. Just open either gallery, move the mouse pointer over a choice to see a Live Preview (see the PowerPoint example in Figure 9.7), and then click the color combo or style to apply.

Change Colors button   Chart Styles gallery

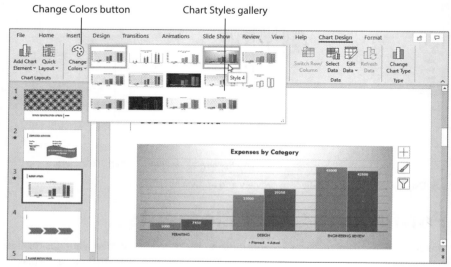

9.7 Update a chart with new colors or a new style.

If you don't need to change the overall layout for the chart but want to add or remove a particular chart element, use the Chart Design → Chart Layouts → Add Chart Element menu. For example, you could choose Chart Design → Chart Layouts → Add Chart Element → Chart Title → None to remove the chart title. Or you could choose Chart Design → Chart Layouts → Add Chart Element → Axis Titles → Primary Vertical to add a placeholder for a vertical (value) axis title, to which you could add the desired text. This menu offers many choices for adding, removing, and repositioning chart elements. For example, you can move the legend to the right side of the chart. Or, you can add a data table to include the data being charted within the chart area, which is handy if you want to include the chart in another document or save it as a graphic image file.

Some elements of a chart, such as an axis, are tricky to select for formatting. The Chart Elements drop-down list at the top of the Current Selection group at the left end of the

212

Format tab (see Figure 9.8) enables you to select a specific chart element prior to format-ting it or otherwise making changes. Choose the item to select in the list, and then use the tools on the Format tab as needed to update the selected element's appearance. You could also choose Format → Current Selection → Format Selection to open a Format pane with detailed formatting choices or Format → Current Selection → Reset to Match Style to remove formatting you've applied to the currently selected element.

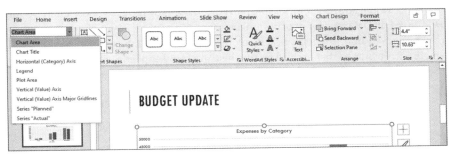

9.8 Select a chart element to format.

Genius

If you've invested a lot of time customizing a chart, you can save the chart as a template that you can use again. Right-click the chart, choose Save as Tem-plate, edit the filename, and click Save. (Do not change the save location.) You can find and use the template in the Insert Chart or Change Chart Type dialog boxes by clicking the All Charts tab and then clicking Templates at the left side of the dialog box.

Some users like to get fancy and add a bold color fill or even a texture or picture fill to the chart area, which is essentially the background for the entire chart. If you go with a treatment like that, be judicious. (Or to put it another way, don't get too crazy.) Make sure that all of the other chart elements remain clear and legible in context with the chosen background.

Changing the Charted Data

A callout in Figure 9.5 shows how, when a chart is selected, Excel highlights the charted data with color-coding and selection outlines, similar to the color-coding used for cell and range references when you are creating or editing a formula. The cells holding the charted data appear in blue, while red is used for series labels and purple is used for

213

category labels. And, as for a formula, any time you change a label or value in a charted range, the chart updates to reflect your changes. This dynamic relationship between the underlying data and the chart ensures that they remain in sync.

That doesn't mean that you can't adjust the relationship, however. For example, if each series or category of the data is held in a column, but Excel assumed each was held in a row, you can flip the relationship by selecting the chart and then choosing Chart Design → Data → Switch Row/Column. In Word and PowerPoint, you have to choose Chart Design → Data → Edit Data (main part of button) before clicking Switch Row/Column (the button may be grayed out). The left stacked column chart shown in Figure 9.9 is an example where Excel assumed that each series was held in a row. I applied Switch Row/Column to the copy of the chart on the right to indicate that the series are held in columns.

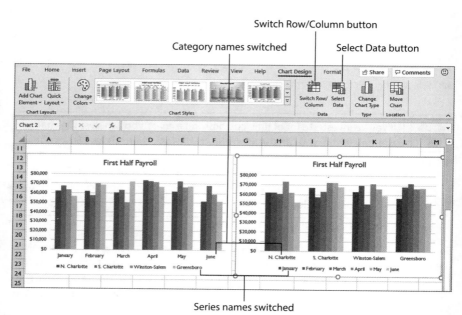

9.9 Adjust series plotting using the Switch Row/Column button.

In other cases, you may need to change the range of data that's charted. Choose Chart Design → Data → Select Data to open the Select Data Source dialog box shown in Figure 9.10. In Word and PowerPoint, the Excel window with the chart data also reopens. Either edit the entry in the Chart Data Range text box or use the collapse button at the far end of the text box to collapse the dialog box so that you select the range (on the Excel sheet or in the Excel window in Word and PowerPoint charts) with the mouse and then re-expand the dialog box. Click OK, and the chart adjusts to show the data from the newly selected range. In Word and PowerPoint, you also have to click the Close (X) button for the Excel window holding the chart data.

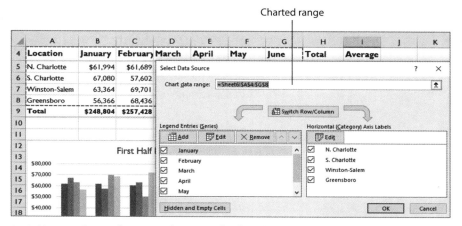

9.10 You can change the source data range for the selected chart.

Genius

With the chart selected in Excel, you also can drag the blue selection handle in the lower-right corner of the blue color-coded data range to change the data included in the chart. In Word or PowerPoint, choose Chart Design ➔ Data ➔ Edit Data (main part of button), drag the lower-right blue selection handle to change the charted range, and then close the Excel window.

Deleting a Chart

You can delete a chart from any page, sheet, or slide. Just click the chart and press the Delete key on the keyboard. Without warning, there goes the chart to the great chart dustbin. If you need the chart back, press Ctrl+Z or click the Undo button on the QAT right away.

You can't delete a chart from a chart sheet in Excel, but you can delete the chart sheet. Right-click the Sheet tab and choose Delete. In the message box that warns that the chart will be permanently deleted, click Delete.

How Do I Manage Emails and Contacts in Outlook?

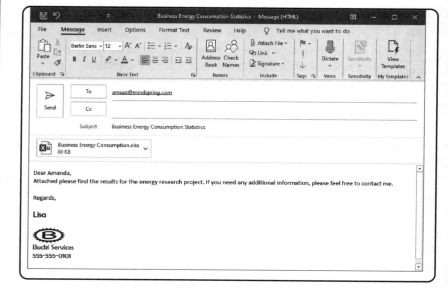

While various messaging apps and platforms are hyper popular, I'm still a fan of good old email. Email messages make it easy to have a back-and-forth conversation with detailed information about the date and time when particular communications occurred. Plus, I trust email more when sharing important documents such as contracts or project estimates. The Outlook app in Microsoft 365 is command central for working with email. This chapter explains how to set up your email account in Outlook, as well as how to create, send, and reply to messages. You'll also get a peek at organizing messages and contacts.

Adding Your Account

Outlook is a desktop *client* app for working with emails, as opposed to being a cloud-based email system such as Outlook on the web or Gmail. That basically means that Outlook can download and store email messages on your computer rather than the messages existing only in the cloud. For this process to work, you have to set up an account in Outlook to enable it to communicate with the incoming and outgoing mail servers for your organization, email provider, or internet service provider (ISP).

You might have an IT person in your organization set up the account for you, but if you don't or you're an independent professional like me, you can first try Outlook's automatic account setup process. (The process varies slightly depending on your email provider.) You'll need your account email address and password. After starting Outlook for the first time, you may see a prompt for setting up an account. If not, choose File ➔ Info ➔ Add Account. Enter the email address for your account (provided by your organization's IT staff, email provider, or ISP) in the Email Address text box of the window that appears, and then click the Connect button. If the process is successful, the next window prompts you for your password. Type your account password in the Password prompt line, and then click the Sign In button.

For a Microsoft-branded email account such as hotmail.com, live.com, or outlook.com, the next window prompts you to specify an alternative address where Microsoft can send a security code for account access. Enter the alternative email address under Where Should We Send Your Code (or alternatively click the Skip for Now (7 Days Until This Is Required) choice), and then click Next. Check that alternative email, enter the emailed security code in the window at the Code prompt, and then click Next. Enter your account password again at the Password prompt and click Sign In. If you see a Mail Delivery Location message box, click OK. At the window titled Account Successfully Added, uncheck or check the Set Up Outlook Mobile on My Phone, Too check box as desired, and then click the Done button. Outlook then retrieves and loads your mailbox settings and any current emails, a process that may take several minutes.

If you don't happen to get lucky with the automatic setup process, you'll need a little more information beyond your email address and password from your IT staff, or email provider's or ISP's online Help information. First, you need to know your account type, with the most common types being POP (Post Office Protocol), IMAP (Internet Message Access Protocol), or Exchange. Here's how they work:

- **POP (or POP3 in some cases).** This older technology downloads emails for offline reading and (usually) deletes downloaded messages from the email server after a period of time. This means that the emails only exist on the device where you downloaded them to Outlook, so you can't read them from another computer or device. This type of account helps keep you within email server storage limits imposed by your provider.

● **IMAP.** This technology both leaves messages on the email server and downloads local copies in the email client app such as Outlook, so you can access the messages from multiple devices. An email remains on the email server until you delete it from within a client app, at which point a synchronization process also deletes it from the server. IMAP accounts typically have much higher storage limits, and in some cases require an account upgrade, which means additional cost.

● **Exchange.** This Microsoft-branded technology works like IMAP and offers message access on multiple devices and message syncing. Many organizations use Exchange email servers, as do other Microsoft-branded email services such as Outlook.com, also called Outlook on the web. Exchange storage limits tend to be very large, but in some cases an organization may set specific mailbox storage limits for users.

You also need to know details about the incoming (POP or IMAP) and outgoing (SMTP) email servers for your provider, including server address, port, and encryption method. (SMTP stands for Simple Mail Transfer Protocol.) For example, for some older MSN-branded Microsoft email accounts, the incoming IMAP server address is imap-mail.outlook.com, the port is 993, and the encryption method is SSL/TLS; and the outgoing SMTP server address is smtp-mail.outlook.com, with port 587 and STARTTLS encryption. Again, obtain this information from your organization's IT person or your provider's online Help.

Genius

Many mail providers enable you to work with both cloud-based webmail and an email client such as Outlook. You can set up an account in Outlook for Gmail, Yahoo!, and iCloud accounts, among others. Consult your provider's online Help to find the correct incoming and outgoing server for your account type. You can also search online for the Microsoft Support article titled "POP and IMAP email settings for Outlook," which lists the IMAP, POP, and SMTP settings for leading providers such as Gmail.

From there, the process is similar to the automatic setup process I described. Choose File ➔ Info ➔ Add Account. Enter your email address in the Email Address text box, click Advanced Options, and then click the Let Me Set Up My Account Manually check box to check it. Click the Connect button. In the next window, click the type of account that you have. For some choices, such as Exchange, Outlook will attempt to set up the account automatically. For other choices, such as POP or IMAP, Outlook prompts you to enter the server and port information. Just follow the prompts that appear to finish account setup. The steps vary depending on the account type.

For some types of email accounts, you can change settings such as the display name or add an organization name. To see the available settings, choose File ➜ Info ➜ Account Settings ➜ Account Settings, click the account on the Email tab of the Account Settings dialog box, and then click Change. (In some cases, you also can click the More Settings button to open a dialog box with additional settings.) Make the desired changes, click Next, and then click Done. For other types of accounts, such as Outlook.com, you have to go to your online profile to change the display name.

Changing or Deleting an Account

To work with the settings for an account in Outlook, choose File ➜ Info ➜ Account Settings ➜ Account Settings. Click the account you want to change in the list on the Email tab, and then click the Change button. Use the choices that appear, including the More Settings button, to make the desired changes, and then click Next, Done, and Close. The available settings will depend on the email account type. When you have multiple accounts set up in Outlook, you can delete one that's unneeded. Choose File ➜ Info ➜ Account Settings ➜ Account Settings. On the Email tab of the Account Settings dialog box, click the account to delete in the list, and then click the Remove button above the list. Click Yes in the message box that warns you about the deletion. The process requires extra steps if you have only one account set up. You first have to use the Add button on the Data Files tab of the Account Settings dialog box to create a copy of the account's .ost Outlook data file (where Outlook saves email messages, calendar, tasks, and other items). Then you can go back to the Email tab and delete the account.

Creating and Sending Messages

Unlike the other Microsoft 365 apps covered earlier in the book, Outlook has two window types: its main window, where you read and organize messages, and a message window, where you compose the contents of an email message. (Outlook generally displays its tools for working with email when it opens.) Each of these windows has its own ribbon. The ribbon contents in the main window may change slightly, depending on what's currently selected in the window. By default, Outlook displays a Simplified Ribbon in both windows. Figure 10.1 shows the Simplified Ribbon for the Main window. To change to the Classic Ribbon, click the Switch Ribbons button in the lower-right corner. The rest of the figures in this chapter show the Classic Ribbon, just to give you a better sense of where to find additional tools in Outlook.

Switch Ribbons button

10.1 Outlook by default displays a Simplified Ribbon.

To create a new message and open it in the message window, choose Home → New → New Email or press Ctrl+N. From there, you can perform the following actions to create and send the message:

- **Choosing a message format (optional).** By default, Outlook creates the message in HTML format. You alternatively can change to plain text (creates the smallest message size but eliminates the ability to format the message contents) or rich text (creates smaller messages with the ability to format the message). The Plain Text and Rich Text options are in the Format group of the Format Text tab.

- **Changing message design (optional).** The Themes group of the Options tab in the message window holds the choices for changing the message theme, theme colors, theme fonts, and theme effects. These choices work as described in the "Understanding Themes" section in Chapter 6. Additionally, you can click the Page Color button in the group and then click a color in the palette that appears to add a page background color.

- **Creating and adding your signature (optional).** Outlook can append your contact information and other contents (such as a logo or brand slogan) at the end of a message if you save those contents as a signature. Choose Message → Include → Signature → Signatures. In the Signatures and Stationery dialog box, click the New button below the Select Signature to Edit list on the E-Mail Signature tab. In the New Signature dialog box, type a name and then click OK. With the signature you just created still selected in the list, click in the Edit Signature area, and then type and format the signature contents as desired. You also can insert a logo or other picture, as in the example in Figure 10.2. Click the Save button to save your changes. Make sure that the signature you just created is selected from the New Messages drop-down list to ensure that it will be included in future new messages, and then click OK. To insert the new signature in the current message window, choose Message → Include → Signature, and then choose the signature name in the menu.

221

New button   Save button

Signature to be included in
new messages

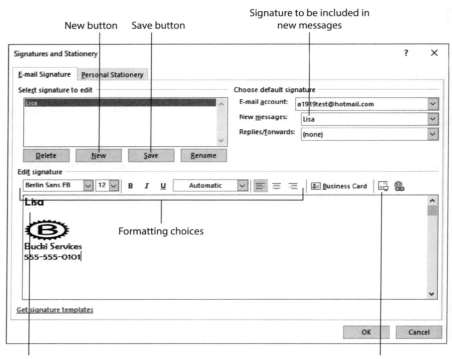

Formatting choices

Editing area   Insert Picture button

10.2 Create your own signature to include with messages.

⬤ **Adding recipients and a subject.** The lines to the right of the To and Cc buttons in the message window are where you can type the email address of your message recipients, adding a comma or semicolon after each recipient when there are multiple recipients. If you've stored the name of any of your recipients as contacts as described in the section called "Adding Contacts" at the end of the chapter, you can start typing the contact name and choose a contact from the Suggestions list. Or, click the To button, click a contact in the Select Names: Contacts dialog box, and then click the To, Cc, or Bcc button. Click OK to close the dialog box when you finish adding recipients. Back in the message window, click to the right of Subject and type a message subject.

Genius

Do your message recipients a favor by using specific subject lines. Rather than just a generic subject such as "Project Update," elaborate more with a subject line such as "Project Update – Phase Two Complete." For a long-running email conversation, it's also a courtesy to change up the subject line when you reply. If I've already replied to a message and have another thought, I'll add something like "//#2" to the end of the subject so that my recipients know I'm raising a new issue.

⬤ **Typing and formatting the message.** Click in the message body area above any signature and type the information for your message. I'm old school and like to include a courteous greeting and closing in most email messages, but whether that's a necessity depends on the norms within your organization or whether you're communicating with a friend or family member rather than a colleague. Formatting the content of the message body works just like formatting in Word. You can use choices on the Message and Format Text tabs to change font and alignment settings and create numbered and bulleted lists; use the Insert tab choices to include tables, pictures, and other graphics; and use the Review tab choices to check spelling, grammar, and word choice.

⬤ **Attaching a file (if needed).** You can attach one or more files to an email message to provide more detail or deliver a specific type of document such as a contract draft, report, project estimate, design sketches, and so on. In the message window, choose Message ➔ Include ➔ Attach File ➔ Browse This PC. Use the Insert File dialog box to navigate to the location holding the file, click the file in the list, and click the Insert button. The file appears above the message body, as shown in Figure 10.3. Clicking the down arrow at the right of the attachment opens a menu of choices, including Remove Attachment to use if you've selected the wrong file.

⬤ **Sending the message.** It's a good practice to double-check your message content before sending it. I often edit and refine message text to ensure my meaning is clear, which is more important in non-verbal communication. You also can use the High Importance and Low Importance choices in the Tags group of the Message tab to communicate the urgency of the message. When you're satisfied with the message, click the Send button in the message window. The message goes to the Outbox folder. Outlook then connects to your email service or provider over the Internet and sends the message.

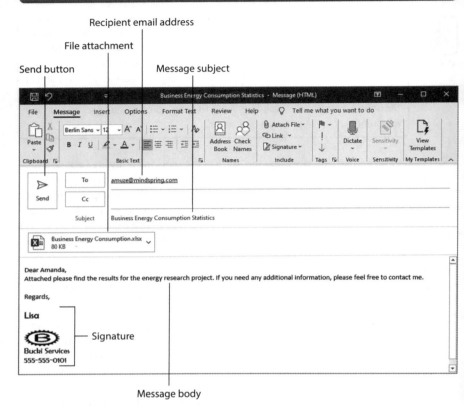

Recipient email address

File attachment

Send button

Message subject

Message body

10.3 An email message in the message window has one or more recipients, a subject, body, file attachment, and signature.

Receiving, Reading, and Replying to Messages

Each time you start Outlook, it checks for messages online. After that, it automatically sends and receives messages every 30 minutes by default. You can send and receive at any time from the main Outlook window by choosing Send/Receive ➜ Send & Receive ➜ Send/Receive All Folders or by pressing F9. The Inbox folder for your account holds all incoming messages.

Note

You can change the automatic send and receive interval if needed. Choose Send/Receive ➜ Send & Receive ➜ Send/Receive Groups ➜ Define Send/Receive Groups. With All Accounts selected in the Group Name list of the Send/Receive Groups dialog box, change the value in the text box for the Schedule an Automatic Send/Receive Every X Minutes text box (under Setting for Group "All Accounts"), and then click Close.

The message list in the middle pane of the main Outlook window shows brief information about each received message. By default, the Focused Inbox feature is enabled, which means Outlook presents the most important messages on the Focused tab of the message list and moves less important messages to the Other tab. (You can toggle this feature on and off using View ➜ Focused Inbox ➜ Show Focused Inbox.) To view the contents of the message, click it in the message list so that the contents appear in the Reading Pane at the right. Figure 10.4 shows an example message in the main Outlook window. You also can double-click a message in the message list to open it in its own window. After you view a message, Outlook marks it as read and no longer displays it in bold in the message list. If you want to change that, perhaps to remind yourself to revisit the message, you can right-click a message in the message list and choose Mark as Unread from the shortcut menu.

When the selected message requires a response, you will typically perform one of three actions:

● **Reply to the message.** Choosing Home ➜ Respond ➜ Reply (Message ➜ Respond ➜ Reply in a message window) or clicking the Reply button in the message opens a message where you can compose and send your response. This message will only be addressed to the original sender.

Note

When you choose the Reply, Reply All, or Forward in the message in the Reading Pane of the main Outlook window, the response message also appears in the Reading Pane rather than a separate message window.

● **Reply All to the message.** Choosing Home ➜ Respond ➜ Reply All (Message ➜ Respond ➜ Reply All in a message window) or clicking the Reply All button in the message again opens a message, but in this case the message will be addressed to the original sender as well as to the other recipients of the message.

225

Forward button

Reply All button

Selected message   Reading Pane   Reply button

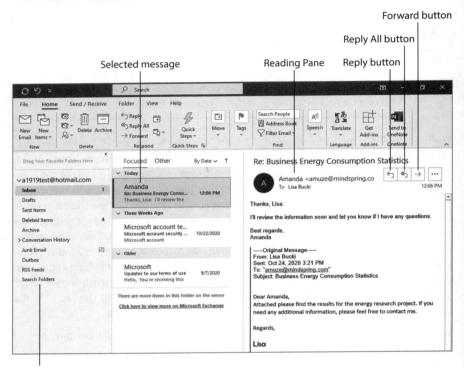

10.4 Read and respond to your emails in the main Outlook window.

- **Forward the message.** Choosing Home → Respond → Forward (Message → Respond → Forward in a message window) or clicking the Forward button in the message opens a message with no recipient specified. This enables you to enter or specify a new person to receive the information contained in the earlier message. Add recipients and message information as needed.

Folder Pane

Note

Some email systems enable message tracking, so you can get confirmation of whether or not your message or reply was delivered and read. To request tracking before sending a new message or reply message, display the message window Options tab. In the Tracking group, click to check the Request a Delivery Receipt and/or Request a Read Receipt check boxes.

After you finish a response message, click the Send button to send it. Note that messages you send temporarily shift to your Outbox folder, and a number beside the folder name indicates how many unsent messages it currently holds. If you need to make sure a message sends, you can perform a manual send/receive as described earlier.

While I find the default appearance of the main Outlook window to be fine for my message management needs, the View tab does offer a variety of settings that you can explore to tailor the screen appearance for your own needs. For example, you could turn off the Focused Inbox feature or the Reading Pane display, or change the sort order of the messages. The Change View button in the tab's Current View group also enables you to change to another view overall, if desired.

Organizing Messages

Messages can pile up fast in your Inbox folder. Outlook handles some of the message madness for you by identifying obvious junk emails and moving them to the Junk folder for your account. This filtering can mistakenly flag an important message as junk, so you should check the messages in the Junk folder from time to time, especially if you were expecting a message that hasn't arrived. Click the Junk folder in the Folder Pane to see any messages in the folder in the message list. Beyond checking the junk, you can use any or all of these techniques to work with received messages:

- **Trashing (deleting) messages.** If your organization or email provider puts a limit on your Inbox storage, then chances are you'll eventually have to delete old messages. To delete an unwanted message, select it in the message list of the main Outlook window, and then choose Home ➔ Delete ➔ Delete. You also can move the mouse pointer over the message in the message list and click the trashcan icon that appears. The message moves to the Deleted Items or Trash folder. (The folder name varies depending on your email provider.) To view the messages in the Deleted Items folder, click it in the Folder Pane. To empty the Deleted Items folder, right-click it in the Folder Pane, choose Empty Folder (see Figure 10.5), and then click Yes in the message box that asks you to confirm the deletion. (If you also look carefully at the bottom of the message in Figure 10.5, you can see that the logo image from the signature is missing. That's because different email systems handle graphics in different ways, so you may encounter glitches like that.)

- **Tagging or flagging messages.** You can assign either a color category or a follow-up flag to a message. To add a basic flag, just move the mouse pointer over the message in the message list and click the flag icon that appears. (Figure 10.5 shows this type of flag.) To assign a category or another type of flag to the selected message, use the choices available via Home ➔ Tags ➔ Tags.

227

Right-click folder

Delete button

Message flag

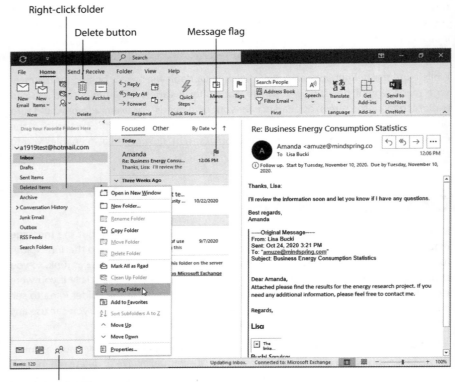

People (contacts) button

10.5 Message organization activities include trashing messages and emptying the Deleted Items folder.

⦿ **Organizing messages in folders.** Creating specific folders and moving messages into them makes it easier to find a particular message when you need to. Historically, I've created a folder for each of my clients and then a subfolder for each project under the client folder. To create a new top-level folder for your Outlook account, right-click the account name in the Folder Pane, choose New Folder, type a folder name, and then press Enter. To create a subfolder of the Inbox folder or another top-level folder right-click it instead. You can then drag a message from the message list into the new folder or select a message and choose Home → Move → Move → Other Folder. Select the destination folder in the Move Items dialog box, and then click OK.

Genius

If you want to automate message organization in Outlook, you can create email rules. For example, you could create a rule that always moves messages from a particular recipient into a particular folder rather than the Inbox. Choose Home → Move → Rules → Create Rule to open the Create Rule dialog box, where you can get started.

Adding Contacts

Creating a contact enables you to store information about a colleague or collaborator, including name, company, job title, email address, and phone number. Among other things, adding contacts makes it easier to specify recipients for email messages. You can just choose a contact from the Select Names: Contacts dialog box as described earlier in the chapter. And a digital contact remains at your fingertips even if you lose the person's business card. To start working with contacts, click the People button (which I like to think of more as the contacts button) at the bottom of the Outlook window Folder Pane, as shown in Figure 10.5. Outlook displays your current contacts and ribbon tools for working with contacts, including these actions:

- **Adding a contact.** Choose Home → New → New Contact. A new Contact window opens. Enter the contact that you'd like to include, as shown in the example in Figure 10.6. To finish and close the window, choose Contact → Actions → Save & Close.

- **Editing a contact.** To make changes to a contact, double-click the contact in the contact list in the middle pane or right-click the contact and then choose Edit Contact. Make the desired changes in the Contact window, and then choose Contact → Actions → Save & Close.

- **Deleting a contact.** Select the contact in the middle pane, and then press the Delete key or choose Home → Delete → Delete. Be careful, though. Outlook deletes the contact immediately without giving you the chance to confirm that you really want to make the deletion.

Other useful contact tasks available for your exploration include the ability to create a contact group to make it easier to address group emails, the ability to forward contact information to others and share contacts, and the ability to set up a meeting and invite contacts.

Save & Close button

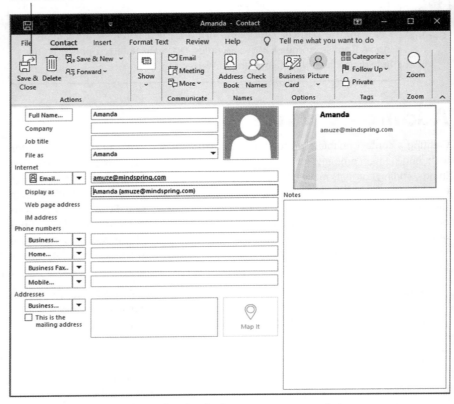

10.6 You can add as many or as few details about a contact as needed.

Click the Mail button at the bottom of the Folder Pane when you finish working with contacts and want to return to working with email messages.

How Do I Print and Share My Content?

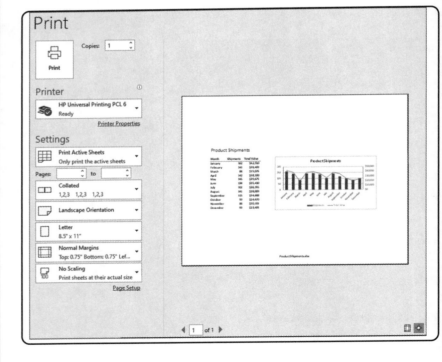

As organizations increasingly digitize document workflows, some situations still justify the convenience or relative permanence of a paper printout. A project estimate you've created in Excel might require the client's signature. You might want to print a Word to-do list for portability. A colleague might want a hard copy of your PowerPoint presentation. You might need a printout of an email message in Outlook. This chapter covers Printout Wrangling 101, from creating headers and footers, to controlling extra settings in Excel, through previewing and printing. I throw in a couple of nonprinting sharing methods as a bonus.

Creating Headers and Footers

To add identifying information to a printout, you can add a header or footer. A header prints in the margin at the top of each page, while a footer prints in the margin at the bottom of each page. Creating headers and footers is one area where the Microsoft 365 apps tend to diverge in approach, so let's take a look at what to do in each of the three main apps:

● **Word.** In the Header & Footer group of the Insert tab, you can click either Header or Footer to see a gallery of preset headers and footers, like the Footer gallery shown in Figure 11.1. Clicking a preset immediately inserts it for further editing and displays the Header & Footer tab, which I'll describe shortly. When Word is in Print Layout view, you also can double-click the header or footer area at the top or bottom of the document to create a header or footer, or you can use the Edit Header or Edit Footer choices at the bottom of the gallery (as shown in Figure 11.1) to start editing.

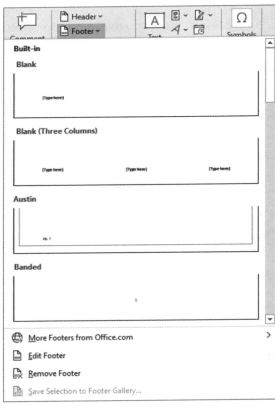

11.1 Word offers header and footer presets.

● **PowerPoint.** Choose Insert ➜ Text ➜ Header & Footer, which opens the Header and Footer dialog box shown in Figure 11.2. It has both Slide and Notes and Handouts tabs so that you can create headers and footers for each. Check boxes as needed in the Include section and change or make any accompanying entries. For example, in Figure 11.2, I've checked both Slide Number and Footer and then entered text in the accompanying Footer text box. (Slides can only have footers, but notes and handouts pages can also have headers.) I've also checked Don't Show on Title Slide, because it's typical to not include a header or footer on a title slide. You can then click Apply to add the footer to the current slide or click Apply to All to add it to all slides in the presentation. The Notes and Handouts tab only offers an Apply to All button.

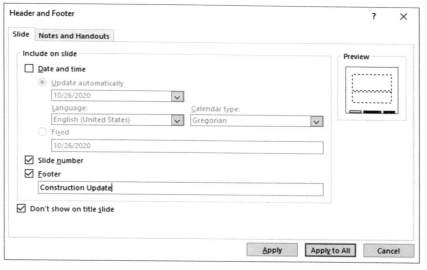

11.2 In PowerPoint, you can create headers and footers for printouts of your slides or your notes and handouts pages.

● **Excel.** Choose Insert ➜ Text ➜ Header & Footer. In Excel, this automatically changes to Page Layout view and places the insertion point in the center box of the header. The Page Layout view shows the page margins and breaks and includes horizontal and vertical rulers. The header and footer both have left, right, and center boxes that you can click in and then type entries or choose a type of content to add. A Header & Footer tab appears, with similar choices to the one that appears in Word.

In Word and Excel you use the tools on the Header & Footer tab to create the header and/ or footer contents, and there are a lot of choices and possible combinations. (Figure 11.3 shows Excel's Header & Footer tab.) If you click either the Header or Footer button in the Header & Footer group, a menu of available presets appears, including page numbers, sheet names, and more.

Presets available
in this group

Individual elements to
insert available in this group

Header & Footer tab

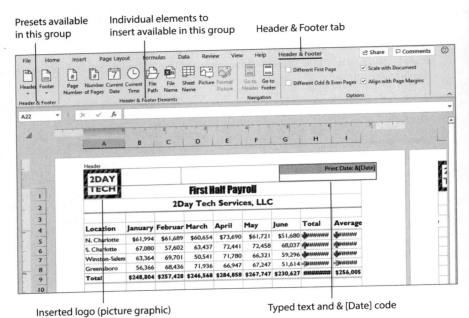

Inserted logo (picture graphic)

Typed text and & [Date] code

11.3 In Excel, the choices on the Header & Footer tab enable you to build header and footer components.

Use the buttons in the Header & Footer → Navigation group to jump between the header and footer. To insert elements manually, first click in the desired area (Word) or box (Excel) in the header or footer. In Word, you also can typically use the Tab key to move to another part of the header or footer. You can type some descriptive text, if desired. Or, click the desired button in the Insert group (Word) or Header & Footer Elements group (Excel) to insert the desired element. In some cases, such as if you click Page Number in Excel, Excel immediately inserts a code for the specified element. The page number code is &[Page].

In the right header box in Figure 11.3, you can see that I first typed some text and then clicked Current Date to insert the &[Date] element. In Word, if you click Date & Time, the Date and Time dialog box opens. Choose one of the Available Formats, click the Update Automatically check box if desired, and then click OK. Word also has a Page Number menu in the Header & Footer group that you can use to choose from various presets. Select the text and element codes in a header or footer and use formatting choices on the Home tab to adjust the formatting. To finish your entry in a header or footer box in Excel, click another box. (If you press Enter, that just creates a line break within the box.) In Word, click in another part of the header or footer.

To insert a picture such as a logo that you want to print on every page, click the Pictures button in the Insert group (Word) or the Picture button in the Header & Footer Elements group (Excel), and then use the choices in the Insert Pictures dialog box to select and insert a picture. The picture appears in the header or footer in Word, where you can resize and otherwise reformat it as needed. In Excel, the &[Picture] code appears in the box, and when you click another header or footer box to finish the entry, the picture appears on the page. (Remember that in PowerPoint, you have to add a picture that appears on every slide in Slide Master view, even for footers. Add the picture to the overall slide master or individual slide layouts as desired.) Even when you're not working in the header or footer in Word, you can use the Design ➜ Page Background ➜ Watermark gallery choices to insert a grayed-out *watermark* image to the page background, such as noting that the document is *Confidential*.

Genius

If an inserted picture looks too big in Excel, reselect the &[Picture] code in the header or footer box, and then choose Header & Footer ➜ Header & Footer Elements ➜ Format Picture. The Format Picture dialog box that appears includes settings for sizing, cropping, and more on its three tabs. Or use a graphics program to resize a copy of the picture file, and then reinsert it into the header or footer. For a logo, a file that's .5 inches high usually fits.

To finish working with the header and footer, double-click in the main document text in Word or click outside the header or footer area in the margin or on a cell in Excel. Or, you can choose Header & Footer ➜ Close ➜ Close Header and Footer in Word. In Excel, you may prefer to choose View ➜ Workbook Views ➜ Normal to change back to Normal view. To edit a header or footer, double-click in the header or footer area in Print Layout view of Word, reopen the Header and Footer dialog box in PowerPoint as described earlier, or choose Insert ➜ Text ➜ Header & Footer again in Excel.

Note

After you work with or view headers and footers in Page Layout view in Excel, when you go back to Normal view, you may see a dashed line over a regular gridline. This indicates a page break.

When you're working with a chart sheet in Excel and choose Insert ➔ Text ➔ Header & Footer, the Page Setup dialog box opens, with the Header/Footer tab displayed. You also can display this dialog box by clicking the dialog box launcher in the Page Setup group of the Page Layout tab and then clicking the Header/Footer tab. You can choose Header or Footer presets from drop-down lists or use the Custom Header or Custom Footer button to open a dialog box where you can insert elements in the three sections. Click OK as needed when you finish using the dialog box(es) to set up the header or footer.

Note

To access the tabs for adding a header/footer or changing paper size in Outlook, double-click a message in the message list of the main Outlook window. Choose File ➔ Print in the message window, and then double-click Memo Style under Settings. Use the Header/Footer and Paper tabs in the Page Setup dialog box to change those elements as needed, and then click OK. From there, you can click Print to print the message.

Changing Page Settings

Like other programs that create various types of documents, the Microsoft 365 apps have default settings for various aspects of the document. In PowerPoint, most of these settings are determined by the theme and slide layout, topics I've discussed in previous chapters. In Word and Excel, margins, orientation, paper size, and scaling settings are most important, so I'll focus on those. The Page Setup group of the Layout tab (Word) or Page Layout tab (Excel) enables you to make these page changes.

Margins

The margins are the white areas between the data and the edges of the printed page. The default preset for this is Normal, which in Word allows for 1-inch margins around all four sides of the page and in Excel allows for .75-inch margins at the top and bottom and .7-inch margins at the left and right. You can use one of two methods to change margins:

● **Choose a preset.** In the Page Setup group of the Layout or Page Layout tab (see Figure 11.4), click the Margins button, and then choose one of the available presets from the gallery.

Margins button

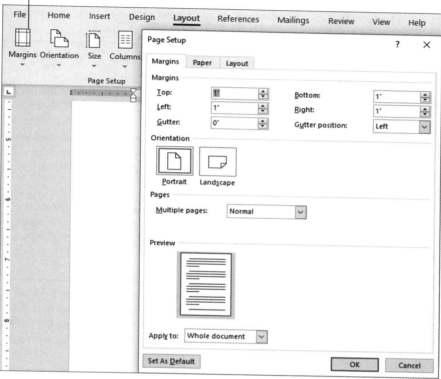

11.4 The Margins button in the Page Setup group enables you to apply a preset or display detailed margins settings.

- **Use the Margins tab of the Page Setup dialog box.** Choose Layout → Page Setup → Margins → Custom Margins (Word) or Page Layout → Page Setup → Margins → Custom Margins (Excel). The Page Setup dialog box opens with the Margins tab displayed, as shown in Figure 11.4. Adjust the settings in the four margin text boxes as needed. Another advantage to using the dialog box is that you also can adjust the vertical area in the Header and Footer text boxes in Excel. When you finish, click OK to apply the changes.

239

Caution

Most printers have minimum margin sizes. Check your printer specs to ensure that you don't set margins that are too narrow, which can cause data to be cut off in the printout or even produce error messages.

Orientation and paper size

Orientation determines the layout of the page. Portrait, the default, means the page is taller than it is wide. Landscape means that the page is wider than it is tall. Sometimes, sticking with the default works. For example, invoice templates and designs traditionally arrange the sheet information in a vertical arrangement meant to fit a standard letter-sized (8.5" x 11") page in portrait orientation. In other cases, you might have many more columns of data than rows, where changing to the wider landscape orientation might save some pages in the printout.

To change orientation, choose Layout → Page Setup → Orientation → Landscape or Layout → Page Setup → Orientation → Portrait (Word); in Excel, choose Page Layout → Page Setup → Orientation → Landscape or Page Layout → Page Setup → Orientation → Portrait.

Note

You can use the Page Setup group dialog box launcher to open the dialog box and then select the desired tab to access many of the settings described here, including the page orientation settings. In Excel, the Scale to Fit and Sheet Options group dialog box launchers on the Page Layout tab also open the Page Setup dialog box.

The paper size relative to the amount of data on an Excel sheet also might impact your choice of whether to use a portrait or landscape orientation. For example, if your printer can handle the 8.5" x 14" legal paper size, a landscape orientation might allow all the data in a sheet to print on a single wider page. Or in Word, you might need to use another paper size by convention for particular types of documents. Use the Size button in the Page Setup group of the Page Layout tab (Excel) or Layout tab (Word) to choose another paper size.

Scaling an Excel printout

True story: I find scaling a printout to be one of the most useful page layout settings in Excel. It's annoying when a stray row or column prints on (and wastes) a whole sep-arate piece of paper. Plus, it opens up the possibility of losing that extra page and the nformation it presents, creating an incomplete picture of your data. I often scale a work-sheet printout to restrict it to a single page.

The Scale to Fit group of the Page Layout tab contains the scaling settings. In Figure 11.5, 've selected 1 Page from the Width and Height drop-down lists to restrict the printout to one page wide by one page tall. Notice that this disables the Scale setting.

11.5 Scale an Excel printout to a set number of pages or to a percentage.

If you try to make a printout scale to a larger number of pages but there isn't enough data to fill those pages, Excel won't scale the document. Instead, you can try increasing the Scaling setting to something like 125% or 150%, but be advised that this scales the font size of the sheet contents rather than just redistributing some of the sheet contents to an additional page or pages.

Genius

In Word, you can control how many pages print per sheet of paper. Choose File ➜ Print. Under Settings, click the bottom choice that initially displays 1 Page Per Sheet. Choose one of the presets, and then continue with the printout. I previously used the 4 Pages Per Sheet preset to print small calendar pages and to-do lists to fit into a pocket-sized schedule binder. Other presets could be used to create and print custom pages for a small journal.

Changing Sheet Settings in Excel

I'm going to veer off even further into Excel territory for a while here, because Excel print-outs offer more challenges and options than printouts from Word, PowerPoint, or Out-look. Beyond working with the page settings for a printout, you can control some aspects of how the content appears within the printed area of the sheet. Further refining the page design in this way can make the printout easier to follow.

Adding print titles

Print titles are rows or columns that repeat on every page of a printout. Specifying print titles helps readers know what the rows and columns of data mean, no matter which page of a printout they're looking at.

Follow these steps to set up print titles for a sheet:

1. **Choose Page Layout ➜ Page Setup ➜ Print Titles.** The Page Setup dialog box opens with the Sheet tab selected.

241

2. **Under Print Titles, use the Rows to Repeat at Top and/or Columns to Repeat at Left text boxes to select the print titles.** You can type in references if you want, but they have to be absolute references to the column letters or row numbers only (recall that you use the $ for absolute references). These text boxes have the collapse and expand buttons at the right, but I've found that you can just click in one of the text boxes and click a column header/row number (or drag to select multiple columns or rows), and the dialog box will collapse and expand automatically. In Figure 11.6, I've specified both types of print titles.

Absolute reference to rows 1-3

Absolute reference to column A

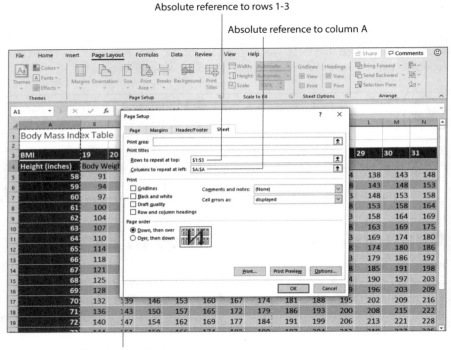

Sheet print settings

11.6 Specify print titles to repeat on every page of a multipage printout in Excel.

3. **Click OK.**

Genius

Some of the settings you choose for printing—such as print titles and the print area—can be saved with the file so you don't have to make those selections again. After applying those settings, use your old friend Ctrl+S to save the settings in the file.

Controlling whether gridlines and other features print

A lot of people overlook these settings, but they can make an important difference in the appearance of an Excel printout. If you look at the Sheet Options group of the Page Layout tab, as shown in Figure 11.5, by default the View check box is checked for both Gridlines and Headings (column and row headers), but the Print check boxes are not. I assume this is because cell gridlines and the headers make it easier to build formulas, but they aren't so useful on a sheet printout.

Caution Sheet formatting can override printed gridlines in some instances. If you have a worksheet with a table or other range that has white borders for cells, printing gridlines will not cause those borders to turn black. To have printed black borders, you'd have to change the table style or border formatting in the range.

That said, there are times when you might want to print gridlines and headings. A good example is if you choose Formulas → Formula Auditing → Show Formulas and then want to make a printout with the displayed formulas. Including the gridlines and headings would give the formulas context.

So, to print the Gridlines and Headings (column and row headers), just click to check the Print check box under each in the Sheet Options group of the Page Layout tab. If you refer to Figure 11.6, the Sheet tab of the Page Setup dialog box also includes a Print section, where you can control not only the printing of gridlines and headings, but also other aspects such as comments, notes, and cell errors.

Working with Page Breaks in Excel

When you print, Excel initially assumes you want to print all of the sheet contents, and it makes its best guess about what area to print and where to break between pages. Some of its guesses can be, well, *awkward* (as a typical teenager might say). You can make better choices by setting the print area and adjusting the page breaks.

Setting a print area

I find that I usually set a print area when my sheet has other contents, such as reference information or an extra table, that I don't need to see in my printout. Or, you might have a project estimate sheet where you want to print the actual estimate portion, but not the detailed calculations further to the right on the sheet, because your client doesn't need those added details.

I'm covering this feature along with page breaks because the specified print area contributes to determining the number of pages and page breaks in the printout. To limit the printout to a specific area to print, select the range and then choose Page Layout ➔ Page Setup ➔ Print Area ➔ Set Print Area. To clear a print area that you've selected previously, choose Page Layout ➔ Page Setup ➔ Print Area ➔ Clear Print Area.

Caution

Carefully review the print preview when you've selected a print area. You want to make sure you didn't leave anything out or include sensitive information that's for your eyes only.

Vertically and horizontally centering the contents of each printout page (see Figure 11.7) adds another dash of professionalism, and it's more important when the sheet contents or contents of the selected print area don't fill the entire page(s). Excel by default jams the printed contents into the upper-left corner of the page. To fix this and even out the whitespace, check the Horizontally and Vertically check boxes under Center on Page on the Margins tab of the Page Setup dialog box.

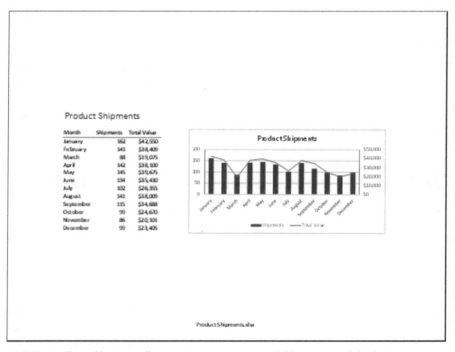

11.7 Vertically and horizontally centering page content yields a more polished printout.

Viewing and moving breaks

At last I get to talk about Page Break Preview view in Excel! This view simply provides a visual method for adjusting page breaks. To display Page Break Preview, choose View ➔ Workbook Views ➔ Page Break Preview. The zoom of the sheet changes and blue page break lines appear, along with a gray "watermark" label for each page. The solid blue lines indicate manual page breaks or breaks resulting from being the bottom- or far-right boundary of the sheet data or selected print area. The dashed lines are page breaks suggested by Excel.

To change a break, move your mouse over the blue line until it changes to a black double-headed arrow pointer, as shown in Figure 11.8. Drag the break to a new position. When you finish, choose View ➔ Workbook Views ➔ Normal to change back to the Normal view.

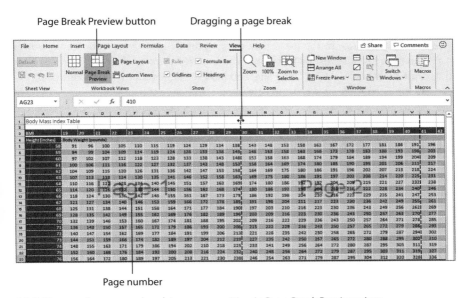

11.8 You can drag a page break to a new position in Page Break Preview view.

Note The Breaks button in the Page Setup group of the Page Layout tab offers a menu of choices for inserting, removing, and resetting all page breaks. You can give this method a shot, but for me, Page Break Preview works in a more intuitive way.

Previewing a Printout and Printing

In working with various page setup and print settings, you may have noticed both Print and Preview (or Print Preview) buttons in various dialog boxes. This strikes me as an anachronism that might go away, because these functions have merged over time. It's likely that some method of changing between page setup settings and preview/print settings will remain available, due to the need to tweak and preview multiple times until you get a good printout.

If you choose File → Print or press Ctrl+P from an open file or an open message in an Outlook message window, the Print screen of the File tab (Backstage view) appears, as shown in the example from PowerPoint in Figure 11.9. The print settings appear below Print in the middle part of the screen, with the preview of the first printout page at the right. If the printout has multiple pages, the information at bottom center shows you the number of pages. You can use the Next Page and Previous Page buttons to navigate between the pages to review them carefully. Clicking the Zoom to Page button at the lower right zooms in for closer examination, and clicking the button a second time zooms back out. (Outlook has Actual Size, One Page, and Multiple Pages zoom buttons instead.) You can use the Zoom slider in Word and PowerPoint to change the preview zoom. Instead of the Zoom slider, Excel has the Show Margins button, which toggles the display of margin lines in the preview. Drag a margin line to a new position to resize it. Black boxes or handles also appear across the top to show the column widths. Dragging one of those resizes the column.

At the top of the Print settings, you can change the Copies entry to print more copies. Choose the Printer to use from the Printer drop-down list. (It must be turned on, have paper, and so on.) The other choices under Settings largely give you a chance to revisit page settings covered earlier, with the exception of the top two. You can choose to print everything, you can specify a range of pages or slides to print, or you can print a selection that you made in Word or Excel before displaying the Print choices. The other options vary depending on the app. For example, in PowerPoint, you can choose to print Full Page Slides, Notes Pages, the Outline, or various handout formats.

When it all looks good, click the Print button at the top. With any luck, your printer spits out the page(s) or slide(s).

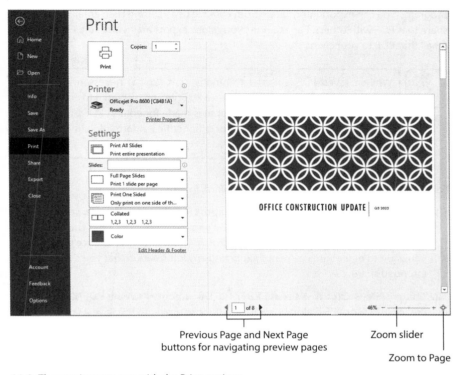

Previous Page and Next Page
buttons for navigating preview pages

Zoom slider

Zoom to Page

11.9 The preview appears with the Print settings.

Sharing Information in Other Ways

You don't *have* to print your documents on your end. You may need to send a file to someone else digitally so that they can print it. (And please, don't even talk to me about snail mailing or faxing. So 1990s.) You have a couple of options for sharing your information with others who need to review it.

Exporting a PDF

A Portable Document Format (PDF) file has been a standard format for sharing documents for decades. You can open and print a PDF file using the free Acrobat Reader app, Word, web browsers such as Microsoft Edge and others, and any number of other programs. You can export information from your file to a PDF and then email or otherwise share that PDF with others. For example, you might export an invoice to a PDF and then email that PDF to your client.

Caution

While a saved PDF is harder to modify, that doesn't necessarily mean the recipient can't edit it. Word can open a PDF file and convert it to editable text, and the full version of Adobe Acrobat is made for editing PDFs. If you email a PDF with financial calculations or other critical information, make sure to verify the contents of the file that you receive back.

Follow these steps to export a PDF file from Word, Excel, or PowerPoint:

1. **If needed, select the pages or text to export in a Word document, set a print area or select the range to export on the sheet in Excel, or select the slides to export in the Normal view in PowerPoint.** This is another instance where you want to make sure you're not exporting any information that you don't intend to share.

2. **Choose File → Export → Create PDF/XPS Document → Create PDF/XPS.** The Publish a PDF or XPS dialog box appears. It looks similar to the Save As dialog box but has PDF selected as the Save as Type choice by default and includes a couple of other PDF-specific settings.

3. **Navigate to the desired save location and edit the filename as needed.**

4. **If you selected the area to export in Step 1, click the Options button; otherwise, skip to Step 6.** An Options dialog box like the one from Excel shown in Figure 11.10 appears. The options in the Word and PowerPoint dialog boxes are similar, but are grouped a little differently.

5. **Under Page Range (Word), Publish What (Excel), or Range (PowerPoint), click the Selection option button, and then click OK.**

6. **Click Publish.** By default, the Open File After Publishing check box in the Publish as PDF or XPS dialog box is checked, as shown in Figure 11.10. This means that after you click Publish, the file opens in the default PDF viewer on your system. This can be Microsoft Edge on a Windows 10 system or another app such as a version of Adobe's Acrobat Reader that's set as the default.

7. **Review the PDF contents for accuracy and then close the PDF viewer app.**

Selection option button

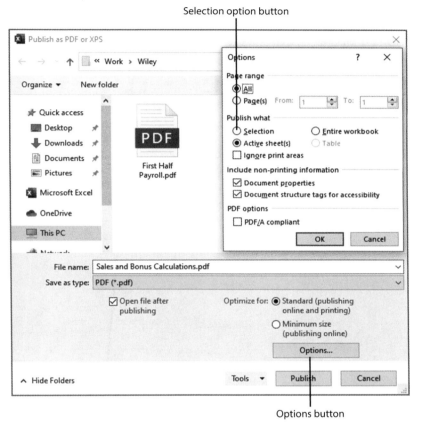

Options button

11.10   You have options when exporting your file to a PDF.

Using OneDrive

From my perspective, Microsoft seems to be increasingly nudging users to save files to their computers' local OneDrive folders so that the files sync to the user's OneDrive account in the cloud. I get it, it's a no-brainer backup method that can save people from themselves. It can stink for some people, however, because if you have limited data for your Internet connection, all that syncing can chew up a data plan quite quickly.

Setting that little gripe aside, once a file has synced to your OneDrive cloud account or you've uploaded it yourself, you can share it from there. In your web browser, sign on to your OneDrive account and navigate to the folder holding the file, if needed. Select the file, and then click Share in the bar at the top. Choose sharing settings. From there, enter a contact name or email address and click Send to send the sharing list, or click Copy Link and then copy the link so that you can email it to recipients as needed.

Thank You, Reader!

Thank you for grabbing your copy of *Microsoft 365 Portable Genius* and for staying engaged through the end of the book. I hope it serves as a useful guide as you hone your Microsoft 365 skills and progress through your career. Sending thoughts of appreciation your way. Check out the bonus coverage in the Online Bonus Appendix for this book, available at www.wiley.com/go/ms365portablegenius.

Index

A

absolute references, 94–97
Accounting number format (Excel), 132, 133
accounts (Outlook), 218–220
active cell (Excel), 21
adding
    accounts in Outlook, 218–220
    animations to PowerPoint slide
        shows, 124–125
    borders in Word, 147–148
    columns to tables in Word and
        PowerPoint, 183–184
    contacts in Outlook, 229–230
    dates in Excel, 23–24
    hyperlinks in Excel, 22–23
    PowerPoint slides, 114–116
    print titles in Excel, 241–242
    rows to tables in Word and
        PowerPoint, 183–184
    slide content in PowerPoint, 26–27
    SmartArt graphics, 173–175
    tables in Word and PowerPoint, 182–183
    text
        in Excel, 22–23
        to shapes, 165–166
    times in Excel, 23–24
    a total row in Excel, 192–193
    transitions in PowerPoint slide
        shows, 123–124
    values in Excel, 22–23
    worksheets in Excel, 64–65
adjusting
    background of PowerPoint slides, 121–122
    cell borders/shading in Excel, 148–149

chart type/layout, 209–211
charted data, 213–215
column width in Excel, 73–75
line spacing in Word and PowerPoint,
    143
margins in Word and Excel, 238–240
orientation in Word and Excel, 240
page settings, 236–241
paper size in Word and Excel, 240
paragraph spacing in Word and
    PowerPoint, 143–145
position of graphics, 168–170
reference type in Excel formulas, 94–95
row height in Excel, 73–75
SmartArt graphics type/formatting, 177
styles, 166–168
table styles, 197–198
themes, 153–154
views, 8–9
worksheet settings in Excel, 241–243
alignment
    applying formatting, 139–142
    for graphics, 170–172
animations, adding to slide shows in
    PowerPoint, 124–125
applying
    alignment formatting, 139–142
    font formatting, 135–139
apps, starting and exiting, 4–5
area chart, 202
arguments (Excel), 97–98
arithmetic operators, 89
arranging lists in Excel, 184–186
at (@), 91
Auto Fill feature, 68–71